Darfur Allegory

Darfur Allegory

ROGAIA MUSTAFA ABUSHARAF

The University of Chicago Press
Chicago and London

The University of Chicago Press, Chicago 60637
The University of Chicago Press, Ltd., London
© 2021 by The University of Chicago
All rights reserved. No part of this book may be used or reproduced in any manner
whatsoever without written permission, except in the case of brief quotations in critical
articles and reviews. For more information, contact the University of Chicago Press,
1427 E. 60th St., Chicago, IL 60637.
Published 2021
Printed in the United States of America

30 29 28 27 26 25 24 23 22 21   1 2 3 4 5

ISBN-13: 978-0-226-76169-5 (cloth)
ISBN-13: 978-0-226-76172-5 (paper)
ISBN-13: 978-0-226-76186-2 (e-book)
DOI: https://doi.org/10.7208/chicago/9780226761862.001.0001

Library of Congress Cataloging-in-Publication Data

Names: Abusharaf, Rogaia Mustafa, author.
Title: Darfur Allegory / Rogaia Mustafa Abusharaf.
Description: Chicago : The University of Chicago Press, 2021. | Includes bibliographi-
    cal references and index.
Identifiers: LCCN 2020027869 | ISBN 9780226761695 (cloth) | ISBN 9780226761725
    (paperback) | ISBN 9780226761862 (ebook)
Subjects: LCSH: Genocide—Sudan—Darfur. | Ethnic conflict—Sudan—Darfur. |
    Sudanese—Sudan—Darfur—Social conditions. | Sudanese—Sudan—Darfur—
    Ethnic identity. | Sudanese—Foreign countries. | Postcolonialism—Sudan. |
    Sudan—History—Darfur Conflict, 2003– | Sudan—History—Darfur Conflict,
    2003– —Refugees.
Classification: LCC DT159.6.D27 A32 2021 | DDC 962.404/3—dc23
LC record available at https://lccn.loc.gov/2020027869

♾ This paper meets the requirements of ANSI/NISO Z39.48-1992 (Permanence of Paper).

For Mona and Hala
And in loving memory of my brother,
Zuhair Mustafa Abusharaf Esq.

History is so unkind to those it abandons and can be equally unkind to those who make it.

SALMAN RUSHDIE, *Two Years Eight Months and Twenty-Eight Nights: A Novel*

Contents

Unmuting Darfuri Voices

> . . . a death space in the land of the living where torture's certain uncertainty fed the great arbitrariness of power, power on the rampage—that great steaming morass of chaos that lies on the underside of order and without which order could not exist.
>
> MICHAEL TAUSSIG, *Shamanism, Colonialism, and the Wild Man*[1]

Umm Kwakiyya: Why Darfur Allegory?

Darfur, the Sudan's westernmost region, is a frontier of violence, a "space of death" in the words of anthropologist Michael Taussig, or, as its inhabitants had appositely termed the violence they endured more than a century ago, an Umm Kwakiyya, a state of damnation.[2] I understood the new iteration of violence that erupted in 2003 as Umm Kwakiyya, a "space of death," for the terms can easily be used interchangeably. This is the allegory that compelled me to undertake this difficult ethnography. In what sense is Darfur a space of death, its state of affairs that of Umm Kwakiyya?

The word for allegory in Arabic is *ibra*, which literally means "the lesson learned." The ibra of Darfur lies in its "lessons" about the impact of multiple and intersecting levels of violence stemming from colonial rule, environmental degradation, and crimes against humanity. This ibra in essence is not very different from the definition of allegory in ethnographic, aesthetic, and cultural studies: "Allegory," writes Andrew Edgar in *Key Concepts in Cultural Theory*, "is a drama, poem, picture or other work of art in which characters and events are used to represent or personify a deeper veiled meaning."[3] Relating allegory to meaning making in ethnographic writing, James Clifford writes, "Allegory draws special attention to the *narrative* [emphasis in the original] character of cultural representations, to the stories built into the representational process itself. It also breaks down the seamless quality of cultural description by adding a temporal aspect to the process of reading. One level of meaning in a text will always generate other levels."[4] Clifford goes on to point out the allegory of the ethnographer:

A recognition of allegory complicates the writing and reading of ethnographies in potentially fruitful ways. A tendency emerges to specify and separate

different allegorical registers within the text. The marking off of extended indigenous discourses shows the ethnography to be a hierarchical structure of
powerful stories that translate, encounter, and recontextualize other powerful
stories.[5]

What do these definitions imply for titling this ethnography *Darfur Allegory*? As we shall see in the chapters that follow, Darfur's deeper meanings—
its ibra—lead us to an understanding of the "encoding, reproduction, and
exposure of political power."[6] From this it follows that the categories typically
deployed for understanding the root cause of the Darfur tragedy have failed
to engage the tactics of political power.

In his formidable account of the Sultanate of Darfur over the centuries, historian Rex Seán O'Fahey exposed us to what Darfuris called Umm Kwakiyya,
referring, he said, to "the damnation of Darfur." He writes, "Umm Kwakiyya
was the Arabic term used by my informants in the 1970s to describe the period
1874–98, when, following the destruction of the first Sultanate, Darfur experienced all the miseries that it is presently enduring."[7] The stories of Darfur that
many of the interlocutors in this ethnography tried to tell, whether in depth
or with economy, represent a kind of a neo–Umm Kwakiyya, an utter devastation that has continued to pound Darfur with astonishing force. In pondering
the enormous pain of Darfuri people across time and location, I thought often
that Umm Kwakiyya is a proper allegory of their experiences, at once evocative of O'Fahey's work and reflective of the underlying situations that I sought
to register here. For underneath the painful experiences I have recorded are
crosscutting stories—about colonialism, local knowledge, the environment,
gender, and especially about the misuse of racial and ethnic categories.

Darfur Allegory is also about a plurality of competing narratives. As a
Sudanese writing about Darfur, I see my role as mediating and prismatic,
yet also adequate to confer some insights through my encounters with Darfur at home and abroad. I intentionally have chosen to present detailed accounts participants shared with me during the course of my ethnographic
research. *Darfur Allegory* then is also about unmuting Darfuri voices. We
need to be wary of the "dangers of a single story," as Nigerian novelist Chimamanda Ngozi Adichie cautions us.[8] The notion of allegory then helps scaf-
fold the stories Darfuri people in and outside of the Sudan have told me in
this ethnography.

In all their competing plurality, the stories in this ethnography pull back
the curtain on a region in ruin. Darfur seems to have perpetually lived on
a knife's edge, in a space of death that has become a classic laboratory not
only for understanding key questions about Afro-Arab politics and society

but also for exposing the tenuous human relations in a postcolonial state that sleepwalked itself into disaster. It is the realm of human relationships produced by the kaleidoscopic power of the state that dominates this ethnography. Although it is important to note that Darfuri people have interacted with the state in highly differentiated ways, with some joining then-president Omar Al-Bashir in an alliance predicated on economic interest and political opportunism, the majority has withstood systematic brutalization. For this reason, explanations of Darfur's mayhem do not lend themselves to a Manichean mode of reasoning based on predetermined taxonomies and prior texts. Within the voluminous literature on the conflict in Darfur that has appeared since 2003, the debate about the root cause of the conflict has turned primarily on race. Put simply, Arabism and Africanism have been thought to be on a collision course in the Sudan. Such a Manichean treatment of Darfur's troubles strips it of productive engagements with the colonial role in inventing those Arab and African identities. Also conspicuously absent are references to Britain's brutal Darfur Campaign, which resulted in the annexation of the region to the Sudan, including the massacre of its last sultan, Ali Dinar.[9] Some of the most significant and messy "traveling concepts" of context and framing are thus lost in the representations of Darfur.[10] Although the politicization of ethnic identity and its ugly consequences are incontestable, I argue that we need to ask more questions about why this is the case.

The ibra here is thus the unyielding marginalization of the majority of Sudanese people, particularly Darfuris and before them the Southern Sudanese. Throughout the postcolonial period, the state (both civilian and military) deemed these populations marginal, thus continuing the "out of sight, out of mind" approach of its predecessor. This neglect continues into the present, its dreadful outcomes evidence of the state's relentless culpability. We must remember, then, that Darfur is a region in a "postcolony" whose leaders have lacked the creativity and imagination warranted to circumvent colonial violence. Mark the poignant words of Achille Mbembe: "The postcolony is characterized by a distinctive style of political improvisation, by a tendency to excess and lack of proportion, as well as by distinctive ways identities are multiplied, transformed, and put into circulation. But the postcolony is also made up of a series of corporate institutions and a political machinery that, once in place, constitute a distinctive regime of violence."[11]

No wonder some of the world's most astute observers of postcolonial societies, among them Césaire, Fanon, Gikandi, Mahgoub, Mbembe, Memmi, Mudimbe, Walcott, and Zuberi,[12] have invited us to reflect on the malaise colonialism has left behind. In the Sudan, the reproduction of the colonial episteme was evidenced in the newly independent elites' mimicry of the British, their conflation of a mythologized Arab past with a politicized Islam, and their systematic negation of the marginalized other. I concur with Simon Gikandi's observation about the movement of African subjects through the anatomy of colonialism[13] and agree with him as well on the egocentrism of elite politics and its self-absorbed leaders. Without understanding these realities, we will be unable to grasp the myriad forms of violence against the Darfuri people or to describe "what happens to the subject and world when the memory of [violent] events is folded into ongoing relationships."[14] Darfur's violence as an allegory of the postcolonial state in Africa suggests an analogy with chickenpox and shingles. "Shingles is a viral infection of an individual nerve and the skin surface that is supplied by the nerve. It is caused by the varicella-zoster virus, the same virus that causes chickenpox in childhood."[15] The colonial chickenpox virus emerged in the postcolonial state's body politic as an excruciatingly painful case of shingles. The state's lack of imagination limited its ability to think independently of the colonial episteme, and hence death, desolation, and scorched earth ensued.

The marginalizing practices of both colonial and postcolonial elites have sustained a state of otherness among Darfuris, as this ethnography shows. This othering and the rendering of Darfur's devastation as unworthy of easing are a manifestation of the state's "fetishization of power," which Enrique Dussel explains as a "will-to-power as domination of the people, of the majority, of the weakest, of the poor."[16] This fact was not lost on Sudanese novelist Baraka Sakin, who commented in an interview with Radio Dabanga: "The war in Darfur is a war over land and power, rather than a war between Zurqa and Arabs. It is fought by the regime in Khartoum in favor of the Islamists."[17] Subsequently I had the chance to speak with him in person. This is what he said to me: "The peace they are talking about is nothing without rooting out the root cause. It is like a corpse of war, planning to rise up like a zombie." The reference to a zombie by this brilliant Darfuri novelist brought to mind once more Mbembe's comment about "the banality of power" in grotesque and obscene postcolonial "regimes of violence" and the logic of the surrogacy relationships that unfolded at independence: "[This] logic has resulted in the mutual zombification of both the dominant and those apparently dominated. This zombification means that each has robbed the other of vitality and left both impotent." By this view, the physical and symbolic violence born out of the womb of colonialism has come to frustrate dramatically the aspirations of Darfuris.

This came home to me forcefully after I had finished an interview with a young Darfuri in Baltimore and was making some notes as I rode the MARC train home to Washington, DC. I reflected on how her recollections of the exertions of life lived in the fringes of a village in Darfur, where basic needs have long gone unmet, revealed so much about the cumulative effect of this marginality in the face of elites' residual sense of ownership. As we spoke, the effects of the ongoing violence she had endured, including the trauma of rape at the hands of the Janjaweed, were evident in her tone, body language, diminished circumstances, and vacant stare. The weight of history, politics, and culture was unmistakable in the powerful emotions permeating her story. Indeed, that story conveyed powerful lessons about the cruelty of a regime that has devastated many women and girls. However, I was also heartened by her will to keep going, for her marginalized identity also involved resistance to the subaltern reality imposed upon her.[18] Just as I was leaving, she spoke of her mixed emotions about Darfur, of a longing, rooted in the acute loneliness of a refugee, isolated in unfamiliar surroundings, for the home where she had nonetheless suffered greatly. Her words reminded me of Oscar Handlin's depiction of the psychological tug of war characterizing exilic experiences: "As I struggled in the effort to spread my wings and labored in the learning to bear my weight, as I ventured to the faraway places and saw what never was seen before, I did not cease to dream of home."[19]

Particularly noteworthy among the various currents that flowed into this ethnography is how the immediacy of violence, flight, and resettlement has shaped daily renegotiations of identity, if not of life itself, among Darfuris, propelling forward the question of what it means to be a Darfuri Sudanese in different contexts and situations. As they critiqued the elite practices of the Arabized few, these Darfuris searched for "self-representation and biographical experiences [that] revised, rehashed, and refigured [identity] through particular strategic uses of language."[20] Some call themselves Blacks in America, B'nai Darfur in Tel Aviv, and (although not discussed in this work) aborigines in Australia. Darfuri refugees have thus come to define themselves not by their tribes or qabila but as people whose identities are reconstructed in the aftermath of crimes against humanity. Darfuri people's narrations of their own definition of who they are and who they are becoming thus challenge the single story characterized by primordial, essentialist representations of Darfur's "tribal" indigeneity, authenticity, and innate identity. Tribe is an interest group whose various interests supersede biology.

As I have tried to unearth the ibra embedded in the allegory that is Darfur, I have also been led to the concept of deterritorialization, or the disappearance of a border as we know it. As Darfuris, like any group in the cusp of change, have continuously negotiated polity and identity, they demonstrate the permeability of such notions as home and nation. No longer constrained by borders and manifestly deterritorialized, Darfuri people have succeeded in breaking silence and resisting the state in ways previously unavailable to political dissidents. Women have been speaking both privately and publicly about sexual violence as a weapon of war. In Doha, displaced Darfuris and community leaders have spoken loudly about atrocities that have devastated their lives. And Darfuri refugees and asylees around the world are taking every opportunity to protest the Sudanese state's sanctioned violence. Finally, social media have opened a thousand horizons for millions of revolution-makers around the world to exercise some measure of a "stateless power in a transnational moment."[21]

I contend that these Darfuris' embeddedness in a byzantine tapestry of local, national, international, and transnational politics become clear in the stories I gathered from the Homestead, Doha, Baltimore, Prince Georges County, and Tel Aviv. At varying levels of specificity, these narratives advance our comprehension of the metaphorical notion of borders as allegories of thought and experience.[22] As they daily negotiated the demands of time and place, they challenged common ahistorical, decontextualized notions of political subjectivity. Even in their occasional brevity, the stories represent a meta-commentary on the perils of simplifying human experience, a reality that shaped my own understanding of the complexity of the Darfur debate in the world.

Chapter Outline

I begin chapter 1 with a description of my own encounters, both personal and scholarly, with Darfur and then present a brief ethnological description of the region. Primarily, however, the chapter engages the interplay of factors that have propelled the crisis in Darfur. At the national level, it highlights competing perspectives on the crisis, including those produced by state and nonstate actors, interviewees from Darfur, and members of Darfuri armed movements living elsewhere. At the regional level, it contends with the issue of borders, including the influx of refugees from neighboring Chad and the incursions of Chadian bandits into Darfur. At the transnational level, it scrutinizes what many organizations have described as the world's worst humanitarian crisis. I emphasize this crisis as a manifestation of the failure of a postcolonial state to imagine a place that is at once diverse and inclusive. Instead, it has reproduced the marginality characteristic of the colonial situation in a region where militarization, environmental degradation, and banditry have become precursors to destruction.

Chapter 2 presents several examples that show the destructive impact of "the violence of representation" in the Darfur imaginary.[23] I historicize the dimorphism of Darfuri identities to uncover their long gestation, extending back to eighteenth-century travel writing and continuing into the colonial era and beyond. The persistence of racial explanations—understood as biological givens—of the conflict blocks any opportunity to look beyond what are considered to be clear-cut taxonomies and obscures fundamental understanding of the socioeconomic forces at play. I argue, therefore, that the knowledge regimes unfolding historically are part of larger sociopolitical histories that enabled the development of certain imaginings about the region's polity and identity. This chapter thus goes beyond the usual innocuous anthropological inquiry into the crisis in Darfur to show how understanding racial categories is necessary—but not sufficient—for understanding its complex reality. The chapter is thus a reversal of the "western gaze, shaped by the western physical encounter with the other as well as the imagined reality of the other."[24]

In chapter 3, I share accounts from several rounds of ethnographic field research carried out between 2004 and 2009 in the Sudan's capital city. I begin by considering some of the most significant events related to the International Criminal Court case against then-president Al-Bashir, describing the solidarity rallies he orchestrated for which attendance was primarily coerced rather than spontaneous. I then discuss competing narratives about the nature of the crisis as articulated by both opponents and proponents of the Sudanese government. Most important among the former are the Sudanese Marxist critiques of the political violence in Darfur, generally and intentionally ignored by commentators on Darfur. I elucidate their oppositional consciousness about elite politics' othering of the majority of the Sudanese people. The chapter concludes with views about the crisis and its personal consequences for residents of forced migrant communities in Omdurman and Khartoum.

In chapter 4, I turn to my ethnographic research in the State of Qatar, which has been a fascinating locale from which to explore both formal and informal forms of engagement with Darfur. As soon as I arrived in Qatar in 2009, I realized that it is host to one of the largest groups of Sudanese abroad, consisting of thousands with various ethnic affiliations and occupational backgrounds, including citizens from Darfur. It is also the locus of numerous efforts to mediate a resolution of the Darfur crisis. The chapter describes my encounters and interactions with numerous Darfuri individuals and groups, in a range of settings, over more than a decade, exploring diverse perspectives on the politics of mediation. Some of those settings were glamorous five-star hotels with lavish amenities, a sublime irony as Darfuris spoke about ongoing violence, death and displacement, and the deprivations of life's basic necessities in desert refugee camps. What emerged most powerfully from these encounters wherever they occurred is that Darfuris are not relying on borrowed power to resolve the crisis, but rather have well-developed solutions shaped by a sophisticated understanding of their history and lived reality. Encountering Darfur in Qatar also demonstrated palpably the fluidity of the field and afforded a rare opportunity to advance the notion of mutuality as anthropology's changing term of engagement, a view advanced by anthropologist Roger Sanjek.[25] The story that emerges so powerfully here transcends the glamorous allure of the venues in which I met and spoke with Darfuris.

Chapter 5 focuses on the story of Darfuri refugees in Israel. It begins in Egypt, where they first attempted to seek refuge, but destitution, desperation, and threats of deportation pushed them to seek out the Bedouin of Sinai, who had mastered the art of smuggling African refugees across the desert into Israel. This chapter asks to what extent this migration represents an ultimate break with a country that identifies itself as Arab, Islamic, and pro-Palestinian. How do Darfuris navigate laws in Israel that define them as members of an enemy state? How are these Black and Muslim refugees received? How do they manage everyday life? This migration is about border crossings, at base an experience of movement across geographic locations, but also a movement across imaginative space, shaping consciousness and identity. Hence the chapter explores such themes as asylum seeking and gender as well as the redefinition of religious and ethnic identity. Although Darfuris continue to talk about the continuing threats from the Janjaweed, of a world turned upside down, they invoke experiences telling of their agency and political imaginings. Stanley Diamond reminds us that the "absolute prerequisite of historical consciousness is an unrelenting exploration of the self, as it exists, and as it may be imagined to exist."[26] These stories fit into this perspective and unveil the resistance to the structures in place.

Similarly, in chapter 6 I incorporate the voices of Darfuri refugees and exiles in the United States, considering ways their various subjectivities and transnational identities have developed in that context and with full recognition of the diversity of Black subjectivities as evidenced in the work of existentialist debates on diaspora.[27] In particular, many of those I spoke with articulate Darfur's dilemma as one of both racial and gender injustice. The chapter also raises several new questions: How have post-2003 Darfuri refugees been perceived by the predominantly white communities where they have been relocated; and how do they perceive American activism, including celebrity activism, on behalf of Darfur? How has the prevailing narrative about the Darfur conflict as one of Arabs against Black Africans transfigured a political problem into one of race relations? How has the preexisting racial configuration in the United States shaped Darfuri subjectivity? Why and how are Darfuri women coming to speak about the use of sexual violence as a weapon of war? Uniting the disparate experiences detailed in the chapter is the notion of voice. These migrants speak eloquently in their own voices about race, rape, and crimes against humanity.

Finally, in the conclusion I argue that the many voices rendered in *Darfur Allegory* communicate both the complexity of the crisis and the sophistication with which Darfuris are navigating the powerful economic and political forces they encounter at every turn. I keep returning back to that notion of the "space of death [as] preeminently a space of transformation: through the experience of coming close to death there well may be a vivid sense of life,"[28] as an allegory for the way Darfuris, thrust into new and transformative relationships, forge new lives and reenact identities in regions far away. Here, another metaphor, that of the horizon, so cogently presented by anthropologist Michael Lambek, equips us for a deeper understanding of the philosophic undertones of Darfuri consciousness of their lived experiences. Together with other definitions of allegory, we can come to know of the intertwined currents of politics and identity, self and place making, and metaphoric and physical border crossings. "Our horizons describe the expanse of the worlds we inhabit, not only in space but in time and in understanding. Horizons are mobile, expanding or retracting in response to social and political circumstances, limited but not limiting, changing as we move towards or away from them or as they begin to merge with those of new conversation partners. Our worlds are not closed off from one another but overlap to the extent that they share an arc or portion of a horizon."[29] In expanding their horizons, Darfuris, who had been forced by unbearable circumstances to keep quiet simply to stay alive, managed to break the silence in their own terms. I recall a powerful passage by American novelist Philip Roth, who wrote: "The trick to living . . . away from all agitating entanglements, allurements, and expectations, apart from one's own intensity, is to organize the silence, to think of its mountaintop as capital, silence as wealth exponentially increasing. The encircling silence your chosen source of advantage and your only intimate."[30] The Darfuris in this ethnography and all the others they represent have emerged as authors of their own history to impart another ibra of fortitude and resiliency in very much in the Nietzschean vein: "That which does not kill you, makes you stronger."

Encountering Darfur and Its Troubles

Where Is the Field? Encountering Darfur

Three distinct memories of Darfur's difficulties have helped to shape my interest in the ethnography of conflict and mediation and contributed to my view of fieldwork as an act of reciprocity. In retrospect, these scattered autobiographical experiences have significantly impacted my understanding of the anguish of the region, a crisis that observers such as Colin Powell have described as "the first genocide of the twenty-first century" and an "African Holocaust."

The first memory was formed in primary school at Teachers' Training College in Omdurman, Sudan, in the 1970s. Founded by the British in the 1930s, the college was located near the tomb of Imam Mohamed Ahmed Al-Mahdi, a revered nineteenth-century revolutionary who fought colonization and in the process mobilized the people of Darfur to rise against the occupying Turco-Egyptians. Its location represents a supreme irony of history and politics in the city many would prefer to replace Khartoum as the national capital. Ringing of the colossal, majestic copper bells in the college's schoolyard always marked the end of the day, as well as the beginning of holidays. I remember the loud clank at the start of the four-day religious holiday, Eid al-Adha, or Feast of the Sacrifice, which follows the end of the Hajj, the annual pilgrimage to Mecca. Eid is celebrated to give thanks to Allah for replacing Abraham's son Ishmael with a sacrificial lamb.

On one particular Eid, the headmistress gathered all the pupils for an important announcement before we dispersed. As I recall, she explained how we could contribute to a project called "Fighting Thirst in Western Sudan Provinces of Darfur and Kordofan," regions hundreds of miles away from Omdurman. She asked us to request that our families donate the skins of their sacrificial lambs to be fashioned as water containers for people dying of thirst. Ordinarily, sheepskins and hooves, with other less desirable parts of the animal, would have been given to the butchers who had slaughtered and skinned the animals. This time, she told us, volunteers would come to collect the sheepskins.

Sure enough, Eid Day arrived, and so did the butchers with their sharpened knives and axes, roaming from house to house in their bloody clothes and uttering a short prayer before they cut the sheep's throats. For three days before the slaughter, we children had watched these animals eating grass, drinking water, and sleeping when night fell. Their slaughter brought only horror to us, but not so to the elders, who exulted at fulfilling a pillar of the faith. Eid brought families and neighbors together, and relatives from near and far joined in feasting to commemorate the solemn occasion. On that cold day, trucks piled high with the skins of lambs in variegated colors, their fatty entrails intact, drove through one neighborhood after another, picking up remains. For me, the cause of saving the thirsty and dying in a drought-stricken land did not mitigate the horror of the frightful events I was witnessing. My memories, even as I write today, stir emotions of horror. In retrospect, the slaughter helped concretize for me the political economy of scarcity. As I reflect on why I am interested in Darfur's anguish, I see that scarcity was stacked on those trucks dripping with blood and spewing exhaust from loud mufflers as they drove through the narrow alleys and bumpy roads of Omdurman.

By the 1980s, the narrative of Darfur's suffering shifted from roaming butchers to human catastrophe in desert regions ruined by drought and desertification. Famine propelled hundreds of thousands of people to flee from Darfur and Kordofan. They arrived in Khartoum in droves, seeking refuge and abode, and settled in an ad hoc camp called Al-Muailh in the southern part of the city, many miles from the national palace where President Gaffar Nimeiri lived in extravagant luxury, oblivious to the tragedy of those living under plastic tents in sweltering heat in yet another merciless desert. This was the context of my second Darfur memory, as my family and neighbors discussed how best to provide aid to the displaced women and children. In due course, clothes, mattresses, bedsheets, food, and over-the-counter medicines were being amassed. We, the youth volunteers, were instructed to inspect donated clothes for wearability before packing them neatly in cardboard boxes. I enjoyed the task. I basked in an atmosphere brimming with a sense of purpose and industry. Although we took pride in the philanthropy of kith and kin, my family emphasized that such effort is necessary but not sufficient. What would have been sufficient was a systematic effort by the state to exercise its responsibility toward citizens who had fallen on hard times. Populations displaced by these climatic conditions are currently referred to as "environmental refugees." The language is far from benign, for it gives the state a rationale for abdicating its responsibility.

These experiences opened up my thinking about the relation of politics to the appalling disparities between my conditions and those afflicting fellow Sudanese. Their memory stayed with me as my thinking slowly matured. As the country's leaders bemoaned "Mother Nature's wrath" over which the government had no control, citizens were left thirsty, hungry, and adrift. I concluded that the environmental factor in the devastation was due to the malignancy of the state's political and economic neglect and the complicity of those within the region whose material interests were aligned with those of the government to which they pledged allegiance. Environmental degradation was, in fact, a combination of "mother nature" and "father nature," the dictators who viewed daily transitions into vulnerability as the natural order of things. The causes of the Darfur crisis, which are multitudinous, with a complex range of narratives, truths, and approaches to understanding, became crystal clear to me even back then.

Upon graduating from college, I joined the Sudan Development Corporation (SDC), the largest development corporation in the Sudan, founded by the late Mohamed Abdel Majid Ahmed, Sudanese ambassador to France and Belgium, in the early 1980s. It was there that my third memory of Darfur was formed. Against incalculable odds, the SDC provided assistance and loans ranging in scale from small amounts of microcredit to large sums for projects such as iron ore foundries, marble quarries, and agriculture. I was appointed a junior development information officer, and my job was to maintain contacts with national, regional, and international partners and donors and create a trilingual (Arabic, English, French) newsletter to report progress on all three phases—feasibility, appraisal, and implementation—of development projects. I participated in field visits with international teams, an experience that exposed me to the economies, discourses, and practices of international development. My work for the SDC allowed me to see how some European companies viewed the Sudan at the time. For example, we received repeated requests from a European company to market asbestos products banned in the West to Sudanese building contractors, to which our CEO responded with a resounding "no!" Through experiences like this, institutionalized disparities on a world scale became obvious to me. Profit outweighed serious health risks to Third World people. Permanent lung damage and pleural disorders were of no concern to the company in question. Although efforts by the SDC were important for development projects in Western Sudan, including Darfur, unfortunately it could not by itself reduce poverty or change decades of institutionalized neglect. Western Darfur, like the South, was an incubator of grievances.

All three encounters taught me much about the underlying and persistent violence Darfuri people have had to endure from the colonial era to the present. Thus was the ibra, the lesson learned. These encounters also signified to me the importance of understanding the particular ways in which Darfur understands its own social, political, environmental, and economic grievances. My SDC experience in particular compelled me to engage in a sustained effort to understand the disparate voices, practices, and representations through which the stories about the Sudan are told. Later, as I embarked on my Darfur project, these memories propelled me to ask myself: Was my fear of the piles of bloody sheepskins on the backs of the trucks misplaced, or was it a sign of horrors to come?

Later Encounters

My experiences with Darfur have continued, and my quest to understand its endless troubles has resulted in more than ten years of ethnographic research in the Sudan, Qatar, and the United States. When I undertook this research, I saw that its purpose was not to create another book on Darfur, but rather to illuminate the wider meanings of the Sudan's fallibility, hence the title of this book. I also see *Darfur Allegory* as a logical extension of my two previous projects on the Sudan's polity: the identity, migration, and displacement of its people; and Sudanese refugees. Similar to these studies, this work is situated within the anthropology of war, forced migration, and broader questions of the global circulation of refugees. All have been envisioned as urgent interventions into the continuous humanitarian crisis in the Sudan, which is emblematic of the crisis in northeast Africa as a whole.

My main preoccupation has been to interrogate the categories used to represent race in Darfur, both historically and in the present. I draw attention to how these categories cannot be treated as a standalone subject, separate from their interaction and overlap within the local Darfuri sociopolitical sphere. I argue that these categories, especially the bifurcation of Arab versus African, derive from particular, culturally specific modes of thinking incongruent with the local understandings of Sudanese communities. Put simply, Arabism and Africanism were not on an inevitable collision course in the Sudan, as many observers have argued in their explanations of the primary causes of the crisis.

Furthermore, when I embarked on my first ethnographic project on Sudanese migrants and refugees in North America in the mid-1990s, Darfuri people were featured as fundamentally Northern Sudanese, no different from their countrymen and countrywomen from every part of the Sudan. No one identified himself/herself as Darfuri; no one used the idiomatic term "Dar-furian" as a singular identity. Everyone was Sudanese first and foremost. The situation has changed, and the term "Darfurian" now signifies a newly as-signed Black/indigenous identity, as opposed to that of a homogenized Arab Janjaweed perpetrator of ethnic cleansing. Journalists, NGO activists, and scholars who have applied earlier accounts of Southern Sudan to Darfur have been in error, insofar as those accounts turned centrally on a racial bifurca-tion that does not obtain in Darfur.

Unlike in my earlier work, my identity and methodology have intersected as this ethnography took new turns conceptually and experientially. It has led me to reflect on my subject position as a Sudanese anthropologist and on my own understanding of the early warning signs of disaster that I had pieced together from this earlier work. As a Sudanese writer, my subject po-sition changed in 2011 after the secession of the South. Now, inescapably, I write as a northerner, with all the connotations of power this implies. Key anthropological debates on "the re-identification of the ethnographer" vis-à-vis ethnographic writing now lie at the forefront of my role.[1] Nonetheless, this involuntarily acquired identity does not diminish my concerns about national self-definition, displacement, borders, political violence, and cross-cultural mediations, nor does it limit my concern with competing narratives of the situation in Darfur locally, regionally, and transnationally. Even more than my earlier work, this ethnography is rooted in the urgency of the pres-ent moment.

Methodologically, my research in disparate locations throughout the world has convinced me of the fluidity of the field as a locus of ethnographic research. Following James Clifford's view that "ethnographic texts are inescap-ably allegorical, and [that] a serious acceptance of this fact changes the ways they can be written and read,"[2] the specific contexts and situations in which I encountered "the field" shaped my ability to consider Darfur as allegory for the realities of a fragile state. In *Anthropological Locations: Boundaries and Grounds of a Field Science*, Akhil Gupta and James Ferguson interrogate the notion of a "field science," thereby opening theoretical and methodologi-cal possibilities for anthropologists to engage with beleaguered societies and global crises. As they write, "Anyone who has done fieldwork, or studies the phenomenon, knows that one does not just wander onto a 'field site' to engage in a deep and meaningful relationship with 'the natives.' The field is a clearing whose deceptive transparency obscures the complex processes that go into constructing it."[3] By constantly navigating and crossing frontiers of thought and experience, I have amassed ethnographic materials that tie the crisis in Darfur to the overall predicament of the Sudanese state and the politics of

Darfuri refugees abroad. Working from life histories and more focused narratives, participant observations, and statements and postings in the Sudanese blogosphere, I have been able to emphasize the competing narratives that drive national and international responses to the devastation of Darfur. As I have attempted to knit together several strands from these disparate field locations in what may be termed cartographies of mutuality, I have come to harbor no qualms as an anthropologist undertaking a prismatic role. For I hope to highlight wider "parallels and paradoxes," even if the task of illuminating my understanding of mutuality warrants an account of who I am. And so while I believe readers can discern my ideological position vis-à-vis the Darfur crisis by reading between the lines of what follows, they might also want a more explicit statement. I have no doubt that the crisis was—and remains—an act of state-sanctioned violence, a "counterinsurgency on the cheap" in the words of Alex de Waal.[4] Darfuris had every reason to rise up against decades of marginalization imposed upon them by then-president Al-Bashir and his predecessors. Yet it is also true the Justice and Equality Movement, which led the insurgency, was Islamist and ideologically not that different from Al-Bashir. Nonetheless, its breakup into two factions, the result of an internal power struggle, resulted in a movement away from Al-Bashir and had much to do with the intensification of violence in Darfur. Having said that, I reiterate that genuine grievances in the region cannot be brushed under the rug. That is why I concur with Abdel Khaliq Mahgoub's class-based analysis, one that does not turn on the Arab/African binary but rather adopts a more holistic view of the state-sanctioned exclusions and enforced silences of those who disagree politically with the ruling elites.

Let me conclude then by saying that through this work I have been made more aware of anthropology's deep engagement, both theoretically and practically, with contemporary predicaments, a move to be expected as we write "ethnography in today's world" and one that is timely and critical in Darfur. I see mutuality and urgency, concepts gaining currency in anthropology, as complementary, propelling us both to interrogate our subject positions vis-à-vis the interlocutors we encounter in fieldwork situations and to move beyond detachment and other "persuasive fictions of anthropology."[5]

Darfur in the Sudan

Darfur, the Sudan's westernmost region, is a frontier society. Its vast territory covers nearly 500,000 square kilometers within the Sahelian zone. Over the centuries, Darfur existed as an autonomous African sultanate like the other Sudanic kingdoms, including Sennar, Wadai, Bagirmi, Bornu, Hausa, and Melle,

among others.[6] It shares borders with Libya, Chad, the Central African Republic, and the Republic of South Sudan. By virtue of miscegenation and shared
communities straddling these frontiers, Darfur's territorial and ethnic borders
have been porous and fluid. Cosmopolitan networks facilitated an impressive
mobility, circulation, and exchange, contributing to the diverse peoples of this
African sultanate. These forms of circularity were evidenced in oral and written accounts before and after Darfur's annexation to the Sudan by the British
in 1916. Since the Sudan's independence in 1956, Darfur has witnessed a size-
able population increase.[7] These populations are invariably Muslim people who
speak a number of languages and hail from different ethnicities.

Darfur's geography falls within four primary zones, including rich savanna
in the south, poor savanna in the middle, arid zones in the north, and desert
in the west. The most prominent topographic feature is the Jebel Marra range.
Darfur comprises the following states: Northern Darfur (capital, El Fashir),
Western Darfur (capital, El Geneina), Southern Darfur (capital, Nyala), Central Darfur (capital, Zalengi), and Eastern Darfur (capital, Ed'dain). Nomadism and agriculture dominate economic activity in the region, although there
are some mixed economies. Land is central to social and economic arrangements. It is important to understand the role the system of land ownership
known as *hakoura* has played in the region's crisis. It is linked to the notion
of dar, meaning abode; Darfur acquired its name as the abode of the Fur.
The dar has historically been linked to sultanic grants of land ownership afforded to the three largest indigenous groups, the Fur, Zaghawa, and Masalit.
Smaller non-Arab ethnic groups and Arabs are not dar owners for the most
part. The Fur enjoy fertile lands stretching from Jebel Marra to Kuttum and
an ample rainfall that they celebrate annually in rain cults and ritual ceremo-
nials officiated by experts called *togonya*. As owners of dar, the Fur invented
sophisticated sub-dar administrative structures over centuries and accorded
titles to their local chiefs.

Darfur is no stranger to political violence enacted against its people. Rex
Seán O'Fahey's *The Darfur Sultanate: A History*, the result of forty years of
research, considered the local histories, anticolonial movements, and governance structures of this African kingdom, including the processes of state
formation in the precolonial period, the boundaries of state power, the end
of Darfur independence, and resistance to outsiders, 1873–74 and 1874–1916.
On this last point, O'Fahey charts a history of insurgencies, resistance to the
Turks, and a triumphal restoration of Darfur's autonomous identity from
1898, when the British colonized the Sudan, to 1916.[8] The euphemistically
termed Darfur Campaign unleashed a fury of colonial violence, ended Darfur's independence, massacred its last sultan, Ali Dinar, and annexed it to its

colonial condominium in the Sudan, which was generally recognized as a bridge linking the Arab and African worlds by virtue of both history and geography. Ever since, Darfur has existed as part of Arabized Northern Sudan, with which it shares the Islamic faith. It is worth noting that Darfuris refer to the history of outsiders' interference in the region as Umm Kwakiyya, the Damnation of Darfur.[9]

Ethnology

> If the Arabs constitute the most important link between Africa and Asia, the Sudanese constitute the most important link between Arab Africa and Negro Africa. There is first the very phenomenon of racial mixture and intermarriage in the northern parts of the Sudan, coupled with the fact a large proportion of Arab Sudanese are in fact Arabized Negroes, rather than ethnically Semitic. For many of them the Arabness is a cultural acquisition, rather than a racial heredity.
>
> ALI A. MAZRUI, "The Multiple Marginality of the Sudan"[10]

When Arab geographers called the region "the Land of the Blacks," they drew upon complexion to label Sudanese Arabs as first and foremost Black Arabs. This, however, had not been the case during British rule (1898–1956), in which the politics of race drew primarily on a taxonomy of Black versus white, a categorization deemed immutable. Complexion was a driving force in colonial policies: the fairer-skinned, whom the British believed superior in both racial and intellectual terms, received preferential treatment. These notions were codified in colonial segregation policies, including the Closed Districts Ordinance (CDO) passed in the 1930s, which limited interactions between the (presumably fair-skinned) Arab North and the (presumably darker-skinned) South and Darfur. This program was the brainchild of Harold A. MacMichael, who joined the colonial service in the Sudan in 1905. He served as political officer with the Darfur Expeditionary Force and was later promoted to sub-governor of the region, where he served until 1934.[11] With this ordinance, British colonial ideology succeeded in inscribing race into history, resulting in overwhelming distortions and contradictions in the sociopolitical organization of the postcolonial Sudanese state.

British colonial anthropologists, who served in the region in diverse administrative capacities, attempted to chart its ethnicities and languages. MacMichael himself, who drew heavily on his own experience in the region as well as the well-known travel accounts of Muḥammad Ibn-'Umar al-Tūnisī and Gustav Nachtigal, divided the population of Darfur into Arab and non-Arab races. His work also showed a high degree of fragmentation among Darfur's various lineages. The extensive charts of these communities' lines of descent are too large to cite in their entirety, but noting the differences within the lineages of the three main stakeholders in the current conflict may be useful for challenging the essentialism with which outsiders have come to see Darfur's diverse population. According to MacMichael, the Zaghawa lineage is divided into more than twenty branches (Arteyt, Mirra, Akaba, Katinga, Kobbe, Kabila, Kugba, Wayra, Bigi, Bursu, and Erla, among others); the Masalit into fifteen smaller lineages (Fokunuing, Misterinn, Asumuu, Serbung, Maratti, Niem, Mingiri, Ajmung, Abdurr, Keriung, Kusube, Forung, Amunung, Dag, and Mundera); and the Fur, the largest group in Darfur, into three primary groups (Kunjara, Karakirit, and Temurka).

Other African sublineages were also noted to include the Guraan, the Midob, the Berti, the Tama, the Tunjur, the Daju, the Birked, the Gimir, the Bayko, the Mima, and the Bedayat. The extent of prevailing divisions within Darfur is thus apparent in MacMichael. Nonetheless, given rigid notions about the racial homogeneity of Darfur's ethnic communities and their labeling as "indigenous black African Zaghawa," "Masalit," and "Fur," it is important to recognize that MacMichael used his ethnographic knowledge to inform policy. O'Fahey has critiqued this work as "entrapping the reader in the mire of Arab pedigrees" and holds that "the genealogical approach has small utility."[12] Although I am in full agreement with O'Fahey about the need to depart from genealogical charts, which fail to illuminate fusions among these groups, MacMichael's work is illustrative of colonial thinking about race and the way it was used to justify ethnic preference. It gives us the seeds for understanding the historicity of marginality and exclusion, which has persisted with terrible tenacity in the postcolonial period.

The Arab tribes in Darfur, mainly pastoralist nomads although some are sedentary, consist of the Habania, Beni Hussein, Ziyadia, Beni Helba, Djawama, Rezeigat, and Maharia, in addition to the Arab urban merchants and government officials mainly of Jellaba origin.[13] It must be stressed that Darfur Arabs are Black Arabs and thus indistinguishable from others in the region. Speaking to the similarities of Darfur Arabs to the other African ethnicities, Lampen notices:

> The Baggara (Arabs) tribes . . . are largely intermarried with black blood due to their proximity to the black tribes of the Bahr el Ghazal [in Southern Sudan]. One sees a small portion of light brown skins, but most of them are very dark. They are not insensitive to the possession of Negro colour and features, and accordingly they pitch the scales of colour low.[14]

Ethnological portraits painted by leading Darfur-born anthropologists illustrate the validity of seeing the ethnological history of these Arab communities as "a history of mixtures and movements, contacts and connections."[15] Lampen's account is useful in our effort to question narratives of innate identity, indigenous or otherwise, on the basis of complexion. These narratives represent Darfuri-Arab identities as dictated by fate rather than politics and therefore as not amenable to change.

Two excerpts from narratives I have gathered can serve as an entry into an interrogation of this notion of Arab as a fixed category. A forty-five-year-old asylum seeker in Europe replied to my inquiry about it this way:

> My father is Masalit and my mother is from the Beni Hussein Arabs. When he asked her family to marry her, he told them that he is a Beni Rashid, another branch of Darfur's Arabs. In physical terms, he was indistinguishable from them. My mother was aware of the truth. Her parents accepted and blessed the wedding immediately. They only found out about the truth of his Masalit identity after my first sibling was born. My maternal grandmother used to joke with us about it. The whole thing passed without incident. My parents stayed married till death did them part.

A woman activist whom I interviewed in Washington, D.C., shared a similar story about her mixed descent when she mentioned tongue-in-cheek that "my maternal uncles are Fur, but my paternal uncles are Janjaweed [meaning of Arab extraction]." These statements and others I have recorded demonstrate that the binary of Arab and African used in various representations of the current conflict did not assume paramount importance in the past. They also represent the best challenge to the essentialism that obscures the pliability of ethnic identification in Darfur.

In my research, it became unmistakable that easy impressions regarding these categories are entirely insufficient for understanding Darfur's taxonomies of power and polity or even identity. In a hybrid society such as that of Darfur, where polygamy helped create multiple identities, both Arab and African people live and breathe the diversity of mixed descent. Invocations of a genealogical relationship to the Prophet Mohammad as Ashraaf descendants are sometimes encountered in both communities. Bad politics rather than biology has been pointed out to me in different contexts as the reason why significant efforts have been made to chart these communities as non-consanguine. Another manifestation of Darfur's diversity is the multitude of languages and dialects spoken in addition to Arabic, the lingua franca.[16] Bilingualism is common, suggesting both regular interethnic communications and a tolerance of difference.

Adding to the complexity of Darfuri identity is social segmentation by occupation and political affiliation, which have helped people negotiate ethnicity and race in ways distinct from that of the colonizers. As anthropologist Sharif Harir tells us: "Despite the apparent separateness of ethnic groups, expressed and misleadingly reified by separate ethnic territories, separate languages, autonomous internal political systems, and considerable variations in cultural and societal forms, they [Darfuri communities] are interdependent as groups sharing the same region which has been subjected to centralization of the state over a long span of time."[17] Throughout my fieldwork, solidarity among Arabs and Africans has been presented as the ultimate organizing principle in a hybrid social formation. Several accounts highlighted large-scale inter-ethnic forms of engagement among Darfuri peoples in commodity exchange and sociality governed by mutually recognized cultural norms and negotiated agreements. Economic forces and the dominant modes of production, which included nomadism and agriculture, necessitated cooperation, for they were seen as complementary rather than competitive enterprises. Farmers traded their products in the marketplace, and the livestock of nomads fertilized everyone's land.

These productive relations have had an important influence on self-identification and "ethnic options," a phenomenon that drew the attention of Fredrik Barth, the most prominent anthropologist of the 1950s and 1960s, who produced cutting-edge monographs relevant to broader anthropological debates about race and ethnicity, ideology, and political economy, developed on the basis of ethnographic fieldwork in Darfur.[18] One of the first generation of historians and anthropologists to recognize the malleability of ethnicity in the region, Barth demonstrated how the process of identity formation is linked to a variety of imperatives, particularly economic conditions. For example, he argued that a Fur whose primary mode of production has been farming can become an Arab upon acquiring enough animals to become a nomadic pastoralist; similarly, if circumstances afford nomads the opportunity to farm, they become Fur. This explanation has been useful not only for understanding Fur-Arab relations but also for developing a social theory that challenges the tendency to abstract social relationships from their economic roots and political context. Quite simply, Darfur does not lend itself to the easy binary of Arab versus indigenous Black African as a grand narrative of its people's identities.

Challenging essentialism is not intended to ignore the mounting political and economic pressures that have entrapped the people of Darfur in intersecting systems of violence since the 1980s. The amicability of group relations notwithstanding, these communities have not been ignorant of their interests and concerns in times of heightened competition over scarce resources. Rather, prior to the 1980s, these quarrels were neither cast in racial terms nor addressed by the brute force with the resulting quagmire characteristic of subsequent years. Neither the politicization of ethnicity that came to figure centrally in Sudan's postcolonial politics nor the broader political, social, and economic realities of a country that emerged as a place of raw violence after independence can be apprehended without understanding this history of racial and ethnic categorization. Darfur's recent history emanates from a lethal and combustible mix of corruption, oppression, and indifference, resulting in something akin to what Douglas Robinson calls "the somatics of postcolonial culture."[19]

Genealogies of Conflict

SOME CONTEXT

It must be remembered that Darfur is a Northern Sudanese region within a fragile state. In the 2018 Fragile States Index it ranked fifth, following the Republic of South Sudan, Somalia, the Central African Republic, and Yemen. Ranking is based on a variety of indicators gathered by the index curators, including mounting demographic pressures, massive movement of refugees or internally displaced persons, sharp or severe economic decline, the degree of the state's legitimacy, progressive deterioration of public services, violations of human rights and the rule of law, a weakened security apparatus, rise of factionalized elites, and intervention of external actors.[20] The conditions that placed the country among the top ranks of fragility and failure have inflicted extraordinary suffering and sorrow on a large swath of the Sudanese populations, including those in the widely perceived "privileged North," as well as in Darfur and the South.

State failure in both North and South is the result of numerous linked events. Following a protracted civil war and with persistent American and African mediation in Naivasha, Kenya, political adversaries in North and South signed a peace agreement in 2005 providing for power and wealth sharing as well as a referendum to determine the future of the South after a six-year waiting period. Accordingly, in 2011 South Sudanese voted overwhelming for independence. Meanwhile, catalyzed by South Sudan's struggle, in 2003 two insurgent groups in Darfur, the Justice and Equality Movement (JEM) and the Sudanese Liberation Movement (SLM), though ideologically opposed—the former avowedly Islamist and the latter secularist—had found common purpose when they decided to attack government facilities in Darfur to protest their exclusion from the highest echelons of wealth and power, thereby catalyzing the latest of the crises that have tormented Darfur since the colonial period. John Ryle, writing at the early stages of the insurgency, suggests further linkages between the South Sudanese and Darfuri resistance movements and sets the latter in broader context:

> The timing of the insurgency in Darfur was dictated by the Naivasha Agreement. Low-level fighting among communities in western Sudan (all of which are Muslim) has been endemic since the late 1980s, when a war broke out between Arabs and Fur, two of the ethnic groups involved in the present conflict. During the 1990s, the apparent impunity enjoyed by militias drawn from Arab communities in Darfur—and the growth of their political influence—confirmed anxieties on the part of the Fur and other non-Arab groups that they were losing political ground.[21]

The Darfuri resistance movement has continued to struggle against the effacement of its region, even as the Sudanese government's response, effected by a proxy militia called Janjaweed (Devils on Horsebacks), has destroyed the region. Official responses have constructed two opposing narratives. The first, developed by the International Commission of Inquiry (ICOI) on Darfur, which was constituted in September 2004, pursuant to United Nations Security Council Resolution 1564, states that the government of the Sudan has not pursued a policy of genocide although crimes against humanity were committed, perpetrated by government officials, militia forces, rebel groups, and certain foreign army officers acting in their personal capacity.[22] The second, advanced by the International Criminal Court (ICC) in response to UN Security Council Resolution 1593, argues that the Sudanese government launched a massive campaign of genocide against the six million people of Darfur. Both positions are represented in the ICC's charges against Sudanese president Omar Al-Bashir (ruled 1989–2019). In an unprecedented move against a sitting president, the former prosecutor of the ICC, Luis Moreno Ocampo, issued arrest warrants on March 4, 2009, and July 12, 2010, the first for crimes against humanity and rape, the second for genocide.[23]

These warrants were in response to the failure of the Sudanese special prosecutor appointed by the government to investigate reports of war crimes in Darfur and to take legal action against the perpetrators, both Sudanese government militias and Darfuri rebels, a fact that itself suggests the impunity characteristic of the country's judiciary. Then-president Al-Bashir refused the ICC's persistent demand to turn over alleged war criminals, declaring unequivocally, "We will not surrender a cat to foreigners, let alone a Sudanese citizen." Although the government received most of the opprobrium for the perpetration of violence, the ICOI report also recognized atrocities committed by the insurgent groups:

Both rebel movements have been party to systematic abuses of human rights amounting to war crimes as defined within international humanitarian law. Rebel human rights abuses followed a pattern. They have included systematic attacks on nomadic communities and the destruction of numerous Arab villages. They have included the murder, wounding, and abduction of civilians and the rape of women. Rebels have also carried out hundreds of armed robberies throughout Darfur, and in so doing killing many civilians. . . . On 27 March 2003, rebel forces led by [forces affiliated] with Abdel Wahid Mohamed Nour murdered twelve soldiers in Buram hospital by burning them alive. Darfur rebels have also murdered several aid workers, foreign and Sudanese, and abducted scores of others. They have also attacked and looted dozens of relief convoys carrying food aid to Darfur's displaced communities.[24]

The warrants against Al-Bashir and his response are discussed more fully in chapter 4. Here it is sufficient to say that this conflict revived the Umm Kwakiyya of Darfur's past. It devastated the region's economy, shredded its fragile social fabric, drove 2.7 million people from their homes, and created an unstable environment filled with fear, misery, and scorched earth. Human rights organizations estimate the death toll at 400,000, although the government of the Sudan challenged these statistics. According to Mahmood Mamdani, total mortality has not been disaggregated to differentiate between deaths caused directly by the military and militia and by displacement and other circumstances related to the crisis and those entirely unrelated to either.[25] Before 2003, Darfur was an enigma to many in the international community, including the celebrities, humanitarians, politicians, and Google publicists who have since taken up a campaign to "Save Darfur." These newly enlightened advocates have too readily cast the conflict in terms of racial binaries inherited from the past, with Arab people of the region depicted as villains and the Black indigenous tribes of Zaghawa, Masalit, and Fur as victims. It is important, therefore, to turn to a brief discussion of the causes of intercommunity violence and the reactions to it. The need to do so is more urgent than ever, as the repatriation of internally displaced persons and refugees has become a top priority for all the stakeholders.

CAUSES OF THE CONFLICT

In 2009, at a sizable rally in Southern Darfur featured on Sudan TV at the height of international attention to the Darfur crisis, Al-Bashir shifted responsibility for it to the supernatural world: "Curse the Satan who got into your midst and wreaked havoc. Brothers, it is Satan who pushed you to do what you have done to one another. Curse him, curse him." While none of the displaced persons, community elders, and refugees I spoke with over the course of my research mentioned Satan as instigator of the crisis, they did seem to have reached a consensus on the genealogies of conflict, prime among them obliteration of native governance, marginalization, environmental degradation, militarization of identity, and banditry. Each of these has merit as an explanation of the conflict, and I consider them in turn below, but with several caveats. First, no cause can be apprehended in isolation from the others, and I have tried to highlight the interdependence of the various problems behind the conflict. Second, these explanations, individually and in their intersections, are replete with complexities and even contradictions, which I have also tried to tease out. Third, I frequently encountered a conflation of causes and effects, but in the context of telling the story this is inevitable. Finally, the various explanations as I heard them were frequently inflected with political undertones and self-interest. Notwithstanding my own interventions, I present the narratives I gathered the way they were recorded, in the voices as I heard them.

First among the stated causes, the obliteration of native governance, is rooted in a long history. Following its annexation to the Sudan in 1916, Darfur was governed indirectly through local leaders (sheikhs, sharatys, meliks, and salatin). Yet the practice had been in place prior to that. As A. B. Theobald has written:

> The [colonial] Sudan Government, itself faced by the formidable problem of administering a vast country which had been devastated by almost continual fighting for seventeen years, and which was certain to be a financial liability for many years to come, was unwilling to undertake the addition[al] burden of governing distant and bankrupt Darfur. Ali Dinar was therefore recognized as the ruler so long as he "was obedient to the Government's authority and complied with its orders," and paid a nominal tribute of 500 pounds annually.[26]

Timing notwithstanding, delegating administrative authority locally was part of a broader pattern of colonial neglect of the region, which according to Martin W. Daly was codified in 1922 when "the first legislation to promote Indirect Rule was enacted. The Powers of Nomad Sheikhs Ordinance, which recognized and regularized the administrative and judicial authority of several hundred shaykhs, was limited to nomadic tribes, where such power—and more—was already wielded."[27] Indirect Rule thus consolidated the region's marginality as the British essentially left the region to its own devices, paying no heed to developing its infrastructure.

Although linked to a colonial calculus, native governance enjoyed considerable support within Darfur, particularly in its approach to administering justice. After annexation, scarce resources led some to take up banditry. Native leaders easily mediated skirmishes between nomads and farmers over water and pasture, for example by summoning together alleged perpetrators, including bandits and criminals, and bringing them to justice after days of deliberations. Tensions escalated over time, but quarrels were immediate and environmental rather than primordial and cultural. This local justice mechanism was known as Judia, and its adjudicators, including tribal leaders, nazirs, and omdas, were referred to as Ajaweed. These mediators, cognizant of the environmental degradation that underlay the increasing frequency of these quarrels, strove to be impartial. With enormous moral authority and the ability to leverage relationships, they served local justice and eased tensions. Sudanese anthropologists Jérôme Tubiana, Victor Tanner, and Musa Adam Abdul-Jalil describe the adjudication process:

> *Ajawid* generally do not impose punitive sanction, and may recommend arrangements of coexistence, such as sharing water resources or agreeing on migration routes and on when to activate them. But in intertribal disputes, and especially when the government is involved, they may impose punishments. Moreover, it seems that historically their power was largely moral, allowing them to order social punishment, especially on someone who refuses the decisions of the *judiya*. He will be labeled *kassar al-khawatir* (breaker of feelings) and ostracized by his own community, to the point he might have to leave the area.[28]

A woman from Eddein whom I interviewed, bemoaning the destruction of the Judia, recognized its efficiency:

> *I have witnessed an event in which a member of the native court responded to a complaint about a conflict between two communities, which was instigated by a belligerent nomad. He stood up and cut off a leaf from a tree. He summoned a man from his community and ordered him, "See this moist leaf? I want you to arrest the perpetrator immediately and bring him to me before the leaf dries."*

Although postcolonial writers have expressed legitimate misgivings about native administration as a colonial remnant, the communities' faith in this institution remained unshakeable over decades, a point taken up in chapter 4. The proficiency of their chiefs served as both deterrence and assurance of little tolerance of aggression. To a great extent a shared moral code militated against defiance of a Judia ruling by either plaintiff and defendant.

In 1971, however, dictator Gaffar Nimeiri (ruled 1969–85) eviscerated native administration by presidential decree under the guise of obliterating "tribal" attachments and kin networks, thereby transforming Darfur's local structures for administering justice. The authority of revered chiefs shifted to unfamiliar administrative and judicial councils populated by government sympathizers, a shift that many Darfuris understand as contributing to the current crisis. In the words of a son of a former Ma'alia chief whom I interviewed in Doha in 2009:

> Long time ago when bandits ran havoc in our community, my father would send people to capture and bring them to him. He worked in counsel with other chiefs and took necessary measures for bringing the stolen animals back. Our native leaders followed all the principles of transitional justice talked about today. No one who is not familiar with the power of native leaders could appreciate the magnitude of loss that our region endured as a result of their marginalization. Right now, no one is competent to catch a rabbit, let alone an armed thief.

Subsequently, Nimeiri further disrupted traditional forms of governance by appointing as leaders loyalists who were invested in self-aggrandizement rather than in addressing the needs of the Darfuri people. These actions, politically expedient for his military dictatorship, enjoyed a wide base of support among his followers. At the same time, they created significant confusion over the neutrality of local authorities in Darfur. The resulting vacuum proved impossible to fill, given the state's long indifference to Darfur. The Declaration of Regional Governance of 1974 further divided a once-unified region. From the start it courted controversy and was met with massive protests in the region.

The failure to recognize the role of the colonial state in sowing the seeds of marginality, itself the second explanation for the conflict, is common to both academic and public writings on Darfur, if not the Sudan at large, a tendency that produces an ahistorical reading of the multivariate indices of marginality and exclusion that "fails to deal with the texted character of [colonial] agents and histories, and the discursively complex nature of their endeavors."[29] Thus when *The Black Book: Imbalance of Power and Wealth in Sudan* was published in 2000,[30] its authors, who until recently were anonymous, emphasized the failings of the postindependence government towards the marginalized areas of the country. Like the 1957 Hutu Manifesto, which polarized Rwandan Hutus and Tutsis along racial lines, the authors attempted to link marginality to race, drawing extensively on statistical analyses to make their case. For example, calculating the identity of ministers serving the government since independence, they concluded that the preponderance descended from Arab Riverain communities and that non-Arab representation was nominal. They questioned President Omar Al-Bashir's interpretation of the correct sharia and promoted democratic reforms, land development, justice, *shura* (consultation), and implementation of divine law, thereby illustrating the deeply rooted Islamist ideology they hoped to reclaim.[31]

The *Black Book*'s emphasis on marginality as a product of racial differences did not succeed in illuminating the multilayered sociopolitical and economic features of the postcolonial state in the Sudan. This, however, negates neither Darfur's marginality nor the fairness of the demand to address genuine grievances over the government's emphasis on the Sudan's Arab—as opposed to African—identity, further politicizing its longstanding neglect of Darfur. An interviewee from Nyala with whom I had extensive conversations expressed justifiable angst:

> *Sudan TV and radio are dominated by people whose Arabization project or their so-called civilization project since this government seized power is geared to Arabs. The shows such as* Sahet al fida *[Battlefields of Sacrifice], which show characters speaking classical Arabic, are imported from Saudi Arabia and commemorate the killings of anyone deemed other or outcast. [These are] coupled with programs on fatwa where Saudi clerics and Sudanese extremists are always ready to volunteer absurd views about proper Muslim and good behavior, what to dress, what to eat, what kind of life you are supposed to lead by looking back at virtuous ancestors* [al salaf al salih]—*all come in one package. Just remember, these are all imported ideologies from Arabia. How can you not feel marginalized or excluded? Gone are the people like Al Tayeb Mohamed Al Tayeb, who decades ago worked hard through popular images of folklore to show the diversity of our country and the richness of our lives and contributions to a diverse, inclusive culture. There is no respect for this heritage; we all have to be brought into the fold of Arabia somehow.*

A more nuanced analysis of the troubles that drove the country to become an "ungovernable space" can be found in the foundational texts of the Sudanese intellectual Abdel Khaliq Mahgoub (1927–1971), which combined textual analysis, a deep knowledge of history, and rigorous critique to probe the iniquities overwhelming the Sudanese social scene.[32] As early as 1947 Mahgoub recognized signs of weakness that have now become reality, including the country's fragmented nationalism, hierarchy and the reduction of colonial forms of power, militancy and militarism, and enforced silences and exclusions. For the current discussion, however, his work gives insight into the enduring marginalization and neglect effected by colonial governance and postcolonial forms of surrogacy in Africa.

As he tells it, Africa's mayhem cannot be understood in isolation from a critical assessment of the emergence of a privileged few who rose as the new epicenter of power and authority in the Sudan after independence. In his view, instead of promoting a more democratic society, this mostly Muslim and Arabized elite, mimicking their colonial predecessors, moved rapidly to acquire power and property in a market in which the Sudanese citizen was the cheapest commodity, to be ignored and disdained. In the northern provinces of Khartoum, Kassala, and Darfur, semifeudal exploitation abounded. In the South, a weakening of the subsistence economy and the failure to promote equality were conscious attempts by the state to accumulate and circulate surplus among the wealthiest, thereby imperiling the entire country. Human rights violations in Darfur therefore need to be squarely situated within this fraught context.

In making his case, Mahgoub understood what he was up against: elite ideology, feudal mentality, existing relations of production, and the deeper impediments created by those invested in the existing establishment. Yet his views were corroborated by careful ethnographic accounts that appeared after his death, when, despite considerable odds, the Left played an important role in advancing a social movement that raised national consciousness and encouraged popular attention to economic and political matters. Nonetheless as the years wore on, conservative forces maintained the status quo. Mahgoub's greatest contribution, the bedrock of his theoretical debates about nation, class, and culture, may be his commitment to deeply analytic thinking. To him this was itself a transformative act, and his confrontations with issues that span national frontiers, such as the persistence of old colonial structures, postcoloniality, modernity, and traditionalism, are germinal to understanding the seeds of state weaknesses.

Third, although often obscured as a factor in the current conflict, the impact of environmental degradation on the conflict between farmers and nomads, whose livelihoods relied overwhelmingly on rainfall, merits a closer look. The impact of drought and desertification in the late 1970s and early 1980s was compounded by the state's failure to gauge the effects of climatic erosion on communities and adopt development projects that could have circumvented natural trends as well as measures to mitigate their deadly reach. Thus environmental devastation was directly tied to political dynamics in the country, and the resulting hunger, thirst, and environmental erosion led to intractable hostilities. Nimeiri's indifference and the indifference of his successors in the face of increasing clashes between nomads and settled farmers over land use, water resources, communal grazing, and pastoral paths triggered immense vulnerabilities including famine, displacement, and refugee flows. The inhabitants of the northern, western, and eastern parts of Darfur, including the Zaghawa, the Berti, the Gimir, the Midob, the Ziyadia, and the Rezeigat (both Arabs and Africans), suffered equally from the intercommunal wrath generated by the environmental crisis. Violence was rampant; to note only a few examples, the Zaghawa both fought each other and against the Gimir; the Turjur fought against the Fur, the Fur against the Arabs, the Taisha against the Salamat.

Rural development specialists in Darfur noted that frictions over natural resources so overwhelmed large areas in Jebel Marra, Garsilla, Kebkabiya, and El Geneina that both local and national governments were incapable of addressing them. Tensions were exacerbated by the arrival of Chadian camel nomads who displayed little deference to existing rules regulating communal systems in the region. Moreover, government actions as noted above had radically changed the prevailing values of cooperation and mutuality, which could have offset some of the worst consequences of the disaster. In the words of Nazir Yehia Adam Madibo:

> Despite the erosion of native administration, it [had] helped reconcile severe conflicts over resources and theft. Even with the politicization of a revered institution, nomadic Arabs and African farmers often resorted to it for resolution. The violence of today is qualitatively different, with tribal militarization and mobilization that changed relationships and fragmented communities to the point of no return.

The ending of native government coupled with militarization had produced an atmosphere in which the rights of citizens to safety and well-being have been lost.

Fourth, the militarization of ethnic identities has been paramount in the metamorphosis of communal disputes in Darfur. As a community nazir told me in Doha, where he was attending a peace conference in 2009:

> It is a huge mistake to talk about 2003 as the exact date for the eruption of violence in Darfur. The region was militarized since the democratic rule of Prime Minister Al-Sadiq Al-Mahdi [1987–1989], who armed Arab groups in Southern Darfur to fight their neighboring Dinka, with whom they share grazing land. He wanted also to expand their duties to fight the forces of rebellion in Southern Sudan. His prejudices against non-Arabs were as detrimental as the policies he put in place to invent militias called displacers [murahleen]. These people were given a wide mandate to attack, kill, and destroy, a duty they heeded fully.

The nazir, who drew on deep memory of the sociopolitical dynamics in his community and its interactions with others in the region, was correct. At the time indicated in his account, both Hassan Al-Turabi, who subsequently headed the Popular Congress Party, and his brother-in-law Al-Sadiq Al-Mahdi envisioned the creation of a so-called Arab alliance, a project they subsequently implemented on a violent scale. In the mid-1980s, Arabized communities in the Sudan had formed what was known as the Arab Congregation, an alliance designed to lobby for official and financial backing from both the central government and the national political parties in support of the cause of the Arabs in the region. Their ultimate political goal was the ethnic cleansing of what they saw as African tribes (Zurqa) in Darfur in order to encourage the settlement of Arabized tribes of the region.

According to Sulieman Hamid, a human rights activist whose work represents the most reliable source on the Darfur tragedy and whose contributions to political theory are discussed in chapter 3, the formation of the Arab alliance prompted the two leaders to look for allies beyond national borders, in Chad and Libya. The actual execution of the project, which came to be known as the Arab-Islamic Security Belt, commenced in 1987 when twenty-three leaders from Arabized communities signed a letter to then–prime minister Al-Mahdi, claiming common Arabic origins in the Sudan dating to the fifteenth century and that 70 percent of the current population of Darfur descended from these ancestors. According to Hamid,

> They demanded to be represented, at the least, by 50 percent of the constitutional positions within both regional and national governments. They warned against neglect of the issue of representation of their Arabic elements; to do so would result in dire consequences. The composition of the new regional government in Darfur in 1988 didn't satisfy their hopes; hence the executive committee of their organization circulated a confidential statement to the membership with a number of resolutions, which were approved and adopted, with all members pledging under oath to implement them.[33]

Hamid goes on to identify these resolutions, thereby exposing the mechanisms by means of which the alliance sought to operationalize the Arab-Islamic Security Belt project. These included increasing the number of volunteers in Zurqa areas in order to destabilize security, halt production, and liquidate tribal chiefs; instigating disputes amongst Zurqa tribes themselves to undercut any tendency toward unified action; concentrating services in areas where the alliance enjoyed authority and influence; excluding members of Zurqa tribes from important positions and placing obstacles in the path of those who held leading administrative positions when possible; and working by all possible means to disturb social stability in the Zurqa tribes' areas.

During Al-Mahdi's tenure as prime minister, the activities of the Arab-Islamic Security Belt increased markedly, becoming organized military activity. Under the leadership of Sheikh Musa Hilal, the chief of the Mahameed Arabs, the recruitment of Janjaweed proxy militias took a highly organized form under the authority of the Arab alliance. This development, coupled with new forms of mobilizing regular troops, furthered political unrest in Darfur. It became obvious to the people of Darfur that their new community leaders were political pawns who pledged allegiance to leaders who violated their right to stability, livelihood, freedom of movement, and access to justice.

The declaration issued in 1992 by the Military Operations Management, a military unit affiliated with the alliance, reflects the scale of the plot against the Zurqa and the organization's goals. Strategies for creating chaos in the region were quite clear, as Hamid summarizes:

> Burn down and annihilate all countryside areas indicated in the plan. The *omdas* [county chiefs] and sheikhs should insure the loyalty of all their subordinates, under oath, in carrying out the instructions and seek the support of volunteers from non-Arab tribes such as the Zaghawa for military procedures and training purposes. In addition, carefully study the geography of the region to make sure that only populations earmarked for obliteration are targeted. Usurp all the cattle and herds belonging to the Fur tribe by all possible means. Physically liquidate all Fur leaders, representatives, and intellectuals; restrict the movement of the remaining Fur in towns and prisons; and revert to assassinations whenever possible. Bring all means of movement or mobility, such as the ability to get to the police or to summon rescue teams, to a standstill and sabotage all means of communication. Locate Arab troop camps high in mountain areas out of reach of enemy troops. Send quick military support to reinforce any Arab movements in areas within enemy territory. Relocate Arab immigrants from Chad in Arab-dominated areas such as Wadi Salih, Makajar, and Wadi Kaja. Distribute the Popular Defense Forces of Arab origin mobilized from Kordofan in areas in the south and southwest such as Kass, Jebel Marra, and Wadi Barry.[34]

Hamid goes on to quote Lieutenant-general Adam Musa, governor of Western Darfur State, as he described the buildup of forces: "The nomads and the Popular Defense Forces were allowed to carry weapons, which eventually led to the spread of weapons and gave rise to armed disputes." It is noteworthy that Musa's statement assumed a merger of Arab alliance militia troops with National Islamic Front forces represented by the Popular Defense Forces into one unified army and that the organization had a free hand to distribute the combined troops according to its own discretion. This development, coupled with the flow and affordability of smuggled weapons, worsened the situation in Darfur over time. The Murahleen militia turned Janjaweed, and their forces were swiftly reinforced by mercenaries from other African countries to crush the insurgency in Darfur initiated in 2003 by JEM and SLM. The resulting acceleration in violence, including genocidal killings, pillaging and burning of villages and farms, and the usurpation of cattle and wealth, forced more and more people from the targeted groups to flee Darfur. Despite the outcry of the international community, the government kept dragging its feet, failing to halt the conflict according to the terms of the peace agreement negotiated with UN Secretary-General Kofi Anan in early 2004, under the pretext that insufficient time had been allotted to do so.

Although Sheikh Musa Hilal's role as militia leader is incontrovertible, he has denied direct association with the Janjaweed by noting in countless media interviews that they are criminals and thieves. Having engineered the genocide against Zaghawa, Fur, and Masalit, in 2012 Hilal gave his daughter in marriage to Chadian Zaghawa president Idris Deby, as a disposition of the spuriousness of the claims against him as perpetrator of ethnic cleansing through his Janjaweed militias. The polygamous president, who at the time of the marriage was in his sixties, paid $26 million in dowry to marry this much younger woman. As reported by the *Sudan Tribune*, the capital city of Khartoum was indeed gripped by these lavish nuptials.[35] Although this move may have cast doubt on Hilal's role in the violence in Darfur, there is no question about the scale of destruction meted out against innocent civilians there. The government's actions represented the peak of the ethnicization and militarization of Darfuri identities under both democratic and military rule. Ironically, it was discovered, on the occasion of his daughter's marriage, that Hilal, although always referred to as a Mahameed Arab, was himself matrilineally of Zaghawa ancestry. His political opportunism was further evidenced when, some years later, he turned against the Al-Bashir government and flirted with an alliance with the Fur.[36]

Finally, in cataloging causes of conflict in Darfur, we find some implausible explanations: for example, Libyan leader Muammar al-Qaddafi was reported as stating to students at Cambridge University, "You may laugh to know that the root cause of the Darfur crisis was a dispute over a stolen camel." His statement, though seemingly absurd, has a grain of truth, as banditry has also figured centrally in myriad accounts of the disorder and terror in the region and the resulting displacement, death, and destruction.

A characteristic of nomadic societies, banditry is deeply steeped in Darfur's history. Early travelers, colonial administrators, scholars, novelists, journalists, and other commentators wrote about it extensively,[37] drawing largely on oral traditions based on descriptions of cattle rustling and camel theft, often attributed to the Zaghawa people. Within Sudanese public culture, this early form of banditry is referred to as *hambatta*, understood to be relatively benign and governed by certain codes such as refraining from robbing the poor. Praised in prose and poetry, the hambatta (men) were lauded for bravery and lionized both for exacting revenge from enemies and for acts of distributive justice, akin to the legend of Robin Hood. However, when these moral codes were not adhered to and robbery and injury resulted, perpetrators were subjected to *haraba* or warfare punishment in accordance with sharia. Over time, banditry came to take on different meanings, depending on whether the catalyst was revenge, tribal feuding, or redistribution of goods.

Historically, local mechanisms for meting out justice helped assuage the spread of lawlessness. As late as 1965, the native administration intervened in fights between the Midob and the Kababish in Northern Darfur related to banditry. From 1989 to 2000, the local government was forced to intervene in Zaghawa banditry against the Gimir and the Mima in Northern and Southern Darfur. Although crimes of banditry are considered haraba and amputations sanctioned according to the judicial verdict of *had al-haraba*, there is no evidence that these penalties were ever imposed. Rather, punishments were limited to the return of stolen animals, compensation for losses, and threats of amputation if the offense was repeated.

Unlike banditry in the past, which was imbued with social meaning, the present version, entangled in the political chaos overrunning the country and across the border, is associated with criminality, war, and militarization. Boundaries between bandits, militias, Janjaweed, and other refugees in the region have been blurred, adding a further layer of chaos to the already complex emergency situation in Darfur. As an interviewee from El Fashir, fifty-six-year-old Isshaq, put it: *"Banditry is happening because of the anarchy all around. Banditry is not about need but about power. It is paralyzing."* It has been consistently pointed out to me as one of main reasons why people flee Darfur and as a major obstacle to the restoration of normalcy in a world turned upside down. In interviews conducted in the Sudan since 2003, I have heard stories packed with violent incidents of banditry. In Al-Radmmia hamlet, Fur women spoke about the violence waged against them by both militias and bandits. In describing her forced departure, a young Fur woman emphasized that banditry was just as dangerous as military operations, as bandits also engage in rape, theft, and even murder. Another woman remarked: *"See my grandmother, sitting here so quietly, she is very heartbroken. The bandits stole her animals and her donkey, which she would never be able to replace. They just came with their weapons and took all of them; she couldn't defend herself because she was so afraid of them."* Yehia, a sixty-six-year-old who had introduced me to this family, added:

> These thieves are ruthless. They do not fear Allah. Now they come in large numbers, all armed and ready to kill if faced with any resistance. They know they can frighten and threaten you with their arms. Today bullets are sold in markets everywhere. It is a lot cheaper to buy a can of bullets than a ball of fava beans. Anyone can buy weapons and steal with impunity. Chadians are also known for their armed robbery. Life changed for people not just because of the war but because of these criminal acts. Bandits are taking advantage of the deterioration and are more emboldened than ever before. Is it our fate? Or is it our bad luck to be there in the wrong place at the wrong time? So many relatives tell us if they go

*to complain to the police, they don't help them at all. Others say bandits have a
lot of friends in the police and sometimes they share the stolen goods with them.*

If in the past people were ready to pin the practice of banditry on specific
groups, today opportunism, political attachment, and national origin make
it more difficult to define the contours of banditry in Darfur and the reasons behind it. Are these bandits in fact Janjaweed militias? Are they driven
by want or by warlordism? Are they Darfuris or Chadians? These blurred
boundaries don't only exist in people's minds; they are rooted in the different
backgrounds of the marauding criminals, a point taken up in chapter 3.

The effects of Darfur's porous boundaries spill over into populations living in a state of total melancholy. *"Long time ago we used to consult religious
men and even fortune tellers to lead us to the thieves, and they used to reveal
to us who they were. Now if they tell me that the thief took my animals outside of the region, how am I to get them, and where would I go to complain?"*
Nafisa asks rhetorically in our conversation about security concerns. I maintain that banditry is a by-product of the systemic devastation of the region's
body politic, consolidated by unyielding deficits in accountability. It is these
circumstances that prompted me to summon memories of my encounters with
the travails of the region as a child and into adulthood.

2

Producing Knowledge, Historicizing Racial Categories

All knowledge is a condensed note in an agonistic power field.
DONNA HARAWAY, "Situated Knowledges"[1]

Darfur like its mother country the Sudan has been the subject of a vast amount of travel writing and historical and anthropological knowledge. Historians tell us of a fiercely independent Muslim Sudanic sultanate (i.e., Sinnar, Wadai, Bagirmi, Bornu, Melle, and Hausa) that stretched across north central Africa from the Red Sea to the Atlantic. With its unique identity, climate, and environment, the sultanate has attracted systematic attention for its shrewd diplomacy and early forms of connectivity with the world beyond its borders going back to the rule of the Keira Dynasty (1580–1660).[2] Early descriptions by the people who traversed this region established its place in world history in wide-ranging accounts that have been canonized as foundational texts.

This chapter considers how both past and present circuits of knowledge production about Darfur have systematically attempted to understand Darfuri identities in binary terms. As discussed in chapter 1, various outsiders, despite having different politically informed frameworks, have divided the region's people into two entities: Zurqa or indigenous Black Africans and invader-settler and migrant Arabs. This bifurcated view not only altered self-perceptions in the region by politicizing ethnicity, but also affected views on the conflict at the national and international levels. What this form of knowledge overlooks is the many variations within these two seemingly opposed groups, each with a different view about its relationship to the state. Furthermore, these two groups are literally indistinguishable in terms of skin complexion. Centuries of intermarriage produced hybrid populations consisting of diverse ethnicities. However, these ethnicities have become highly politicized and militarized in the context of political violence, scarce resources, and interventions from neighboring countries such as Chad and Libya. Among the questions addressed in this chapter, therefore, are: How has knowledge been produced about Darfur in the past, in ways that have promoted this bifurcated view? How does this view linger in the present, with what implications for the current crisis? How does it inform the evolving truth regimes purporting to provide definitive explanations about the causes of the conflict? Also, how do newer circuits of knowledge via electronic media lend themselves to the complexity of this exercise, and what do they bring to it?

The groundwork for the racialized violence that has affected the region since 2003 was laid by generations of travelers, historians, ethnographers, and colonial administrators[3] who produced an enormous amount of knowledge about the region. This chapter does not claim to provide a comprehensive account of these knowledge regimes. Rather, in alignment with the postcolonial critiques of African historiography developed by Talal Asad, Achille Mbembe, V. Y. Mudimbe, and others,[4] it highlights continuities in the representational discourses forged at particular moments of Darfur's history, drawing upon illustrative examples from the earliest forms of travel writing to the relatively recent colonial knowledge. These knowledge regimes are situated within particular sociopolitical histories that enabled certain imaginings about the region's polity and identity even as, in this frontier society, many were grappling with the blurred boundaries and the shifting alliances created along economic and political strategic interests. What is clear is that even as Darfur's identity has been a victim of the violence of representation since travelers started to roam the vast territory, colonial administrators, by representing Darfuris as inferior to the more favored Arabs, exercised a particular version of racial violence with ramifications for the current crisis. My goal in this chapter, and perhaps its inherent ambiguity, is aptly stated by James Faris in his book *Navajo and Photography: A Critical History of Representation of an American People*: "It is to deconstruct (or to challenge without program) the conceptual space, the rule of being, the representation. Framing is, then, in this sense, censoring. It is not, however, a simple aesthetic gesture, for an alternative power might rest in what does not appear."[5]

Four Travelogues

Early records are important because they inform later historical accounts of Darfuri society and polity. From the time of the Keira Dynasty, the sultan ruled over a number of "tribes," but the most numerous and powerful was the Fur, so the region became known as Darfur, the home of the Fur. Commenting on the region's independent spirit, Sir J. A. Gillan, British administrator in the Sudan in the early twentieth century, noted: "Darfur, as befits a child born as a long afterthought to a large family, has always had an identity very much her own. Dongola, the first born, may become a part of the Northern Province; Bahr el Ghazal may be submerged in Equatoria; but Darfur remains Darfur, and woe the man who tries to tamper with her integrity."[6] It took the British Royal Flying Corps, mounted infantry, artillery batteries, mules, and the Imperial Camel Corps Brigade to bring such integrity to an end with the massacre of Darfur's last sultan, Ali Dinar, in 1916 in what was euphemistically called the Darfur Campaign. As we shall see, the defeat and subsequent annexation of Darfur spawned significant British knowledge regimes that proved critical for the colonial government.

But first it is important to consider the travel accounts upon which colonial administrators throughout British Sudan relied heavily for their knowledge of the region. Four travelogues, covering a large swath of the Darfur sultanate across its north-south and east-west axes and frequently accepted uncritically by scholars, are especially important. William George Browne, Muḥammad Ibn-'Umar al-Tūnisī, Gustav Nachtigal, and Robert Felkin traversed the African sultanates of Wadai (present-day Chad) and Darfur and published detailed accounts on the region's flora and fauna, ethnology, and polity. Their travelogues contributed to the broader knowledge regimes revolving around preconceived assumptions about African people as a whole. In addition, their work contributed to the later ethnographic documentation of Darfur by colonial administrators, many of whom were trained anthropologists. The discussion below addresses both the political inflection of this travel genre and its influence on later forms of knowledge.

Many historians and ethnologists of Darfur and Wadai claim that William George Browne, who arrived in Darfur in 1793, was the first European to set foot in the region and the first to systematically collect material about it. A medical doctor and self-defined explorer, Browne's visit was motivated by scientific curiosity, including an interest in medicinal plants. His voyage, chronicled in his *Travels in Africa, Egypt, and Syria* published in 1806,[7] began when he joined a caravan of slave merchants crossing the Sahara along the Darb Al-Arba'in, the Forty Days' Road connecting Assiut, Egypt, to Darfur.[8] W. B. K. Shaw, who served in the Sudan Forest Service in the 1920s and was a member of the Royal Geographical Society, describes this voyage as passing through "over a thousand of the most barren miles in Africa." Writing in 1929, he noted:

> Traffic on the Arba'in Road is now reduced to a minimum; probably no caravan has passed along its entire length since the beginning of the twentieth century, though sections of it are still in intermittent use. . . . But it was at one

time a highway between Egypt and Darfur, whence roads radiated to Wadai and Bornu in the west and to the happy hunting-grounds of the slave dealers in southern Darfur and the Bhar el Ghazal. . . . The traffic on the Road was closely connected with the slave trade, and for thousands of unfortunates it was a "one-way street" at its worst. From south to north travelled slaves, and from north to south the merchandise wherewith to purchase them. . . . Kobbé, the real terminus of the Arba'in Road, lay some 35 miles north-west of El Fasher. It is now deserted and the 1:1,000,000 map of Darfur marks only the hill of J. Kobbé. But it was once the chief city of the western Sudan. . . . Browne describes it as lying in a wide plain, a long narrow town of scattered houses.[9]

Characteristic of travel writing about Africa, Browne attempted to establish his authority and cultural superiority from the outset, asserting his intellectual supremacy and scholarly skills to document an alien cultural world for a Western audience. He begins his narrative by describing in minute detail the Darb Al-Arba'in caravan he joined, from his encounters with the Jellaba slave merchants to the health of their camels and their negotiation of prices in slave markets, and also gives details about the slaves who were part of this journey. He goes on to describe the suspicion that met his arrival in the sultanate, which he tried to dispel with flattery and by emphasizing his ethnographic and scientific interests. He described his encounter with Sultan Abdel Rahman Al-Rasheed: "Melek [King]," said I, "having come from a far distant country to Misr, I was there made acquainted with the magnificence, the extended empire, and above all, the justice and hospitality of the king Abd-el-rachmân, whose dominion be eternal! . . . Having been used to wander over various countries as a *derwish* [dervish], to learn wisdom from the aged, and to collect remedies for diseases from herbs that spring in various soils, I grew desirous of seeing Dar-Fûr."[10]

Like most travelers, Browne describes the sufferings he endured for the sake of discovering a kingdom in the interior of Africa. Disease, an inhospitable climate, abstinence, and "unruly" natives all contributed to his misery. Of the last he writes with exasperation:

A stranger is here not a little incommoded by the impertinent and obstructive curiosity of the natives. A passion that operates with them most powerfully, but which is too indiscriminate . . . has hitherto been too little directed, to have produced any beneficial effects toward their advancement in society. The habitations being open to all the world, I was at first constantly harassed with visitants, sometimes to the number of twenty, of every description, who came with no other view than to gaze upon objects that appeared to be new to them. Their remarks were made without restraint, and occasionally afforded me some diversion; but I more frequently lamented the difficulty of being private. . . . For the spectators are not always contented with feasting their eyes. Whatever is exposed before them, they wish to have a part of. Snuff and tobacco are indispensable; and I have more than once been remonstrated with for not offering a watch, of which I had two, or a turban of which I had several, to my neighbor who was un-provided with these articles.[11]

In addition to the pain visited upon him by the natives' unruliness, he laments the theft of his property and especially the sultan's empty promises of protection: "I was told that my person and property would be secure, and that permission would be given me to go wherever I might think proper. Since my arrival within the confines, I have found that all these assurances were fallacious; my inclinations have been thwarted, my person treated with indignity, and my property plundered, while compliance has been refused even to my reasonable demands."[12] And again:

I complained of the injuries done me, and he [the sultan] assured me of redress for the past, and protection for the future. At the same time it was clear that he esteemed the present [I had given him as] a tribute, and conceived that personal safety was more than I could reasonably expect. His conduct afterwards was a further proof of his sentiments: for though I remained at El-Fasher three entire months, I saw him only when I forced myself on his notice, and experienced no return of civility, much less any compensation for what I had already suffered.[13]

With a grim resignation to the situation, Browne became accustomed to insulting the local population: "The misrepresentations which had been made concerning me, and which had by this time reached the Sultan . . . prevented my remonstrance from having any effect."[14]

Browne's observations revealed more about his racial and androcentric views than they did about the actual transactions being described. About slaves he encountered he wrote, "Candour and ingenuousness have no part in the character of slaves; and the ancient observation is most just, that 'when a man becomes a slave he loses half his virtue.'"[15] Consider also the misogyny evident in his remarks about a manumitted slave whom he met in Cairo: "In the caravan, I observed a black woman advanced in years, who had been long a slave in Kahira [Cairo]. Having been enfranchised, and having amassed some property, she was returning to her native place. Supine, helpless, ignorant, and sensual, as this description [sic] of females generally is, and habituated to a quiet and luxurious life, that she had encountered the difficulty and danger of such a voyage would seem surprising, if daily instances of a similar kind did not evince the strength of attachment to their native soil."[16]

In yet another example, his description of a thwarted attempt to sexually assault a slave girl is, in its very casualness, equally an expression of his position as a powerful white man encountering the most vulnerable of populations:

> After waiting in fruitless expectation at El Fasher, as the time of my depar-
> ture was drawing near, an accident happened, which, though not of the most
> pleasing kind, contributed to make me noticed, and obtained for me at length
> an interview with the Sultan. The slaves of the house used frequently to col-
> lect round me, as if to examine a strange object. I joked occasionally with
> them, without any other view than that of momentary relaxation. One day as
> I was reading in the hut, one of them, a girl about fifteen, came to the door
> of it, when, from a whim of the moment, I seized the cloth that was round
> her waist, which dropped and left her naked. Chance so determined that the
> owner of the slave passed at this moment and saw her. The publicity of the
> place precluded any view of farther familiarity, but the tumult which suc-
> ceeded appeared to mark the most heinous of crimes, and to threaten the
> most exemplary vengeance. The man threw his turban on the earth, and ex-
> claimed, "Ye believers in the Prophet, hear me! Ye faithful, avenge me!" with
> other similar expressions. "A Caffre[17] has violated the property of a descendent
> of Mohammed." . . . When a number of people was collected around him,
> he related the supposed injury he had received in the strongest terms, and
> exhorted them to take their arms and sacrifice the Caffre. He had charged a
> carbine, and affected to come forward to execute his threats, when some one
> of the company who had advanced farthest, and saw me, called out to the rest
> that I was armed, and prepared to resist. It was then agreed amongst the as-
> sembly that some method of punishment might be found, that promised more
> security and profit to the complainant, and would be more formidable to the
> guilty. The man whom I have already mentioned as my broker was to take the
> slave, as if she had really been violated and agreed to pay whatever her mas-
> ter should charge as the price. The latter had the modesty to ask ten head of
> slaves. He was then to make his demand on me for the value of ten slaves, and
> if I carried the matter before the Cade [judge], which he supposed I should
> hardly venture to do, he had suborned witnesses to prove that I had received
> of him property to that amount.[18]

Browne attributed the sudden interruption of his attempted rape of this pubescent girl to both Muslim scorn for the "Caffres" and the "prejudice and machinations of . . . [my] enemies" in the region.[19] As a result of this at-tempted rape, he was immured by the sultan, which he claimed was the result of the distrust and disdain of a Muslim society towards his Christian faith, noting that since Sultan Abdel Rahman's "elevation to imperial honors, [he] had been enforcing with increased severity the laws against infidels" out of a desire to cultivate ties with Muslim leaders elsewhere.[20] In the end, Browne's frustration with his experiences in Darfur prompted him to request safe passage to Ethiopia, which he described as "a Christian country rich with gold, medicinal herbs and abounding in slaves."[21] When Browne departed Darfur, he left with an egotistical story that centered on his suffering and victimization by the natives.

One cannot help considering the way Browne's disparaging views of the Fur later came to the aid of British colonials. They relied heavily on the image of "uncivilized" natives to promote a Pax Britannica, which sought to subdue, discipline, and annex the natives into the fold of empire.[22] For these approving foreigners, Browne thus lay the groundwork for further knowledge, new expeditions, and imperial policies. Johannes Fabian's critique of early travel in Africa well accords with Browne's legacy: "The actual encounters that paved the way for imperial rule or established it in embryonic form were often inherently contradictory—indeed anarchic—so much so that their true nature had to be concealed or better, negated by projecting to the world images of a purposeful oeuvre civilisatrice."[23]

In 1803, nearly seven years after Browne's departure from Darfur, the region received the Tunisian Muḥammad Ibn-'Umar al-Tūnisī, an Arab, who was to remain there for eight years. He dictated an account of his travel chronicles to Dr. Nicolas Perron, whom he befriended in Cairo upon his return from Darfur and to whom *Voyage au Darfour*, finally published in French in 1845, is credited. Years later *Voyage au Darfour* was translated into Arabic as *Tashidh al-adhan fi sirat bilad al-Arab wa el-Sudan*, and it became among the most widely read travel accounts of his generation. Unlike W. G. Browne's, al-Tūnisī's travels were prompted by neither the quest for scientific knowledge nor personal drive. Rather, his motive was simply to follow his father, who was knowledgeable in Islamic law and had been invited to join the sultan's court as religious figure and consultant. However, al-Tūnisī's long stay in Darfur afforded him valuable opportunities unavailable to Browne. Similarly, comparing al-Tūnisī to Browne and Nachtigal, the editors of *Tashidh al-adhan fi sirat bilad al-Arab wa el-Sudan* noted: "Regardless of the motives behind these European travelers' arrival into Darfur and whether they were prompted by the quest of knowledge or service to the colonialists, al-Tūnisī's purpose was never questioned as a Muslim."[24]

In a narrative that combined rhymed poetry and prose, al-Tūnisī told the story of his travels to Darfur and gave detailed descriptions of the region's natural history, topography, kings, rites and rituals of succession, marriage customs, gender politics, practices of concubinage and castration, folktales,

spirit possession, cannibalism, magical beliefs, dispensation of justice and revenge, and health and healing practices—in addition to a plethora of maps,
figures, and genealogical charts of the sultans of Darfur.[25] Especially noteworthy among the cultural and political themes he addressed are the structure
of government, customs of the sultans, Fur sexual behavior, and ritual practices. He described the existing political and administrative hierarchy, with
the sultans at the top followed in order by kings, governors, and various sultanic appointees, all of whom constituted the administrative body of the sultanate. Al-Tūnisī was particularly drawn to the way sultans exacted revenge,
which he understood as a natural reaction to those perceived as traitors. As
he describes it, once the sultan learned the identity of a traitor, he pronounced
a death sentence upon the person by presenting him with a red cashmere
cloth. Before his execution, an alleged traitor was made to eat knowingly the
chopped-up flesh of preadolescent children mixed with animal meat. It is no
wonder that accusations of betrayal to the sultan and community were not
taken lightly. As we shall see below, fear of this fate deterred many from form-
ing controversial alliances with other travelers.

In describing the sexual practices of Fur society, al-Tūnisī portrayed Sultan Mohammad Tairab as a man of guilty pleasures, with an insatiable lust
for women[26] and in possession of countless concubines. Al-Tūnisī observed
that the sultan frequently brought young men and women to dance for him,
after which the dancers paired off and secluded themselves to speak of love,
marriage, and dowry prices. The mixing of the sexes and gender parity in this
devout Muslim society was, according to al-Tūnisī, the norm rather than the
exception. He further remarked that "it was not uncommon for someone to
walk into a man and a woman copulating. They didn't care and neither did
the person who caught them in the act." This attitude was in accordance with
the prevailing custom that mandated a man would not take a wife without
impregnating her once or twice, after which point he could affirm, "Oh, she
is fertile."[27]

About spirit possession al-Tūnisī wrote, "One of the most bizarre things I
have heard [is] that in Darfur people hire *jinn* [invisible spirits] to shepherd
their cattle. This jinn, the spirit guard, was known as *damazooqa*. Their hiring is facilitated by a shaman to whom you bring fresh milk to signal your
interest in jinn guards for the animals. These damazooqa could also be hired
to guard your property from theft." He also notes that the protection accrued
from jinn and also amulets worn around one's arm were common methods
of recovering from stabbing wounds.[28] Spirit possession, some forms of gender mixing, and forced cannibalism all shocked al-Tūnisī, for these practices
transgressed basic social norms as he understood them.

Nonetheless, al-Tūnisī seemed to have been particularly appreciative of the hospitality shown to him, as evidenced by gifts bestowed upon him by Mohammed Kara, a famous eunuch and a confidant of the sultan. These included "green cashmere cloth, an Indian cotton garb, two concubines, and vegetables."[29] He explained that the gift of slaves and concubines, often numbering up to a hundred, was the ultimate sign of welcome bestowed by the sultan and notes with satisfaction that the sultan ordered slaves to serve and obey him as "Allah's guest." Admittedly, al-Tūnisī's identity as a Muslim may have mitigated the doubt and skepticism that met others. Yet he was no less racist and misogynistic than W. G. Browne. His prejudices became clear as soon as he joined the caravan from Egypt to Darfur: "When I found myself among strangers of whose language I didn't know but a few words and among whom no single beautiful face was to be found, I recalled the poem, 'your body, your clothes, your face, blackness upon blackness upon blackness.' I regretted injecting myself in the midst of the sons of Ham and recalled their hatred of the sons of Sam. My fear was indescribable."[30] Despite his regret at embarking on the journey, he was determined to venture forth, as he saw in this difficulty a test of his endurance, a virtue that proved his manliness. Descriptions of his encounters with bandits, whom he described as a people dispossessed of dignity, became opportunities to emphasize his fortitude in the Sahara.

Like Browne, al-Tūnisī embraced a European aesthetic in describing Fur people as a negroid folk lacking physical beauty. Their wide noses, thick lips, red eyes, protruding teeth, and course hair were all noted as markers of a perceived racial inferiority. He emphasized the propensity towards hate and revenge among people whom he continually referred to as "savages": "When we arrived at the town of Kabkabia, we came across a plentiful marketplace, where we stopped before heading to Jebel Marra. Once we arrived we spent the night in the midst of savage people, hateful of guests especially if these guests were Arabs. We suffered greatly from them. We only stayed to spite them for we knew they were hateful of us."[31] Al-Tūnisī seemed to have been particularly exercised by the Fur response to his fair complexion. He wrote:

> My companions who traveled with me all of a sudden surrounded me. I wanted to know why they did so. "Because they [Fur] are foolish," I was told. At that time my knowledge of Fur language was minimal. My friends heard people say, "Look at him, he has not cooked long enough inside his mother's womb. Look at his red color; even if a fly lands on his skin she would be able to suck his blood." Another aggressor said, "His blood will gush out when I stab him with my spear." My friends said, "These people are determined to kill you, we surrounded you to save your life."[32]

Unfavorable descriptions like this abound. Even his favoring of the Berti people, whose presumed decorum and generosity he attributed to their long relationships with the nomadic Arabs, is framed in contrast to the "savage" Fur[33] and to the Zaghawa people, whom he abhorred for their involvement in banditry and crime.

Although Browne and al-Tūnisī are similarly biased, the latter's unfettered access to the royal forecourt as well as to the communities in which he settled enabled him to gather in-depth information. During his eight years of residence in Darfur, he also learned local languages, which made him particularly adept at capturing minute details about many aspects of life in Darfur. His observations about social customs and rituals opened a window into nineteenth-century Darfur, and perhaps for this reason he has been valorized in many circles as the only traveler able to capture the dynamism of the culture. Perhaps too it is for this reason that his attitudes were never critiqued as they should have been even by today's readers. Al-Tūnisī's continued, blatant displays of both prejudice and discrimination vis-à-vis his coreligionists, contrary to the principles of equality taught by his faith, remain deeply troubling. In many ways, his racialized account informed other travelers and explorers in Africa.

During a time when the Sudanese peoples viewed the presence of foreigners with suspicion, Gustav Nachtigal, a German physician, explorer, and ethnographer, crossed the Libyan Desert to arrive at Darfur through its western corridor in 1874. Nachtigal was by no means treated as Allah's guest, and in *Sahara and Sudan*, his account of his adventures from Wadai through the Masalit Mountains,[34] he, like Browne and al-Tūnisī, reveals the depth of his repugnance for the native Fur. Although his English translators have written favorably about him, noting that "reading *Sahara and Sudan* today, one is immediately struck by the lack of pretentiousness in the account, the absence of any condescending or patronizing tone,"[35] Nachtigal's own depictions of the Fur and Daju people contradict this reading of his work. Consider his descriptions of the region and his account of its political history:

> The population of Darfur may be divided on the one hand into Negroes and Arabs, or on the other into its original inhabitants and the conquered peoples or foreigners. In our historical sketch we have already seen the influence which in the course of the centuries the Arab elements have had on the native tribes, and how, according to local tradition, the last dynasty itself arose from a grafting of the Tunjur, undoubtedly an Arab tribe, on the original masters of the country, the Forawa. . . . The Tunjur, to whom, because of their higher standard of civilization, the Daju more or less voluntarily conceded first place, appear to have entered the country some four centuries ago, and claim to be

descended from the Beni Hilal, who are said to have lived in the highlands of Arabia at the time of the Prophet.[36]

The Daju also represent themselves as having immigrated from the east, and it is worthy of note that most of their rulers had Arab names. Tradition does not, however, impute to them any connection with Arabs or Arab blood. On the contrary, it is stated that they were extraordinarily uncivilized, and had fallen so far short of the claims of Arab custom that the transfer of power from their hands to those of the Tunjur was to be ascribed only to the superior culture of the latter. . . . The intellectual superiority of the immigrant Tunjur, and their more refined customs (their hospitality was especially celebrated), wrested power from the Daju without any fighting or violence.[37]

The Fur, or Forawa, have fairly dark skin, grey-black or black, are of middle height and with undistinguished features. Their character is arrogant, hot-tempered and revengeful, and they are much given to quarreling and out-breaks of violence. They can scarcely lay claim to any reputation for real brav-ery. They have little talent for industry, almost as little indeed as their western neighbors, the people of Wadai, and like all mountain dwellers, hold tena-ciously to their ancient manners and customs, so that Islam itself, of which in the larger villages they are fanatical adherents, has not been able in the more distant regions to suppress Paganism completely.[38]

He also complained of his treatment at the hands of local people, even as he continues his racialized categorization:

The difficulty lay in the ill will and the hatred entertained towards me by the inhabitants, which indeed was generally in accordance with their proud, arro-gant, religious-fanatical character, but was especially increased by the political developments which threatened in their country.[39] . . . Wherever I appeared, I was insulted and derided by those who met me, and even in the king's palace I was subjected to the grossest insults. . . . In the royal forecourts or in the streets people often came to me with the scornful enquiry whether I could say that "la ilah ill' Allah," and tried to induce me to add the second part of the text.[40] On one occasion in the forecourt of the palace, which was filled with people seeking an audience, a surprisingly light-colored Banda slave passed me, who in the dim surroundings appeared even fairer than she actually was; for a moment, I almost thought she was a European, and could not suppress a movement of astonishment. She was thereupon brought to me, and pressing hard and mocking at me on all sides, the people proposed to me that I should marry her. I saw herself at last compelled to tell the king that I should have to forego the pleasure of visiting him, since he was obviously in no position to protect me and my dignity against the common people.[41]

Native ill will was rooted in Nachtigal's identity as a European, as well as suspicions about the reason for his presence in the region, given prevailing fears of the Ottoman colonial project extending into the Sudan and impending Turkish aggression. Concern that Nachtigal might be a foreign operative extended even to those with whom he associated. When he asked a gentleman whom he had befriended to introduce him to the sultan, the man was unequivocal: "If I do, I will be accused by my people of being a traitor and a spy." Natives did not take lightly the accusation of being a Turkish operative. It represented a betrayal of the community and the sultanate, and the consequences for both were brutal, entailing imprisonment and death.

Despite his racist views and the scorn and wariness of the local population, Nachtigal's occupational identity as a physician opened many doors for him, as al-Tūnisī's religious identity had done for him. So did his adoption of certain local customs. He wrote:

> Since I was summoned from several quarters to see the sick, I also visited the town without giving the impression that I wanted to explore and take notes. Although for a long time I had been without any medicines, I did not reject this opportunity to get to know the town and its people innocently and without being exposed too much to the glances of the curious. I was, however, rather surprisingly, less exposed to this unpleasantness than some other foreigners, for through my connection with the Jellaba I had become so like them in clothing, speech and behavior, that if they did not already have knowledge of the fact, only very few suspected me of being a Christian or a European.[42]

For all his biases, Nachtigal provided detailed descriptions of the region, ranging from its history to its people to the organization of the state. His attention to detail at a time when few written documents were available reflected his skill as an ethnographer. He drew charts, recorded popular traditions and oral narratives, and reviewed what existing manuscripts there were. Primary among these last was the *Book of Dali*, which later came to capture the imagination of historians and legal scholars interested in the dispensation of justice and the adjudication of disputes.[43] This book, which has been attributed to Delil Bahar (n.d.), whom Nachtigal viewed as the most brilliant prince of the Keira Dynasty, laid the foundation for the principles of power and wealth accumulation, the codification of criminal laws, gender relations, and rules of precedence that successive sultans followed to the very end of independent Darfur. They regarded it as an inviolable document.

Nachtigal was especially keen to document the importance of kinship ties for maintaining political power and preempting dissent. He remarked, "To keep the numerous members of his family well-disposed to him [the sultan], the richest regions of the country were securely in the hands of his brothers, sisters, cousins and favorite slaves."[44] He notes the ascendancy of female family members, including the sultan's sister, Zemzem, "whose character was very much that of a man":

> She exercised so much power that she could with impunity give herself over to that unbridled arbitrariness to which she was by nature inclined. She moved around the country at the head of her armed men, plundered the districts placed under her control, and easily got from the weak king those hawakir [land lots] which she particularly liked. Feared and hated throughout the whole country, she could indeed do nothing better than die at the same time as her royal brother. It is said that, immediately after the death of King Hasin, she fell into such deep depression that she refused all food and likewise died forty days later.[45]

Later in his career, Nachtigal's work in Wadai and Darfur earned him prestigious posts in Tunisia. In addition, German chancellor Otto von Bismarck promoted him to the position of a special commissioner for Germany in Togo and the Cameroon, which had been annexed to the German imperial territories in Western Africa in 1884, where he continued to produce reductive explanations of identity and society. His views on the bifurcated Darfuri identity were broadly accepted throughout the colonial period, and his travelogue considerably influenced British ethnographies of race and ethnicity at that time.

The last of these four travelers to arrive in Darfur was Robert William Felkin (1853–1926) of Nottingham, England. A fellow of the anthropological societies of London and Edinburgh, this Freemason medical missionary in Central Africa was well-known in the field of tropical medicine as a pioneer in relating disease ecology to geography and population studies. Unlike the three travelers discussed above, Felkin and his companion Charles Wilson, also a missionary, entered Darfur in late 1879 through Bahr El Ghazal in the South, not through the well-traveled Darb Al-Arba'in. Felkin did not travel as widely in the region as his predecessors, and his stay in the region lasted for only nine days in the village of Dara, Southern Darfur, as part of a broader journey. His observations about Darfur thus constituted a small part of the travelogue in which it appeared, *Uganda and the Egyptian Soudan*.[46] Although Felkin's remarks on the Fur, based on his observations in Dara village, were brief, his tone exuded confidence and authority. To the untrained eye, his descriptions had the air of truth, thereby enhancing their power to shape cultural perceptions.[47]

Two tasks seem to have absorbed him: describing the physical characteristics of the Fur and mapping out key cultural and social-structural features of Fur society, especially gender relations. He was cognizant of the limitations of his narrative, but with a steely resolve he ventured forth, presenting customs and traditions, mythology, fables, even greeting customs. Given an intense interest in physical anthropology and the prevailing views of his time and environment, his account was infused with the logic of the Fur's presumed racial inferiority. Lamenting his inability to spare time for "taking measurements of the For [Fur] people," he nonetheless offered measurements of "my boy's head"—referring to a young Fur boy who had entered his service while in Darfur—"as better than nothing." Calculations such as the breadth of the boy's nose and mouth and the length between his cheekbones demonstrated a fixation on physical characteristics. In addition to his decidedly social Darwinist schema and an accompanying emphasis on color and body odor, Felkin experimented on Furs' five senses, concluding that "their sight, hearing, and smell are very good, but the sense of touch is not very acute, and their sensibility to pain is decidedly less than that of Europeans."[48]

Felkin's attention to women and to gender relations, more extensive than in most other early travel accounts, reflects notions of a biologically driven social hierarchy similar to his racial views. However, unlike his racial views, his views on gender did not comport with local knowledge. He maintained that the Fur did not see women as humans. They were thought to be lacking in mind and religion; when they "die they are buried without prayers and without much ceremony."[49] Unlike men, they do not enjoy a sex life after death since their only life was that which they had on earth. Despite the absence of sexual segregation, these discriminatory gender ideologies placed women in the lowest position in the social order. On this topic, Felkin's observations concur with previous accounts, although they vacillated between understanding promiscuity as transgressive and as not particularly problematic.

Writing about marriage and sex, Felkin projects an exoticized sense of difference onto the lives of women. He displays a tendency towards voyeurism not uncommon in ethnographic writing, but at the same time writes with a certain dispassion, displaying an ethnographic curiosity. Marriage, he writes, "takes place at the age of seventeen. The women are prolific. I saw a good number of women with seven, eight and nine children. . . . Polygamy exists. Barrenness is common in Jebel Marra district, where the men always make sure of a woman's fertility before marriage."[50] This last observation echoes al-Tūnisī, who noted that customarily marriage occurs only after a woman has had one or two children by the intended husband. Felkin continues, describing the social arrangements to ensure ongoing support for children born out of wedlock: "If a girl should have a child before she is married, and its father will not marry her, he has to pay a fine of cows to the chief of the village. The child belongs to the mother's father, and when she subsequently marries it remains [with] him."[51] Felkin makes no reference to honor killing for fornication or whipping the unmarried woman in accordance with sharia law. The child's adoption by the maternal grandfather tells us about the fluidity of the notion of illegitimacy, which is clearly irrelevant in this community when sex is consensual. This is markedly different from the response to rape and elopement, which resulted in the harshest of punishments:

> If a rape should be committed upon a very young girl, a circumstance of extreme rarity, the whole of the offender's cattle is confiscated. If a man runs away with a girl, both his and her parents have to pay a fine to the chief. Seduction in our sense of the word is unknown. If a woman is caught in the act of adultery her husband is allowed to kill the man and beat the woman. It is very common for a married woman to fall in love with another man and ask him to kill her husband; if this gets found out, as is usually the case, both guilty parties are executed.[52]

The execution in this last example is less about transgressing morality through the act of extramarital sex than it is about punishment for murder.

The brevity of his stay notwithstanding, Felkin shared significant commonalities with the travelers before him in his mode of representing Darfuri identity and society, in the fellow anthropologists, gentlemen scholars, and colonial administrators to whom he directed his work, and especially in his intent to create and disseminate knowledge about the people of Darfur. He was, however, unique in his reliance on what then seemed like scientific methods to attempt to prove the biological basis of racial differences.

These four travel accounts by Browne, al-Tūnisī, Nachtigal, and Felkin present certain similarities despite the different historical periods during which the authors visited the Darfur region. All four travelers shared certain views regarding race, and a common denominator of their accounts certainly is the ways in which they depicted racial differences. Rather than understanding race as a cultural and political construct governed by wider political, economic, and social processes, they treated it as a biological reality. Relying on traditional taxonomies that divided populations into immutable, mutually exclusive categories, they classified the sultanate's population as either Negro or Arab. They systematically noted distinctions between "negroid" and "Arab" peoples of Darfur, based on what anthropologist Marvin Harris has described as the belief in "a particular assemblage of hereditary traits that always made it possible to determine racial origin on the bases of external

characteristics" including skin color, hair texture, body mass, and facial features such as the shape of the nose and the thickness of lips.[53] This archetypal
view, dominant at the time, especially in Europe, and rooted in the "racial
taxon" of evolutionary biology, not only ignored and denied the "ephemeral-
ity of the races"[54] but also helped set in place a racial hierarchy of superior
Arabs and inferior Africans. And these views in turn reinforced the thinking
of those Europeans, primarily British, French, and German, who were introduced to the Sudan by Browne's, al-Tūnisī's, Nachtigal's, and to a lesser extent
Felkin's travel writings. They also had an impact on the people of Darfur, who
began to see the ways in which they were treated as a fact of nature. The observations of all four of these travelers were accepted at face value in contemporary reviews of their work, but the continuities in their representational
approach to Darfuri people's ethnicity may well be another opportunity for
critical inquiry.

    Browne, al-Tūnisī, Nachtigal, and Felkin also were hardly unique. I con-
tend that their mode of representation pervaded descriptions of travel in
Africa throughout the African-European encounter. Furthermore, following
Johannes Fabian, who questioned the premise that travel writing was predicated on a disinterested quest for knowledge and instead found that it was
undertaken for patently political reasons, it can be argued that writings about
Darfur played a central role in the unfolding of the British Darfur Expedition
of 1916 and its aftermath.[55] The depth of travelers' depictions also aided in the
later construction of the ethnographic record. All the details to which travel
writers devoted attention, ranging from topography, history, and government
to manners and customs, slavery, diseases, animals, and plants, figured prominently in the diaries of British colonial officers in the Sudan; clearly they
drew from the earlier work in composing their own ethnographies. These
earlier accounts also informed a policy of population segregation, codified
in the Closed District Ordinances of the 1930s and 1940s, which restricted
travel between northern and southern Sudan, thereby effecting the division
of Africans and Arabs. The policy was the invention of H. A. MacMichael,
who served in the Sudan from 1905 to 1934, was a member of the Darfur Expeditionary Force, and authored the voluminous *History of the Arabs in the
Sudan: and Some Account of the People Who Preceded Them and of the Tribes
Inhabiting Dárfūr* (1921). MacMichael was of the opinion that the racial differences between Arabs and Africans were so vast that separating them and
limiting their interaction was good colonial policy.[56]

    In the introduction to his edited volume *Anthropology and the Colonial
Encounter*, Talal Asad draws attention to the way that the production of ethnographic knowledge in the colonial situation was facilitated by established

inequalities between the colonizer and the colonized. According to Asad, "The colonial power structure made the object of anthropological study accessible and safe—because of it, sustained physical proximity between the observing European and the living non-European became a practical possibility. It made possible the kind of human intimacy on which anthropological fieldwork is based, but ensured that that intimacy should be one-sided and provincial."[57] The archaeological, historical, ethnographic, and environmental knowledge about Darfuri society and culture amassed by colonial administrators and filling volumes of *Sudan Notes and Records* exemplifies the intense colonial desire to know every minute detail about Darfur. Indeed, British colonials adhered closely to fundamental anthropological methodologies as they considered every element of society and documented political and social transformations. As with MacMichael, this work informed their colonial administration. Given the vast number of these studies, the works of A. C. Beaton, G. B. Paul, Reverend A. J. Arkell, and others are discussed below as examples of what can be viewed now as an almanac of anthropology in Darfur.

"Their Archive, Our History": *Sudan Notes and Records*

In his *Castes of Mind: Colonialism and the Making of Modern India*, Nicholas B. Dirks writes: "The archive, the primary site of state monumentality, is the very institution that canonizes, crystalizes, and classifies the knowledge required by the state even as it makes this knowledge available to subsequent generations in the cultural form of a neutral repository of the past."[58] Although Dirks is writing about the British invention of caste, which became conjoined with India itself, a similar legacy obtains in Darfur vis-à-vis the invention of the dualistic racial categories of Arab and African. That this is the case is due not only to the shared British imperial history in both colonies, but also to the colonial practices of historiography, ethnography, and politics imported to the Sudan from India.

Sudan Notes and Records (*SNR*), which was launched two years after the British annexation of Darfur to the Sudan in 1916, is arguably the most comprehensive source of published knowledge about the region. Its authors were primarily British governors and district commissioners in the Sudan, many of whom were Cambridge- and Oxford-trained anthropologists. As A. H. M. Kirk-Greene pointed out in his work on the sociology of imperialism, "The Sudan Political Service enjoyed a reputation of efficiency equaled only by that of the Indian Civil Service. [Its] emphasis on the recruitment of what was believed to represent the epitome of British imperial leadership"[59] helps explain the range and depth of knowledge this elite corps advanced in an enormous number of essays on Darfur's culture and politics. From these accounts, readers came to know about the relics of Christianity in local religious practices, tribal genealogies, the practice of magic, stone worship, Tora palaces, and slaves' adventures. Colonial administrators also kept diaries and wrote letters, memos, and memoirs, all with exemplary attention to detail and contributing firsthand knowledge about Darfur to British archives. *SNR* was also the first journal intent on institutionalizing and disseminating a codified Sudanese history and ethnology to the British public, an agenda that required the production of a written history in the English language. Sudanese history, a once-contested sphere in which many competing and contradictory oral narratives coexisted, thus became a codified site that was rendered inaccessible to the Sudanese people as it was made legible to the colonial government.

The journal's paramount significance was not lost on Sir Reginald Wingate, baronet and governor general of the Sudan, under whose watch the independent sultanate was defeated and who wrote the forward to the journal's inaugural issue:

> It was with the liveliest satisfaction and pleasure that I learned that the proposal to establish a scientific journal for the Sudan has matured. The need of such a publication is a very real one and the field of its study will be wide and, in great measure, virgin soil. . . . Knowledge is power, in Africa and elsewhere, and if, as I confidently hope, this journal will be the means of recording and disseminating information that will conduce to a clearer outlook on the country and a better understanding of its natives, their past history, social conditions and future development, it will confer a lasting benefit not solely on those responsible for government, but also on the community at large. There is one corner in particular of the wide field of research to which I suggest early and careful attention should be paid if valuable material is to be rescued from oblivion. The creeds—I refer of course chiefly to those parts of the country untouched by Islamic culture—the superstitions and the folklore of primitive tribesmen are subjects of the deepest interest in themselves and, apart from their anthropological and ethnological values, are of importance as contributing to the people and their mentality which is so essential to a successful administrator.[60]

Wingate certainly understood that greater knowledge of the Sudan would enable the British to rule it more effectively. The body of work published in *SNR* was thus a special genre of ethnographic knowledge that enabled the British to devise stratagems of governance capable of beating the natives into submission.[61] In particular, ethnographic knowledge about the "marginalized territories" of the Nuba Mountains, Darfur, Southern Kordofan, and the Blue

Nile figured prominently in the large-scale pacification policies in the British Sudan. A. C. Beaton, a district commissioner of Darfur, was well aware of the purpose of the ethnographic knowledge he produced about aspects of Darfuri society:

> Since the government's main function is to regulate public life and to satisfy the legitimate desires of the people, it requires a knowledge of not only the facts but also the motives of the public, and since the sanctions of conduct lie both in past tradition and present practice, it is at least of interest, if not of value, to know what beliefs are held and what customs are current among the various tribes that inhabit the Sudan.[62]

Beaton was not ambivalent about his relationship to Darfur or the British authority he sought to serve. However, his colleague H. G. Balfour-Paul, a historian turned anthropologist on the advice of Wingate, a family friend, had undergone a temporary soul searching upon being invited to join the Sudan Service. He wrote in his unpublished memoir:

> The outlook of the professional Anthropologist and the professional Administrator cannot help but be miles apart. To take a hypothetical case (and, perhaps, not quite such a silly one as it sounds) suppose there was a tribe which had the custom of killing and eating its grandmothers before they reached the age of fifty years. The Anthropologist would consider this custom as both interesting and important as it was clearly an attempt to conserve for the tribe in general the wisdom and experience of these ageing ladies before they vanished into senility. He would advise strongly against modifying, let alone abolishing a custom on which the whole stability of the tribe depended. The Administrator on the other hand, would be obliged to inform the tribe that it was his duty to lead them into the 20th Century where the eating of grandmothers was strictly discouraged and that if he found anyone even looking sideways at his grandmother and licking his lips, he would hang him as high as Haman.[63]

This reluctant colonialist's account clearly raises questions about the position of anthropology in the colonial project in the Sudan and elsewhere in the colonial world. His awareness of this tension, however, did not prevent Balfour-Paul from making detailed observations about everyday social and political life in Darfur.

Others, however, reflected neither on their subject position vis-à-vis Darfuri communities from which they extracted ethnologic materials nor on the circumstances within which these knowledge forms were produced. For instance, Beaton was a firm believer in the civilizing project of colonization, in several instances comparing precolonial practices unfavorably to the state of affairs after annexation. About marriage in Fur society he wrote: "In pre-government days a girl who refused to marry a man chosen for her in her infancy, was beaten and handed over by force, but nowadays the matter is settled by the repayment of any advance of bride wealth made by her rejected wooer."[64] Drawing upon Felkin's travelogue, he noted:

> Premarital chastity is enjoined on, but not necessarily observed by both sexes. Fur morals are loose and promiscuity not uncommon. . . . Felkin reports that the father of an unmarried girl's child had to pay a fine to the chief if he refused to marry the girl and that the child then belonged to the girl's father, who retained it if the girl is subsequently married. Nowadays however a subsequent husband will adopt the illegitimate child, bring it up and give it his name.[65]

"Pre-government" practices were simply inconceivable to the British, who, following a Eurocentric logic, painted African societies as irrational, uncivilized, and so deserving of the brute force of civilizing repression. Upon learning about the practice of female infibulation described by all travelers to Darfur, J. A. Gillan wrote in the *New Statesman* and the *Nation* in language dripping with contempt: "We have supped so deep of horrors that most of us believe we are beyond being shocked."[66] Elsewhere, I have argued that that these kinds of visceral responses highlight the emotionality underlying the colonialist desire to assert control and reinforce preexisting structures of dominance throughout colonial Sudan and Darfur.[67] This sense of outrage was clearly evident in the ways colonial administrators included here spoke of Ali Dinar, Darfur's last sultan, the topic to which we turn next.

BRITISH ANTHROPOLOGY NARRATING ALI DINAR IN *SNR*

High-ranking British officials regularly published accounts of the sultanate in the pages of *SNR* from premedieval and medieval times to the Turco-Egyptian occupation through the Mahdist revolution of the late nineteenth century. Prepublication notes and administrative papers maintained in the Sudan Archives at Durham provide extensive support for the insights into diverse people, events, and movements in and out of the sultanate presented in *SNR*. This is especially the case for Darfur's last sultan, Ali Dinar, whose reign extended from 1898 to 1916. Impressions of Dinar were far from favorable throughout the British colonial service. Through the body of knowledge about Dinar produced by colonial recorders, readers were introduced to a sultan who not only clubbed people to death but also had an extreme fetish for women, slaves, and concubines. Moreover, according to historian John Slight:

[A package] of stridently condemnatory and negative views of Ali Dinar's government was transmitted to ordinary Darfuris just before the [1916] British invasion. Propaganda leaflets in Arabic dropped on El Fasher stated that "Ali Dinar has killed your chiefs, plundered your property and sold your women and children." The rhetoric used in these leaflets was designed to discredit the Sultan to his people. In a letter to Ali Dinar, his "evil deeds" were cited as the cause of the British advance to "relieve the country from your . . . oppression."[68]

These views were derived in part from a public culture in the region that emphasized the sultan's alleged ruthlessness. In promoting them, the British relied on the knowledge amassed from travelogues as well as oral narratives that supported a mythology about Dinar that came to be treated as a fact. According to popular belief, Dinar had executed hundreds of his adversaries by putting them in a giant mortar and crushing their skulls. This myth has been canonized in proverbs, and to this day whenever people complain of authoritarianism, domestic violence or in-laws' maltreatment of women, or tyrannical bosses in the workplace, they invoke the sultan and his alleged style of execution by saying, "We are squished in Ali Dinar's mortar." Whether or not this myth has any basis in fact, Dinar did promote a particularly violent mode of governance, and pervasive public awareness of that reality predisposed them to believe it. As Beaton noted: "Ali Dinar reserved the death penalty for himself and weakened his viceroy's powers. . . . The last of the sultans is variously credited with clubbing murderers to death, beating to pulp inefficient tax collectors, lopping off the hands of thieves and castrating adulterers."[69] Publicizing—and perhaps exaggerating—these atrocities by what the British called a fanatical, militant despot who alienated his own people "formed part of a propaganda effort that sought to justify the impending advance of Sudan government forces into Darfur."[70]

Although horror at Dinar's alleged clubbings and beheadings may have played a role in the colonialist decision to advance into Darfur, the British were not ready to invade in the years immediately following their colonization of the Sudan. The Fur themselves had their own reasons to fear Dinar, who had raided and attacked their villages. According to Boustead, himself a colonial administrator in the Sudan, after Dinar had murdered his cousin Sultan Abul Khairat to proclaim himself sultan, "by reason of his harsh and violent temper, and the general fear which his record of brigandage had inspired, the Fur peasantry fled from him to Dar Masalit, to Dar Sulu and even to the East. He found himself with only his armed followers."[71] In this Fur view, Dinar's avowedly nationalistic fervor was undercut by functionaries defecting from his royal court.

Although British colonial accounts reflected marked resentment towards the sultan and his relationship with colonial authority was cold, he was allowed

to stay in power so long as he met the British demands for loyalty and obedience. However, Dinar was clearly a cause for concern, not only because of his
cruelty or belligerence but also because of his opposition to the colonial regime, including allegations that he had conspired with external powers against
the British government. He was eventually massacred in the course of Darfur's annexation in a decidedly violent imperialist encounter, which the British
tried to downplay by calling it "the Darfur Campaign" of 1916. Photographs
taken by the British during the campaign graphically tell of the terror meted
out to the people of Darfur: we see military transport motor vehicles, rifles
and weaponry, and members of the Fur royal family, including Ali Dinar's
sons and other notables, surrendering to the British forces. We see Hubert
Huddleston, one of the commanding officers, on a horse overseeing the attack on Ali Dinar's last camp in Kulme; Sir Reginald Wingate bidding farewell
to the officers of the Western Frontier Force during his visit to Nahud; local
people watching the first airplane to reach Rahad Abyad; and Fur causalities
on the battlefield.[72] From Gillan's account we learn about a camp of nearly two
thousand displaced people who, upon the approach of British forces, had run
for safety: "[We] reached Kulme without loss to find it just deserted. Pots were
still boiling on the fires and there were all the signs of a hurried evacuation."[73]
He proceeded to describe Huddleston's subsequent actions: "[He] dashed after
what looked the best dressed party just disappearing round a hill. A few shots
were exchanged from ridge to ridge, and after about the third rise we came
on a thick built form, with a strong and dignified face marred only by cruel,
sensuous lips, with a bullet hole drilled through the center of his forehead. It
was Ali Dinar."[74] Dinar was "killed at Zulli by a patrol operating in Dar Zami
Toya under the command of a young officer who later, as Major General Huddleston, became Governor-General of the Sudan."[75] The number of deaths resulting from this episode of colonial violence remains unknown. Instead, the
rationale advanced in most historical narratives turned centrally on British
aversion to the slave trade widely carried out by Ali Dinar.

In sum, the pages of SNR presented knowledge about the last sultan's sin-
glemindedness and fierce nationalistic passions in ways that strained credibility. His keen interest in the autonomous status of his sultanate, his recognition of the importance of its boundaries, and other acts manifestly averse to
colonial intervention became the perfect storm for his downfall.[76]

ANTHONY JOHN ARKELL (1898–1980)

To A. J. Arkell, who joined the Sudan Service in 1921 as assistant district commissioner of Kuttum and El Geneina and served until his retirement in 1948

as deputy governor, we owe a great deal of the rich ethnographic descriptions of Darfur. Trained in archaeology at Oxford, in 1939 he was appointed commissioner for archaeology and anthropology in the Sudan, a post he occupied well into his retirement. In addition to his voluminous contributions to *SNR*, rich archival sources housed at the special archives at Durham University[77] and the University of London School of Oriental and African Studies shed significant light on the man's experiences, sentiments, and challenges in Darfur as both anthropologist and administrator.[78] It is important to note that colonial archives are not immune to critique.[79] He was, however, a colonialist apart: his work represented a departure from his colleagues' association of Darfuris with racial inferiority. In his contributions to *SNR*, he never imposed racially coded, hierarchical systems of classification upon the people of the Sudan. Rather, through systematic observation and research in which he tried to historicize current cultural manifestations, he came to recognize the creativity inherent in Darfuri culture and society. True to his training, he believed in cultural relativism and refrained from passing judgment on local practices and mores. I include him here to recognize how even within the colonial corpus of knowledge, there have been important exceptions to the normative Western view of Africa and Africans.

Arkell's archives and essays illustrate his singularity in spite of the fraught circumstance of their production. He can be credited with creating a robust ethnographic record, all the while taking stock of his position as an anthropologist who produced knowledge as "a sympathetic outsider who . . . recognized the fact that he was an outsider."[80] His knowledge of the region was encyclopedic, and his archive provides a framework for understanding the patterns and processes through which cultural realities of Darfuri communities came to be understood by British and Sudanese alike. While there is no doubt that the knowledge he amassed was used by colonial officers in ways that did not necessarily reflect his scholarly perspectives, he cannot be responsible for how his work was used by others.

Arkell laid open the very anatomy of Darfuri knowledge regimes, thereby foregrounding the variety and significance of its rituals,[81] ideologies, and beliefs. His descriptions were prudently drawn, with a keen recognition of the importance of historically grounded internal variations in the social organization of the region's structures and communities. Because any attempt to address all of the many subjects he tackled is futile, I will focus on two themes that illustrate the cultural, religious, and political currents to which he devoted attention: Darfur's Christian and non-Muslim heritage, which he was able to pinpoint through historical tracings and archaeological excavations,[82] and Darfur as a society of circulation and external ties across its geographical frontiers. These two subjects are not mutually exclusive. His treatise on archaeology and anthropology uncovered the intercultural experiences running deep through history, creating layers of connectivity that sculpted Darfur's distinct identity and polity.[83] He wrote:

> My ideas on this subject were thrown into the melting pot, when I learned that pottery, that must have originated in Christian Nubia . . . was found 30 years ago in what has hitherto been considered a mosque at Ain Farah in Northern Darfur. . . . It is now clear that Ain Farah was not a capital of a Moselm [sic] sultanate, but that it was a Christian monastery, which dated back to A.D. 700 in Transjordan. Ain Farah was certainly not built A.D. 1585 for King Idris Aloma of Bornu.[84]

Arkell's work was anomalous not in its examination of cultural syncretism, but in placing that practice within the context of a sophisticated cultural dynamism. Other British district commissioners examined Christian relics in the context of the persistence of the symbolism of the cross in ritual practices among Islamized communities.[85] Indeed, several years prior to Arkell's search for Christian vestiges and residues, other colonial anthropologists had explored not only these influences but also the remnants of a pagan past on Darfur's religious cosmology.[86] Arkell's commentary on Fur spiritualities brings to mind the words of Nachtigal who noted: "The people . . . like all mountain dwellers, hold tenaciously to their ancient manners and customs, so that Islam itself, of which in the larger villages they are fanatical adherents, has not been able in the more distant regions to suppress Paganism completely."[87] Anthropologically, eclecticism is not solely a characteristic of Fur religion. Even today, throughout the Sudan and in spite of the fundamentalist discourse promoted by the government, Sufists visit tombs and shrines, utterly rejected by fundamentalists, to seek blessings (baraka). As anthropologist El-Sayed El-Aswad observed in an Egyptian village, shrines and tombs are powerful symbols "embodying a link between this world and the other world . . . a symbol embodying peoples' concepts of kinship, including those of descent and affinity . . . of blessing and honor [and] of solidarity."[88] They link the living to the dead saints in a singular spiritual field. But unlike his predecessors, Arkell argued that these symbolic representations came to be deeply rooted in Darfuri imagination as they navigated momentous transformations associated with the introduction of Islam.

Arkell developed these cultural connections in his work on Mani magic, which was a mysterious power practiced by the Zaghawa, Bedayat, and Zande in Northern Darfur and is believed to unfailingly kill anyone who swears falsely by it. There are various ways to swear by Mani; he describes one as the Spear of Mani (*Ku Mani*) and another as using a clay model and spears. Arkell's informants were a Zaghawi Mirra from Anka in Northern Darfur, a Zaghawi Mirra from Eastern Darfur, and a Kaitinawi and a Zaghawi Geni-gargera from Northern Darfur, who all assured him that "many Bedayat were more afraid of an oath on Mani than one on the Koran."[89] Arkell cites the long account given by Evans-Pritchard on Mani magic among the Zande of South Sudan, who practiced different versions of the custom, and argued that parallels between the different tribes' practice of Mani magic is not coincidental; rather, it is evidence of cultural contact between the Bedayat and Zaghawa and some sections of the Zande. Based on this evidence, Arkell hypothesized further parallels between the Zaghawa and the Zande to support his notion of Darfur's exchange with communities beyond its frontiers. There is also evidence of Mani magic among the Berbers, who reached central Africa through Libya and founded the empire of Kanem.

Arkell's work on Darfur's antiquities presents additional examples of the circulation of ideas and objects to and from the region. He investigated early transactions with a world beyond the sultanate in mythology; in double spiral amulets, sacred drums, stones, and the like; and in the practice of removing the uvula in infants. In his essay "The Double Spiral Amulet," Arkell exposed the root of this pattern in amulets found near the ruined town of Uri in Northern Darfur.[90] Although the amulets were no longer worn by the peoples of Northern Darfur when his essay appeared in 1937, he noted that they still were prevalent in other societies on the Indian Ocean rim, including among the women of the Aulad Suliman, Magharba, Urfilla, Bedur, and other "Arab Kanem" of El Fashir, and in Libya via Kanem. He also found evidence of these amulets being worn by pregnant women and children to the age of seven in Northern Nigeria and among the Mumuye and Yakoko in Yola Province. They are commonly worn as an ear pendant among the Jalno in Nyanza Province, Kenya, and as far afield as in Sumatra, at the southeast end of the Caspian Sea, and in the Naga Hills of Assam. Amulets were also found at the Muski market in Cairo in 1935. In all these localities, people shared similar beliefs in the magical powers of amulets resembling those worn in Darfur. Arkell concludes that their significance lies in the typical spiral pattern: it appears as a line without an end, which, it was hoped, would confer life without end.[91] In his essays on the surviving examples of steel structures (*zinat* in local Arabic), referring to flint and tinder in 1935 Darfur,[92] Arkell identifies the pattern of a "steel" purchased in Bazaar Tizi at Ouzou, Algeria, as strikingly similar to that of two "steels" from Darfur, suggesting the diffusion of steel patterns from North Africa to Darfur.

Arkell also considered the symbolism of Darfur's built environment, specifically the sultans' palaces as vessels of power. His study "Darfur Antiquities II:

Tora Palaces in Turra at the North End of Jebel Marra" assessed the relationship between social hierarchies and architectural features of six distinct palaces. Again, he provides detailed descriptions of the site of each palace, its surroundings, and its inner structure and imagines the arrangement of the various living rooms and huts. He infers that the destruction and renovation of a palace site was a result of internal strife and competition. In what he described as "a provisional conjecture as to the origin of the ruins of palaces," Arkell maintains that the exceptionally strong walls of the palaces are evidence of deteriorating security in the face of the raging civil wars that had destroyed existing forts in these sites.[93]

Arkell's rich record of Darfuri culture was an unusual contribution to the ethnographic knowledge of the region. By marking out the significant social life of material goods, historical sites, and cultural practices, he shows that Darfur was by no means a cocoon inhabited by insular indigenous tribes. By tracing cultural connections throughout the world with passion and seriousness, he produced a corpus of work that demonstrated that this was a cosmopolitan community rich in intellectual faculty and creativity. In doing so, he reminds us that there were exceptions to the distorted and injurious body of knowledge about Darfur amassed in the colonial period, that it was not solely a homogeneous monolith built on a set of false assumptions.

Exceptions like Felkin and Arkell notwithstanding, we can trace a straight line from the social categories imposed upon the Sudanese population by early travelers, to the racial assumptions governing the ethnographic observations and the policies of the British colonial regime, to the politics of Arab-dominated governments of the postcolonial period. Throughout this history ethnic differences have been codified into a racial hierarchy: darker-skinned Darfuris, defined as African, have been deemed inferior to lighter-complected Arabs. This categorization has also had political consequences: during the colonial period, the British effected policies that divided the Sudanese people into the more privileged Arab-dominated north and the marginalized African south. Since independence in 1956, the Sudanese elites who inherited power from the British—and their underlying racial assumptions—persisted in a pattern of marginalizing the south. Given this history, it is no surprise that both the elites and the marginalized of the Sudan have embraced an identity grounded in ethnicity, with profound consequences: as northern elites have continued to think of themselves as superior, worthy of political and social power, the peoples in the south and west have been increasingly restive in the face of continuing economic and political marginalization. These divisions erupted in 2003 and have driven the continuing crisis in Darfur. Most recently, nongovernmental organizations operate within the framework of these longstanding ethnic and racial binaries; as they work on behalf of Darfuri victims of ongoing violence, they fail to address the underlying issues of power and resource allocation. It is to this that I turn in the final pages of this chapter.

Pax-Humanitariana: NGOs' Manicheanism after 2003

The many NGOs that have flooded into the region since 2003 have represented the current crisis in Darfur as, to a large extent, a war between Arabs and Africans, two highly charged and overgeneralized categories defined entirely by ethnicity. It should be recalled that the troubles in southern Sudan (now the Republic of South Sudan) were similarly represented in binary terms, as a confrontation between Arabs and Black Africans. What then does this bifurcation of identity mean for individuals and communities living in and outside the region—the people the NGOs call "Darfurians"?

As these organizations have striven to transform knowledge into what philosopher Michael Welbourne has called "a kind of public commodity, something that may be available to anyone,"[94] they have drawn upon eugenicist notions of race in the Western imagination as essential and inborn and based on a physical appearances index (in fact, physical differences between Sudanese Arabs and non-Arabs are minimal). For what purpose? In this case, the universal application of presumably clear-cut ethnic identities has led many to conceive of all people who identify as Arabs as Janjaweed, those "devils on horsebacks," or as Janjaweed sympathizers. Janjaweed and Darfurian as oppositional identities have thus been coined, circulated, and consumed as givens—even as not all Arabs are Janjaweed or their allies and some Janjaweed are Darfuri. Despite the inaccuracy, however, the essentialization of identity has legitimized calls by the NGOs and their supporters for the rescue of the indigenous Black tribes, the Fur, Zaghawa, and Masalit, highlighting a persistent pattern of humanitarian organizations' embeddedness in and contribution to a broader international order supportive of the reductive labeling of victim and villain.

The focus on biology at the expense of political and economic factors in the interpretation of the conflicts in the area also ignores significant ethnographic knowledge produced by Darfur-born anthropologists. As early as 1979, anthropologist Musa Adam Abdul-Jalil wrote a dissertation in which he called into question the concept of ethnicity as an immutable biological fact by linking it to occupation, genealogy, and language.[95] More recently, Sharif Harir's 2004 dissertation addresses the difficulties created by environmental degradation as it relates to racial and ethnic identities.[96]

A reliance on racialized binaries also fails to recognize a major fact on the ground, i.e., that Darfur is an integral part of the Arabized Muslim Northern Sudan. Prior to 2003, there was no reference to "Darfurian" as a singular identity distinct from other ethnicities in the country. Rather, the term is a foreign designation born out of specific patterns of representation and cultural production imposed on a people who previously viewed themselves as Afro-Arabs and Sudanese citizens. It now signifies a newly assigned Black identity as opposed to a homogenized Arab Janjaweed. Similarly, the word "Janjaweed" may have existed in Darfur in reference to outlaws or bandits or even to naughty little children. However, its current meaning only gained currency in the context of intra-Muslim violence in the region. It is part of political processes that have shaped its invention since at least the 1980s, due largely to Al-Bashir's racism and the militarization of ethnic differences, a discussion taken up in chapter 3. This categorization severely inhibits NGOs' ability to grasp events in their totality, even as their presumed expertise, based on direct encounter with conditions in Africa, makes them producers of truth-claims. NGO staffers working in Darfur have also relied on images of victimization and suffering to garner support as their relationship to conflicts on the continent has changed from the delivery of emergency aid to support for military intervention, a transformation Michael Barnett has argued is a characteristic of humanitarian organizations working around the globe.[97] Celebrities throwing their weight behind these new forms of power also reinforce the enduring image of the African as primarily a victim. Recasting the plight of populations in crisis in terms of the moral language of a Western corpus of knowledge thus exploits humanitarianism for political advantage and the corporate interest of the humanitarian organizations. As a consequence, only violence inflicted by Arabs against Africans is reported, whereas violence meted out by JEM and SLM insurgents, which include "African" Darfuris, against Darfuri civilians is not. For instance, a Dutch humanitarian team accompanied by a Sudanese translator was in Darfur collecting stories about rape perpetrated by Arabs as a weapon of war. When an interviewee mentioned that she was sexually violated by a fellow internally displaced person, the team coordinator rejected the translation as she did not hear the word "Janjaweed" in the translator's retelling.[98] In other words, a perpetrator from among the presumed victim category doesn't fit this Dutch humanitarian's categories, and the complicated politics of the situation are again obscured.

In sum, NGOs have embraced the same binary ethnic categories described by early racist travelers and codified by British colonial administrators as the sole framework for understanding the conflict in Darfur. By ignoring the fact that people have flexible identities that do not rely on narratives of origin and essentialist tribal and ethnic affinities and using these narratives and affinities as a basis for bestowing aid, humanitarians have forfeited a core ethos of neutrality.

With a Click of a Mouse

> Knowledge is a fiercely contested site in modern societies. Questions of who possesses it . . . elicit strong emotions. The intensity generated by issues of evidence, of authority, and of expertise reflects a way of thinking of knowledge, which has become so familiar that it is difficult to see alternatives. Although it is an abstraction, knowledge seems a remarkably solid part of our world—a secure end-state, even a product—standing independently of the cumulative struggles of its achievement.[99]

So far, I have provided examples of the various knowledge regimes that have been produced on Darfur in the course of history. I conclude with a few thoughts on how knowledge about Darfur is being produced in the digital age. Digital platforms, powered by technology, carry with them considerable power. They have consolidated the story of binary opposition that I have tried to highlight. Note, for example, the digital activism of a campaign called Darfur Is Dying. This video game was developed by a team at the University of Southern California's School of Cinematic Arts "to share the experience of the 2.5 million refugees in the Darfur." Its designers said that their intention was to raise awareness of the genocide taking place in Darfur and empower college students to help stop the crisis. The game won the Darfur Digital Activist Contest sponsored by MTV; its creators claim that the game was developed in cooperation with "humanitarian aid workers with extensive experience in Darfur."[100] Here is how they describe the game:

> *Darfur Is Dying* is a web-based, viral video game that provides a window into the experience of the 2.5 million refugees in the Darfur region of Sudan. . . . The content and the creative are woven together throughout the game, beginning with the first phase where the user selects an avatar [note that all avatars are black with African features] to forage for water. Upon success or failure, they learn that their chances of succeeding were predetermined by their gender and age. The navigation system . . . enables a player to learn about the situation in Darfur, get involved with stopping the crisis, and understand the genesis of the project [game].

Darfur Is Dying helps make activism intuitive in the digital age. Action items are embedded within the game, so that the user may send an automated note to President George W. Bush to support the people of Darfur or petition Congress to pass legislation that aids Darfur's refugees, and by doing so increase the overall health of the camp. To further enhance the reach of the game, Darfur Is Dying was designed to be spread virally. Players can contact everyone in their email address books and social networks about the game with a click of the mouse.[101] Curiously, several of the Darfuri children depicted in Darfur Is Dying have South Sudanese names, suggesting that the game developers use the category "Black" to represent people, unaware of the difference between Darfuri and South Sudanese. Still, in itself, this game is by no means the most atrocious thing that Darfuri people have had to contend with. Its significance lies with the 800,000 players of the game who have come to form opinions based on essential categories (Black African vs. Arab) that are then deemed effective for guiding social and political action.

Similarly, the Save Darfur Coalition posits that what is occurring in Darfur is a form of ethnic cleansing targeting Blacks, analogous to Nazi Germany's extermination of Jews. It eschews a more comprehensive understanding of the politics at play, thereby rendering invisible sources of differentiation other than race and ignoring Mahmood Mamdani's understanding of the distortions that occur when drawing upon overdetermined racial categories to explain events. This simplistic view has nonetheless raised millions of dollars to draw public attention to the crisis in Darfur. However, it has changed nothing on the ground, nor has it helped the Darfuri people.[102] When challenged about this, the movement's creators claimed that aid to the people of Darfur was not their mandate. Their only purpose was to raise awareness of the conflict. Similarly unencumbered by doubt about the likelihood of transforming words into action, digital activists in the United States have persisted in creating forums such as Darfurian Voices,[103] 24 Hours for Darfur, and Darfur Now, as well as countless YouTube uploads in which Blackness is constructed as an explanation for narrating events in Darfur. This is rendered especially clearly in the YouTube video "Brooklyn Darfurians," in which a number of Black men from Darfur introduce themselves, describe what they term "genocide" against the Black people of Darfur, and ask the United States and the United Nations to respond. "In 2003 the government of Sudan and its allies, the Arab Janjaweed, they burned my village to the ground. In that village, the government and the Janjaweed killed more than fifty-two people in one day, and they loaded everything [stole people's belongings], raped women, and destroyed the wealth. Since that time, my family, my parents they are displaced in camps, some of them until now I don't know where they are," says Hamza Ibrahim from Anka village, Northern Darfur.[104] Videos like this exemplify how groups of activists with access to the internet are able to publicize their point of view. All these race-based descriptions of the conflict are extremely appealing to a large swath of people who do not understand the complexity of "race" in postcolonial Africa. They do not comprehend how ethnicity intersects with class, deprivation, and poverty. In fact, Darfuris who have reconciled with the ousted Al-Bashir are among the wealthiest people in the country and are, indeed, part of the Sudanese government.

We cannot ignore the fact that many Darfuris both inside and outside of the country have bought into the binary, race-based nature of the conflict. And the postcolonial elites in the Sudan, including especially Al-Bashir, have certainly benefitted, even exploited it to their political advantage and personal gain. Indeed, their internalized sense of supremacy is nowhere better expressed than in the term Al-Bashir used when he described his Arabization project as a "civilizing project." Yet the Darfuris are not just victims of erroneous thinking; they are also producers of knowledge. As Sir Reginald Wingate noted in 1918, knowledge is power, and a significant amount of power derives from knowledge of any sort. There are Darfuri scholars, as noted above, producing robust and nuanced knowledge about the crisis. The International Criminal Court actively listens to victims of the violence meted out by Al-Bashir's regime, providing a forum for both a measure of personal empowerment and the dissemination of public knowledge. More vernacular producers of knowledge are also claiming the power to define their own stories via social media. While their knowledge of the dynamics of the current crisis in Darfur may be limited, it is no more partial—and perhaps less so—than the grounds of Al-Bashir's knowledge. Their work has the power of shaping perceptions, as their often-defiant responses to the crisis take hold via social media. Impressed with South Sudanese secession activism, a group of young Darfuri artists have used social media as a platform for channeling their energy and voicing their opinions. Since its early days, rap has been used as an instrument of political expression and a medium for self-determination, and thus dissent and opposition are woven into its cultural representations. A band called the Darandoka Boys has been active on Darfuri-run social media and has recently promoted their song "Almoostatinoon Aljoddod" (The New Settlers). In addition to furthering the perception of the Darfur crisis as a "genocide" and "humanitarian disaster," the song contributes to existing categorizations by painting a picture of conquest in which Darfur is occupied by "new settlers." The song speaks of invaders who come in without any "identification" or "résumé" and take over villages otherwise peacefully inhabited by native residents who have lived in their land for centuries. The Darandoka Boys are part of a group called Darfur Youth for Secession, which, as its name suggests, supports Darfur's secession from the Sudan. The song reinforces popular rhetoric among Darfuris on social media that the resistance and regional loyalty of Darfur's people will only continue to grow the more the invaders attempt to divide and destroy them. The deployment of the rap genre in this context is therefore a conscious appropriation of a popular medium of expression to promote a particular discourse predicated historically on power relations, racial conflict, and systemic structural injustices.[105]

For Sudanese and non-Sudanese alike, the internet has the potential to offer an anonymous public sphere in which individuals can discuss issues more openly than they normally would in everyday life.[106] But in reality, this ideal rarely plays out. People are not entering this public sphere on an equal footing. Some players (for example, celebrities) are so powerful that they drown out the others. Moreover, the location of these online forums on Facebook, for example, means that individuals are required to have existing accounts in order to join these groups. A user's profiles, which often feature the account holder's picture, also give the individual's name. For people still living in the Sudan, criticism of the government's policies, such as its failure to provide services, exposes commenters to significant danger of retaliation or bullying. Darfuri bloggers and YouTubers persist, but the truly open conversation that the medium could support has not developed. Thus, when bloggers in the Sudan used WhatsApp to call for acts of civil disobedience in September 2017, the media message sent shudders of horror through the authorities in the government. In a crescendo of rage, President Al-Bashir resorted to bombastic dares: "Those cowards who hide behind keyboards, why don't you meet us in the streets?" and a blogger struck back, "Why don't you meet us keyboard to keyboard?" In an equally hyperbolic pitch, Al-Bashir's right-hand man Nafi Ali Nafi added, "Lick your elbow," to suggest the impossibility of radical change. So far, these bloggers have not faced personal repercussions, but the danger is always there.

My interpretations of the knowledge created by social media—and indeed of all the knowledge regimes discussed in this chapter—were generated by a series of questions raised by V. Y. Mudimbe in what he refers to as "the invention of Africa." He asks: "Who is speaking about it? Who has the right and the credentials to produce it, describe it, comment upon it, or at least represent it?"[107] And, I would add, who owns the knowledge that has been produced about Darfur? It is clear that circuits of knowledge production profoundly affect identities, both how you are seen by others and how you see yourself. Transnational technologies exacerbate and often distort these processes.[108]

The production of knowledge about Darfur, as we have seen, has a long history, from the observations of early travelers to the voluminous ethnographic chronicles in the colonial era in *Sudan Notes and Records*, and continuing in the present in the knowledge regimes of NGOs and digital platforms. While the travelogue afforded us an opportunity to historicize the production of knowledge, the colonial successors to these wayfaring men drew on their earlier work to construct cultural and political profiles of the sultanate and its people in binary categories of Arab and African and to construct policies based on them. NGOs who arrived in the region in 2003 have used the same categories to understand the conflict and thereby to claim a place in the world community as arbiters of truth about the root cause behind the conflict. Most recently, both Darfuri and non-Darfuri activists have illustrated the tenacity of this oppositional framework on digital platforms.

This discussion of the production of knowledge about Darfur nonetheless leaves us with more questions than answers: What is at stake in the knowledge produced by the dichotomous thinking that still obtains? What regional, class, and gender politics are overlooked by this form of knowledge? What is the effect of enduring representations that pivot on race and ethnicity? The exploitation of ethnic differences to mobilize political violence in the struggle for power must be situated within the politics of a postcolonial failed state that has allowed its elites to become among the most ruthless and richest people in the world today. Understanding in depth how economic and class differences transect with power is critical for understanding the terrible tenacity of the Sudan's political violence, a phenomenon that cannot be attributed to a single all-embracing cause.

Some Views from the Sudan¹

When I finished my ethnographic work in 2018, I and many of my interlocutors would not have anticipated the meteoric rise of Mohamad Hamdan Daglo (Hemeti) to the highest echelons of political power following the Revolution of 2018. A man who was at the center of mobilizing the militia in Darfur is now a revered and feared member of the governing Transitional Sovereign Council. By all accounts this is not the council the revolutionaries who raised the slogan "We are all Darfuris" wished to see, and at the moment disappointment and disenchantment are running deep in the entire Sudanese body politic. No doubt relieved that Al-Bashir is gone, they need an accounting for current conditions and the justice they have long waited for. Many find it paradoxical that someone whom many have blamed for atrocities is now in charge of ratifying the appointment of former Darfuri opponents to ministerial posts in the newly formed government. Photographs of Hemeti with exiles have traveled across time and place on Facebook and in Sudanese newspapers to show elites closing ranks around their class interests. This imagery goes to the heart of not viewing Darfur in binary racial categories and serves as a lead into this chapter. Those who have treated the "sliding signifier"² of race as dogma are having to revisit their positions in light of the scenarios presently unfolding. Still, predictions about what mayhem is coming down the pike are hard to make.

In this chapter I present wide-ranging and contested perspectives on the Darfur crisis, including narratives approving of Al-Bashir's regime, critical counternarratives particularly from a Marxist perspective (translated from Arabic scripts), and voices of the displaced in the capital city of Khartoum describing the experience of dislocation and making do in the bustling city. I conclude with a discussion of recent government efforts to encourage internally displaced people (IDPs) to return to Darfur. It is important to be clear at the outset that while I do relay narratives of Al-Bashir's supporters that justify political violence in the region—views to which no one has paid systematic attention to date—my intention is not to legitimize either these views or their supporters, but rather to present important voices in Sudanese politics. No single representation can be accepted at face value; indeed, among both Al-Bashir's supporters and his opponents, views and opinions differ vastly. For example, Khalil Ibrahim, a former minister in the Al-Bashir government and a staunch Islamist, was one of the two leaders who started the insurgency in Darfur, a fact that some would claim is evidence that renegade Islamist opponents of the government initiated the violence. I have juxtaposed these views with powerful Marxist critiques, which those writing about Darfur have also effaced, largely because these critics defied preconceived racial explanations of the conflict in Darfur. In both cases I felt it imperative to bring these voices forward, for they are important sources for understanding ongoing debates on Darfur. Finally, as I stated in the Prelude, at an early age I became aware that Darfur had long been systematically ignored and marginalized. It is my view that this indifference cannot be isolated from right wing conservative politics that grew out of the womb of colonialism.

Given the multiplicity of competing views about who and what is responsible for the Darfur crisis and hence the difficulty of pinning down a single explanation, I yield to the wisdom of Yahia Adam Madibo, the *nazir* (leader) of the Rezeigat tribe of Southern Darfur, who said to me, "The Darfur problem is definitely reminding us of the bad omen we attach to a crowlike, flesh-eating bird named *umm kulu'lu'*. When it lays its egg, everyone is forewarned: don't come near this egg, because if you lift it, it will kill your mother, and if you leave it alone, it will kill your father."[3] Nazir Madibo's analogy captures the agonizing dilemmas facing Darfur today: To a great extent, competing narratives about the nature of the crisis and the language used to describe it render it unsolvable. Of primary importance is the government's denial of its role in the violence meted out by the army and its proxy militias, the Janjaweed. Additionally, government sympathizers claim activism on behalf of human rights in Darfur to be a signifier for imperialist intervention in the Sudan's internal affairs. Nowhere has this charge been made so clearly as in the discourse questioning the Janjaweed's identity and political alliances. This became apparent with the issuance of an arrest warrant against the Sudanese president on March 4, 2009. In the case of the *Prosecutor v. Omar Hassan Ahmad Al Bashir* (ICC-02/05-01/09), the International Criminal Court (ICC) charged Al-Bashir with five counts of crimes against humanity, two counts of war crimes, and three counts of genocide against the Darfuri people.[4] In a 2009 broadcast of the BBC's *The Doha Debates*, moderator Tim Sebastian moved that "Arab governments should hand over President Omar Al-Bashir to the ICC." Ghazi Atabani, at the time an adviser to the president, voted against the motion, arguing that "the case is weak. We need to know that the prosecutor of the ICC has never set foot in the Sudan. He collected evidence by proxy, and this evidence itself is flimsy." He added, "The ICC is an instrument of politics, not of justice."[5] Statements like this are uttered frequently not just in the Sudan but throughout the African continent, a position whose reductio ad absurdum suggests that these Janjaweed are nothing but an urban legend.

Solidarity Rallies, Fatwas, and Chants

The blood being shed is from Muslims, and we absolve ourselves of shedding Muslim blood and of whatever is perpetrated by [Islamist leader Hassan] Al-Turabi. . . . There was a certain person who used to be our sheikh and leader, but we have come [to] realize that he was but a liar and a hypocrite. . . . The enemies of our country and enemies of our people do not want this war to stop. They do not want the carnage to end. They want to tear our country apart and incite Muslims to kill their fellow Muslims.

So spoke President Al-Bashir, at an event in which he appeared, in full military attire, before hundreds of people who had come to hear one of his numerous speeches on Darfur. His words, which I have translated from Arabic, were reported as follows: "The problem of Darfur was engineered to abort our joyful anticipation of imminent peace. The problem in Darfur is essentially a traditional dispute over meager resources."[6]

In a climate saturated with the emotions of both proponents and opponents of the ICC's indictment of Al-Bashir, the High Supreme Council of Sudanese religious leaders issued fatwas, or religious opinions, against the warrant. These fatwas differed markedly from those issued in years past and not necessarily applied in the Sudan. Those against the ICC, however, heightened Sudanese citizens' attention to Al-Bashir's fate. One such fatwa prohibited Al-Bashir from traveling abroad for fear he would be arrested and the government be destabilized. Al-Bashir ignored their warning, presumably to avoid losing face among the Sudanese people and other Arab nations. He appeared in solidarity rallies dancing, swinging his ebony cane in the air, and declaring loudly and clearly, "Tell [ICC Prosecutor Luis Moreno] Ocampo to soak his warrant and drink its water," and "Ocampo and his followers are all under my shoe."[7] Cavalier about both the fatwa and the ICC, Al-Bashir took several trips to Eritrea, Qatar, Libya, South Africa, and Zimbabwe. In South Africa, attempts to arrest him were thwarted by then-president Jacob Zuma. Robert Mugabe, at the time the Zimbabwean president, declared that his country had no obligation to surrender its controversial visitor to the ICC.

Mugabe's response must be situated within African politics and in relation to threats from African nations to withdraw from the ICC because of its allegedly unfair treatment of Africans and Arabs. Al-Bashir, now considered a fugitive from justice by the international community, is a bona fide hero to his Islamist supporters, for whom he personifies Arabism, Africanism, and Islamism rolled into a single narrative of resistance to "arrogant states." He and his supporters contend that his powerful defiance of the ICC symbolizes the end of neocolonialism and that his fate lies within the purview of the divine. They conveniently cite the Quran: Allah "can bequeath the throne to whomever he wishes and uproots it away from whomever he wishes."

However, there has been no unified position among Islamists about the ICC warrant. While Al-Bashir's supporters continued to pass unfavorable judgment against the ICC prosecutor, his Islamist opponents, including Hassan Al-Turabi, accepted the political realities of the ICC. Another fatwa, more controversial and potentially more consequential than its predecessors, authorized the shedding of Ocampo's blood by Islamists on the grounds that his decision represents an inexcusable assault on African and Muslim leaders who have refused to perform rituals of obedience and loyalty to Western hegemony. A poster widely displayed in rallies in Khartoum and Darfur featured Ocampo as a pig, a symbol of filth in Muslim cosmology, and stated in bold letters, "Ocampo, you coward, Al-Bashir is in the battlefield." An alliance of organizations, the Martyrdom Jihad Movements, embraced this fatwa and disseminated it publicly, with the warning that it would execute suicide missions against countries championing the ICC's decision (e.g., the United States, France, and the United Kingdom).[8] Supporters of the warrant were threatened with retribution as traitors of faith and nation. In one case, members of Doctors without Borders in Darfur were abducted by Nosoor Al-Bashir, a member of the alliance, under the pretext of protecting the country from spies masquerading as humanitarian workers. Inflaming nationalist, Islamist, and jihadist sentiments, Hassan Nasrallah of Hezbollah and Khalid Mishaal of Hamas embraced the view that Al-Bashir was pursued because of his unyielding resistance to imperialist discourses on global security. In a long television speech, Ayman al-Zawahiri, the second-in-command of Al Qaeda, pushed for a jihad against individuals and countries that supported the ICC warrant, asking the Sudanese to prepare for a guerrilla war and comparing the resistance with situations in Iraq, Afghanistan, and Palestine.

These statements essentially evacuate the ICC's jurisprudential legitimacy, describing its chief officer as an activist rather than a jurist and accusing him of weighing justice with two scales. It is worth noting that Sudanese history brims with nationalist passions that are linked to questions of sovereignty and that sovereignty can be staged as a performance of political authority. As a participant in a pro-Al-Bashir solidarity rally asserted, "*The servant of the holy man is forced to pray.*" A Darfuri in Doha seconded this view as he described how crowds are mobilized in Darfur: "*If you bring people in cars you are paid a certain sum of money. You are also paid handsomely if you get people to a rally location on a horse, a donkey, or a camel.*"[9] In other situations, those who joined rallies cited nationhood as a reason for their decision to stand against the presumed double standards of the international community.

How then do we understand the solidarity rallies that flooded the streets from Khartoum to Darfur as depicted in the Sudanese media? What were the emotional investments of those who rallied for Al-Bashir? And how do we ascertain the significance of solidarity rallies as evidence of public opinion under constraining circumstances? To navigate the terrain of media, we do well to summon Edward Herman and Noam Chomsky's *Manufacturing Consent*; it offers a powerful analysis of how political and economic forces prompt individuals and media organizations to mold the landscape of knowledge and belief.[10] For several months after the warrant against Al-Bashir was issued, Sudan TV's daily program *What They Are Saying about the So-Called ICC* broadcast demonstrations across the Sudan protesting the ICC decision to audiences within and outside the country. According to Ibrahim Hamdi, these televised rallies elevated morale to new heights and, during a speech before thousands in war-torn Zalengi, one of the most politically charged towns in Darfur, gave Al-Bashir the confidence to promise—falsely—to track down war criminals in Darfur.[11] While skeptics argue that under political dictatorships public opinion cannot be measured by massive demonstrations and, as we have seen, participation is sometimes quite expedient, nonetheless the extent of political mobilization in favor of Al-Bashir has been unprecedented. Media analysis suggests that these televised rallies have played a role in shoring up support for Al-Bashir, even as they exemplify the performance of sovereignty and resistance to neocolonialism.

In the Sons of Southern States Solidarity Rally, which took place in 2009 before the secession of the South, Al-Bashir appeared in a feathered headdress, leopard skin skirt, ox horns, beads, and amulets. Huge speakers in the yard of Sadaqqa Hall by the Nile in Khartoum transmitted chants of "Hallelujah" and "Allah Akbar." Millions of southerners vowed that they were willing to die for the Sudan if Al-Bashir were targeted by the ICC. Southern leaders, sultans, and politicians voiced their solidarity with a "man who brought peace to the south" and concluded the six-hour event by taking a solemn oath to stand by him. A Sudanese TV correspondent reported that "there was no obvious sign of opposition at the rally where Al-Bashir arrived on the back of an open truck, as streams of white-robed Darfuris rode past him on horses and camels. On the edges of the crowd, people climbed trees and stood on the raised scoop of an industrial digger to get a better view."[12] A southern Darfuri explained the fervor of these rallies to me plainly: "*We spared no effort to offer our lives in sacrifice for jihad in the path of Allah. We were at the front lines in the war in southern Sudan. When the Islamists recruited us, we obliged. The majority of those who joined jihad in southern Sudan did so of their own volition. In fact, we revered the cause and the people like Sheikh Hassan Al-Turabi [at that time an Al-Bashir supporter]. At one point if he asked us to pray facing west [in opposition to the Islamic practice of facing east toward Mecca to pray], we would have gladly prayed facing west."*

Considering these responses, political leaders in opposition parties who stood by Al-Bashir noted that whether or not people have rallied in his support is quite peripheral to broader concerns about the adverse consequences of neocolonial interventionism. To assert that these rallies indicate Sudanese rejection of the ICC is likewise insufficient; rather, their strong links to nationalist passions and questions of sovereignty must also be understood within the context of what is largely perceived as a neocolonial confrontation. Worldwide, rallies drew thousands who denounced the double standard of international law and rebuked the ICC. While the majority of Darfuris were supportive of the ICC, a few departed from this position by remonstrating against any possible international intervention and opposing what they argued was selective and compartmentalized justice. These responses, whether in support of or in opposition to the ICC, cannot be treated as homogeneous. Similarly, contestations within the Sudan over the Darfur crisis take place at the nexus of several interrelated topics, including the responsibility of the government and Janjaweed for the crisis, the government's responses to the crisis, the perspectives of internally displaced persons and government apologists, and peace activists' visions of enfranchisement and empowerment. Below I provide examples of views from the Sudan about the origins of the conflict. The official script attempts to disavow the link between the Janjaweed's counterinsurgency activities and the government. In opposition is an account that illuminates the transformation of the Janjaweed militias from "displacers" to chief perpetrators of the violence in 2003. To this latter category belong Sudanese Marxist critiques of the state, also discussed below.

Albino Crocodiles, or Devils on Horsebacks? Some Views on Janjaweed

When the fighting started, we all tried to run away with our children. The men fled after seeing others getting killed and beaten by the Janjaweed. These people acted like devils. They don't have good hearts and are not pious Muslims. They burnt villages, attacked, and caused a lot of pain and death.

How can they kill and rape like this? Every time we listen to the radio or read the newspapers, we hear about thousands of displaced people on their way back to their old villages. These people were forced to leave in 2004 and continued running away for years. They lost their independence.

Since the start of the violence, the Janjaweed's provenance, genealogy, ethnic and national identity, and actions in the region have received considerable attention in literary circles and films, and among celebrities and faith-based groups. Before 2003, the word "Janjaweed" was a sheer enigma, a satanic sprout that sprang from the middle of nowhere. In Darfuri vernacular it refers to "the devils on horseback." In the course of this ethnography, I have heard of other less nefarious meanings as well. To Haj Alkhalifa, a man knowledgeable about local and border politics whom I interviewed in 2004, "Janjaweed" as a vernacular Darfuri Arabic word migrated from Chad. It has no correspondent in other parts of northern Arabic-speaking communities, hence its incomprehensibility. He noted an interesting triangulation of banditry, Chadian politics, and borders:

> The usage of this term in Darfur has always been associated with criminals, hence jin in Arabic. But sometimes it was used to describe naughty people, unruly children, and the like. In political terms, a friend told me that he first heard it uttered by the late Chadian president [François] Tombalbaye, a French-speaking Christian from the Sara ethnic community who faced fierce opposition from Muslims throughout his fifteen or more years of rule. He called those who gave him a hard time "these Janjaweed." That is what I heard. I don't know this for sure. Am I shocked? No. So many ugly things came to us from our neighbor Chad—bandits, soldiers, smuggled weapons, and disasters, even the encroaching desert. I won't be shocked if the word also crossed the border.

In Abdal Aziz Baraka Sakin's novel *The Messiah of Darfur* a conversation between the protagonist and a relative who served in the military gives us many elements of the Janjaweed's origin and identity:

The Janjaweed live in huge camps on the outskirts of Nyala. They would come downtown on Land Cruisers, trucks with Dushka cannons on their backs and the ugly RPG machine guns dangling on the sides. They sit on the back, wearing filthy dresses soaked in sweat and dust, wearing amulets and big helmets. They have bushy hair that reeks of the desert and homelessness. The GM3 on their shoulders is ready to shoot for any silly reason. They have no respect for human life and barely see any difference between human beings and stray dogs. They are distinct in their strange dialects known as "Dajar," the colloquial Arabic of Niger or Western Sahara. They have no women or girls. Nor have they among them anyone who is civilian, religious, enlightened, teacher, student, manager, or craftsman. They have no village, town, or even a state. They have no homes that they long to return to at the end of the day. They work for one single objective: that creature with long legs and strong humped back and belly big enough to store a barrel of water. They imprint its image on their flags, eat its meat and fat, drink its milk, live on its back, and use its hair as accommodation. It's the creature that carries them for long distances to where they kill or get killed for the sake of securing grazing land for it. It's their master and slave at the same time: the so-called camel. It's not clear to anyone why the government selected those people in particular, of all the nations of Africa, to launch the war in Darfur on its behalf.[13]

In my own exchanges with him, Sakin told me that he tried to give the reader a better understanding of both the complex identity of the perpetrators and that, contrary to the assumed Arab/African binary, "not all Arab Darfuris took part in the carnage."

Among the useful discussions about the origins of the Janjaweed and its connection to the Sudanese government is Mohamad Badawi's *The Harvest of Gunpowder*, published in Arabic, which traces the emergence of the Janjaweed within a context of political violence, social disarray, and contested international borders. He divides the Janjaweed into several interlocking groups to identify the layers of their politicization and subsequent incorporation in Darfur's proxy war:

> In tracing the origin of Janjaweed, we have to look at the political context of Darfur since 1989. Since the region was under Emergency Law, the authorities there were given exceptional mandates to establish special courts for trying dissidents and opponents of the Islamist regime. But the pretext [for using the courts] at the time was that of fighting banditry . . . and when the governors of the three states in Darfur decided to release bandits from their prisons, they armed these convicted felons and renamed them as the repentant troops. These bandits formed the kernel of Janjaweed in 2001. With the escalation of conflict over scarce resources between the farmers and the nomads, the governors hastened to call upon this troop in El Fashir, especially from the camel-owning bandits. . . . At the time Janjaweed had multiple usages, which spawned significant debates. The media played a role in changing the word from Janjaweed to al-Janjaweed.[14] . . . Previously, these Janjaweed were camel herders. With the new change it became a military base with the specific objective of militarizing specific ethnicities who hailed from camel-herding groups. Under the supervision of the Sudanese military intelligence, the government decided to call these militias by another name, Border Security and Intelligence, to consolidate their position as a unit of the army as well as to decrease the attention of the international community to the issue of Arab identity questions around the Janjaweed. The government proceeded to recruit from the ranks of the African ethnic Berti in 2006 as reserve army with the same mandate as the border patrol.[15]

Badawi thus offers insights into internal differences within what numerous Western representations have considered a singular, undifferentiated tribal Arab entity.

These categories, recognized by Darfuri writers and activists in my conversations with them, deserve further consideration. First are the militias recruited within Darfur itself, which include Arabs and non-Arabs from Chad; second are ex-felons and mercenaries. A Sudanese from Darfur whom I also interviewed about Janjaweed identity said a great deal in support of the above accounts: *"The government enlisted from among the Tuarig people of Niger as well as common criminals from the Cameroon. Their desperation pushed them to enroll as mercenaries, soldiers of fortune who have no emotional attachment to Darfur and its people,"* adding, *"just another crowd of outlaws that Darfur had to reckon with."* Through my conversations, I came to understand the origins of the Janjaweed militia as connected to complex social, economic, and political circumstances. According to a Sudanese of Berti heritage, *"The Janjaweed learned the lesson of draining the pond to kill the fish. The attack against villages was undertaken in this spirit. They knew that insurgents need to return home, to eat, bathe, and rest. But by destroying their homes, they ensured that rebels had nowhere to go."* Nonetheless, whether or not Janjaweed were bandits from Chad and irrespective of the conceptual and political contestations over their origin, the acts they committed prompted those who survived their attacks to see their flight as tantamount to fleeing *"from under the shadow of the sword,"* as a woman told me.

Juxtapose these views with a text titled *The Janjaweed Legend: An Excuse for Foreign Intervention and Destruction of Darfur Society* by Shams E. Idris. To Idris, like the rest of the regime's supporters inside the country, the Janjaweed is merely a legend, akin to albino crocodiles in New York City sewers. As if woven from his imagination, the author spares no effort in promoting the age-old alleged conspiracy that the Sudan is targeted by outsiders for its strategic location and supporting it with stories gathered in different locations as he traveled in Darfur:

> The name Janjaweed surfaced through the Western media and the international organizations that have a special agenda to destroy the country. These equated them with Arab tribes in Darfur. When I visited Northern and Southern Darfur to ask about the identity of the Janjaweed, a sheikh in his seventies mentioned that the man who doesn't own a horse (since the Janjaweed are associated with horses and known as devils on horsebacks) has no standing in the community. Horses are means of transport. "We are used to racing, it is a symbol of dignity," [he said]. . . . When I commented by saying that these tribes are using the animals to attack other people and to steal their money and animals, he explained that "the rebels from South Sudan used to attack their area in Bahr Al-Arab to steal, kill, and take hostages. We had to protect ourselves. So we recruited knights to enter the rebel zones to bring back our stolen cows. The real name for these horseback fighters is knights, not Janjaweed." "Where did they get their arms from?" I asked. [He told me that] arms are easy to obtain from Central African Republic and Chad: "After

the Southern rebels attacked us in 1987, we asked the government for help. It provided us with weapons to protect ourselves from those Southerners who used to attack us from Bahr Al-Arab."[16]

Idris goes on in this vein to comment on his conversations in Kass, Nerttiti, and Zalengi, elaborating on the presumed distinction between the Janjaweed, who cover their faces, and the people with whom he had spoken in Wadi Salih, who claim not to be the Janjaweed and veil for other reasons:

In this station in Wadi Salih, the inhabitants are mainly Fur although some Arab tribes also live in the western regions of Jebel Marra. . . . We found horses and camels owned by some people and kept together as if parked in any marketplace lot. I asked the people there about the reason behind the use of the turban [which is wrapped around the face in burqa-like fashion]; they told me, "We veil to protect ourselves from the heat and the dust and from the retaliation of Chadian people. We used to trade with them in arms, which we carried back on our camels' backs. When we cover our faces with these turbans, which are also worn in Chad, we avoid vengeful acts."[17]

Heat and dust aside, Idris fails to challenge the veiled men's explanation, refusing to see their identity as marauding bandits implicated in the political violence in Darfur. To him, the stakeholders in the region and abroad who recognize this proxy militia as a horde of mercenaries, displacers, and executioners believe in a fiction they helped to create and then embrace as true. By disavowing its existence, Idris thus simultaneously absolves the Janjaweed of any responsibility for its acts and empowers it to continue doing the state's dirty work.

An army deserter whose story on YouTube I translated opposed this view. Its veracity is unconfirmed, yet it is still worth noting:

The commander gives us [the] order to do everything. Kill them. Destroy their villages. Rape the women. This happened at the beginning of 2003. The attack would start at six in the morning, and we would destroy the village. We don't leave anything behind. The government army would start the attack. Then the Janjaweed would follow on, coming on horseback [the word before horseback is unclear], and chase those who managed to slip through the army cordon and seize any livestock. These orders came from above, and if we refused to do it, they would shoot us. At the end of the day, we are fighting our own people in our own country. This is why I had to abandon the army and the government and leave Sudan. This is what is happening in Sudan. But if you are not living there you don't know it is happening.

When they asked me to go on a second patrol, I refused to do it. They then accused me of knowing the rebel leaders and tortured me for information.

They would burn a tire and hang it from a tree so the hot rubber would drip on your body. I have got scars all over my body, on my back and on my legs, and you can also see where they hit me with the back of a rifle. The pictures that remain in my mind and appear in my nightmares are of torture and attack on innocent people, destroying their homes and killing them. And very young children being raped. They're all innocent. And the suffering of people in Darfur. The government isn't giving them anything, and they haven't committed any crimes. Then the government came and attacked their villages, burned them, and destroyed them. The government says it has only killed ten thousand people. So, who are responsible for the rest? They deny killing many, many people. It would be very good if President Bashir was arrested now. The whole universe would be happy.[18]

The actions this deserter describes rang true for a group of female combatants in Darfur whose sophisticated political awareness of the chain of command was apparent in a parody of a protest appearing on a YouTube video that went viral on WhatsApp. Armed with their own AK47s, they crooned:

> Omar Bashir, we're looking for you, to make you wish you were dead.
> We're looking for you to take out your eye.
> We're looking for you to beat the religion out of you.
> We're looking for you but we can't find you.
> Give up or run!
> We're the killers of those who exploited Sudan.
> We won't bow to the Janjaweed!
> We won't bow to Bashir!
> We won't bow to anyone![19]

In a completely different tone, other research participants told stories of the troubles they have experienced at the hands of the Janjaweed. One interviewee told me, "*These veiled men covered their faces because they refused to be identified, but can they hide from Allah?*" An interviewee from Tawila spoke of the terror this way: "*We ran away in the pitch-dark night, awakened by the smell of war that rose like a grey thick cloud over the sky. My heart was racing, and I thought it was going to stop right [then]. I am still alive, thank Allah.*"

The Smell of War: A Leftist Meditation

Given the systematic marginality of the Darfur region, Marxist observers in the Sudan warned against its bleak future well before the onset of the current conflict. Sitting at the lunch tray at an early age, I recall my late aunt Khalda Zahir, a physician, women's rights advocate, and Marxist, discussing the situation in South Sudan with my parents. Suddenly she switched to the topic of Darfur, saying "the successive governments have maltreated and abused South Sudan, and the poor southerners are left totally destroyed. But let them wait and see when Darfur rises." Elsewhere I have discussed how growing up in a progressive household shaped my views and familiarized me early on with different meditations on a plethora of issues related to justice and equality in Sudanese society.[20] Increasingly I became interested in the views of Marxists about ruptures between state and society in the Sudan. I still find class-based Marxist critiques useful in understanding elite politics vis-à-vis the marginalized people of the Sudan. They represent a powerful foil to the conservatism of the Sudanese political leadership of all ethnic stripes, arguing that the latter's primary obsession is to grab power and wealth by any means necessary. However, the primary concern of these Marxists is the material conditions of a person's life. In particular, I turn to *Darfur: The Definitive Answer* by Sulieman Hamid, a Sudanese Arab who appeared in chapter 1. Published in Arabic in 2004,[21] Hamid's work has not been translated into English, so I am presenting its main ideas to acquaint readers with a counternarrative characteristic of Sudanese Marxist analyses of elite politics and classism and critiques of official state policies on marginality, ethnic minorities, and constitutionalism.

The Definitive Answer is an expose of Islamist politics, which the author charges figured prominently in the creation of the situation in Darfur, understood within the context of the intersection of race and class. Hamid writes, "Documentary evidence indicates that the National Islamic Front (NIF) is to be held accountable for the Darfur tragedy."[22] The work demonstrates a leftist commitment to understanding Muslim politics within the context of the marginalization of the region as well as its embeddedness in border politics reconfigured in the government of the Arab-Islamic Security Belt. Additionally, it draws attention to the involvement of diverse ethnicities in this project. Hamid notes that not all Arab tribes were involved in the conflict and that, conversely, some Fur were deeply entrenched in the government project. What readers can glean from this narrative is that binary representations of Arab and African are political rather than essential identities, formed by political alliances and solidarities.

Hamid's perspective parallels many of the interpretations offered during my fieldwork in the Sudan. In forums about Darfur in which history, politics, and culture are debated, there is general consensus about the development of a belligerency that ruined a country once thought of as a microcosm of both the African and the Arab worlds.[23] As discussed in chapter 1, Hamid tells us that the formation of militarized ethnicity, which morphed later into the Janjaweed, can be traced to the political period in the Sudan known as the Third Democracy (1986–1989), the transitional government formed after President Gaffar Nimeiri's overthrow. Armed groups matured under Sheikh Musa Hilal, the chief of the Mahameed Arabs, as a highly organized proxy militia with all the trappings of an army and escalated the "resurrection of a warrior tradition in [an] African political culture."[24] This militia, although represented as identical to Arab "tribes," is highly differentiated internally in rank, national origin, and political ideology. Hamid highlights the significant role of Islamist leaders in organizing and arming the militias, including Imam Al-Sadiq Al-Mahdi of the conservative Umma Party and prime minister during the period 1986–1989, and his brother-in law the late Dr. Hassan Al-Turabi, whom he appointed as attorney general during Al-Mahdi's premiership. Hamid exposes their political and ideological core and their motivations for arming the Moraheelin. It is perhaps worth noting that I was present at a well-attended event in Doha at which Al-Mahdi was speaking about political reconciliation. A Sudanese man from Darfur challenged him: "Please don't talk of democracy and reconciliation. You aborted democracy and made a pact with the devil when you worked in the Socialist Union of the murderer Nimeiri. You worship power. We all know it, and you know it." Stunned, the imam paused for a moment. You could hear a pin drop before he uttered an absurd response: "I joined the Socialist Union for one month only." While the audiences burst into laughter, a participant sitting next to me turned his head to say, "He will never learn. He will just continue to talk nonstop," adding, "Yes, the art of haranguing and sermonizing is what this power-obsessed man is known and will be remembered for in our history books."

Hamid also addresses the effort by Darfuri activists and delegates to Khartoum to avert escalation of the conflict in the region following Al-Bashir's rise to power, noting the arrival of three hundred delegates of various ethnicities[25] in the capital in February 2004 to initiate negotiations for a peaceful resolution of the conflict. Their effort was unsuccessful, and their warning against politicizing "tribal identities" scorned. True to his Marxist-Leninist views, Hamid asks: What is to be done? He suggests that policy recommendations that do not confront the deep structural violence inflicted by the state on society at the economic level are neither acceptable nor effective. In the end, his views remind us that Darfur's predicament cannot be separated from the history of violence—economic, political, and military—in the Sudan's relations with its peoples. Darfur is a summation of the elites' refusal to relinquish wealth and power, even if doing so entailed closing ranks around their parasitic capitalist identity. The consequence of this was the dispersal of its citizens all over the world as exiles and refugees, as well as internally as displaced citizens.

Notes from the Homestead

Today I visited a family in the Homestead. This was a female-headed household consisting of my interviewee and five children ranging in age from fourteen to five years. Upon entering the house with a friend of mine from Omdurman, I saw colorful, newly washed clothes hanging neatly on the clothesline catching the sun's rays and dripping water, methodically wetting the earth beneath. The tiny brick home was spectacularly immaculate. We were greeted warmly and then offered tea and water. The room's three beds were neatly made. Placed on the window were several promising-looking plants cultivated in tin cans. I knew right then and there that my hostess's green thumb had a lot to teach me about her fortitude and agility and her own extraordinary vision of the proverbial "putting down roots."

Between 2004 and 2009, I carried out several rounds of ethnographic field research in the Sudan's capital city, to my knowledge the first attempt to study the experiences of displaced people there by scholars, who instead have focused considerable attention on refugees in neighboring Chad. I conducted most of my interviews in Omdurman, my birthplace, although on occasion a research participant requested that we meet at some other place for their convenience. Omdurman has hosted the overwhelming majority of arrivals to the capital region since 2003, as it had in the 1980s for those escaping the environmental crises in Darfur and Kordofan. Some of the views of these displaced citizens, gathered in both individual and focus group interviews, are presented here. The location where I carried out most of my ethnographic research is a slum that bears all the characteristic markings of urban poverty and the state's lack of empathy. I call this place the Homestead.

From the outset, I recognized that doing interviews about political violence in Darfur entailed constraints unlike those I encountered during my previous research on the impact of drought. Although the reasons for the difficulties may be obvious, they are necessary to note. Telling the story from inside the country is qualitatively different from telling it from a refugee camp or a country to which a person has immigrated. In the context of immigration, providing detailed testimony about one's harrowing experiences is key to a successful bid for asylum. In contrast, no one can afford to tell their story so freely from a makeshift dwelling or a poor urban neighborhood. Fear of being arrested or evicted inhibits people from sharing stories about crime, including gender crimes. I contend that location dictates the discursive frames through which Darfur is talked about across geographies. Also, unlike in research on other African civil wars, it was impossible to gather the point of view of perpetrators of government-supported terror. Except for a few postings in the blogosphere from army deserters, no systematic accounts exist, attesting to the absence of a truth commission or tribunal. In this the Sudan is unlike Rwanda, where such accounts have been recorded by the National Unity and Reconciliation Commission. However constrained the narratives that IDPs did share in this ethnography, I am convinced that the events they lived through will remain etched in the region's memory and that victims' stories will be transmitted over generations. In their own articulate silence, narrators imparted a great deal.

My observations in the field suggest that the majority of IDPs are women and children with no formal education. In this they are unlike men, whose gender, education, and occupation created significant opportunities for seeking asylum in the United States, Israel, Europe, and elsewhere. Thus, gender identity and freedom of movement are intertwined, leading to different migratory biographies for women and men. Yet I found it particularly difficult to interview women, whose suffering was specific, disproportionate to that of men, and rooted in the grim realities of being female in a war-torn community. My research participants constantly reminded me of their discomfort in talking about sexuality and gender crimes—and this even though gender-based violence is among the most pervasive of the vast range of difficulties catalogued by the participants in this ethnography. Although it is commonly understood as a spoil of war, this is only partially true. Fundamentally, gender violence is emblematic of the unchecked power of men, which they exercise with impunity. Perhaps this is why research participants focused centrally on the devastation of the region, only occasionally uttering a brief sentence like "sometime they attacked and beat women and girls" in the course of a three-hour conversation.

I did not press them on the subject because I did not want to come across as intent on pursuing a pointedly personal or political agenda. Because I am Sudanese, most prefaced their stories with "you are a Sudanese, you know the situation" or the like. At the moment of these utterances, I recalled Lila Abu-Lughod's experience when she wrote: "The confluence of principle, personal predilections and circumstance, [and] my unwillingness to pursue questions aggressively . . . limited the extent to which I could study some matters systematically."[26] Likewise, I fought the urge of conventional ethnography to probe with the apparent goal of adding to a lengthy catalogue of afflictions and sorrows. Women told their stories in their own terms and on subjects they deemed proper. Our conversations, therefore, varied from very long to rather short. My goal became more focused on the quality of specific content rather than on using the interviews to make sweeping generalizations about the whole universe of the capital's residents from Darfur. Indeed, within this universe, there are significant differentiations based on class, educational attainment, and political solidarities and affiliations. Among these residents are college students, government employees, cabinet ministers, and members of parliament. However, my focus is on those who were dispossessed, displaced, and forgotten, people with few material resources or social capital. Aware of my position as a "dialogic partner" doing ethnographic work in my own country, my intention was to amplify perspectives they wished to contribute.[27]

Participants' repeated statements of "as you know well" and "as you know the situation" beg the question of what from their perspective was allowable and not allowable to share, thereby calling into question Strathern's and Jackson's skepticism about doing "anthropology at home."[28] Narrators' comments, while reflecting their conviction that I should understand, for instance, the limits of speaking about sexual violence, also point to an important debate about anthropology's deconstruction of the notion of a shared understanding of social structure or of home.[29] Nevertheless, I felt that their statements succeeded in conveying a panoramic view of the conflict as well as the urgency of their own experiences. They often spoke of these experiences as "when the troubles started in our village," wording that served to situate their subsequent struggles in an urban world.

WHY WE CAME HERE

Participants' accounts reveal that the primary reason they and those with whom they are acquainted left the refugee camps to seek residence in the Homestead was that they deemed camp conditions unbearable. I knew about these conditions, but they were brought home to me most poignantly on a Qatar Airways flight heading to Khartoum. I was seated next to a South African United Nations–African Union Hybrid Operation in Darfur (UNAMID) staff member, listening as he explained the woes endured daily by civilians in Darfur's camps. How did this conversation start? When the attendant came by to offer Jolly candy, the man asked if he could take the whole basket, explaining that "I need to bring candy to the children in Darfur." He turned to me to explain further: "I am not staying in Khartoum as I have to rush to El Fashir and then to the camps. Once I arrive at my station, I will have something to give the little kids." His request revealed exceptional kindliness and opened a door for me to ask him his thoughts as a peacekeeper in the region. He was generous with his knowledge and proud of the mission he was part of. He remarked on the composition of the camps, including innocent civilians, spies, opportunists, and people who have no business living in a camp. He was aware that "some people are professional IDPs," but then went on to clarify wider misconceptions. If anything, his remarks mitigate the essentialism with which "victims" are perceived in the political and social imaginaries about war and its effects. Mostly, though, he talked about camp conditions.

Since 2013 the number of IDPs has risen exponentially. That year marked the mapping—to the extent possible—of the extent of displacement and the location and names of camps. A population census conducted by the United Nations Office for the Coordination of Humanitarian Affairs (OCHA)[30] reported an estimated two million Darfuris as recipients of humanitarian aid. Of the seventy-five IDP camps in Darfur that OCHA surveyed, twenty-five are home to over ten thousand people each. Others house more than five thousand, and a small minority have between five hundred and three thousand residents.[31] Comprehensive documentation of camp conditions in Darfur conducted by the UNAMID monitoring team in 2010 revealed 1,286 allegations of human rights violations and abuses involving 3,358 victims, including 2,108 women and 299 children. The allegations related, inter alia, to violations of the right to life and personal integrity, sexual and gender-based violence, arbitrary arrests and detention, abductions, and violations of the rights to freedom of movement, expression, peaceful assembly, and association. Data collected by UNAMID show that IDPs have remained a major category of victims due to their vulnerability and the prevalent weakness of state mechanisms to protect them.[32]

My interviews corroborate the evidence of official reports, painting a bleak picture of the camps and emphasizing the lack of security, the competition and hustling among residents, and the pervasive fear of strangers. Everyone who had lived in a camp had a story. One woman described her journey to the Homestead in terms of a flight from camp conditions:

> Our situation in my camp was a real disaster. We had fled from our homes on foot in a very difficult journey to the first place to which we could find transportation. [We left the camp and] now we are staying with people from home who came to Khartoum a long time ago. Like us they don't have a lot, but they allowed us to stay with them in these small houses. We don't have money to buy food. We are also very worried about work. We cannot find work since this place is very far [from transportation]. Now the rainy season created added problems because this area is flooded.
>
> We depend only on Allah to change our situation. Our children are in danger too. We don't know what has happened to other relatives and neighbors. We hope that they are still alive. We are also worried that we will not be able to go back. When our people tell us the news they hear on the radio, it makes us even more accepting of our situation. You see others' disasters and you start to wonder how easy your own disaster is compared to them. The camp is the worst. Every day we just prayed for mercy. We could not even sleep at night. Just sitting there thinking, thinking, thinking. We live with the hope that others can join us here.

Women in particular find camp life inhospitable and unsafe, especially for raising children, and prefer life in the Homestead. As a social worker in the Homestead told me:

> *Of the women I work with, fleeing their homes is the most important psychological factor. To leave family members and neighbors behind is something every one of them mentions as a great problem. Coming to the Homestead for the majority of women is not an easy decision, given the distance they had to travel. But most of them have known people who came here recently or had already been living here for years.*
>
> *We are all from one region, but most of the women mentioned that they did not want to stay in the camp and that life in the camp is very difficult. It is crowded, and it brings them into contact with total strangers. The camp is itself a country within a country. Because of these realities, they wanted their children to lead an ordinary life in a neighborhood, to go to school and just be like other children living far from fighting and chaos. The camp life is not one you can speak favorably about. If you have children especially, you don't feel safe, you just don't know whether or not children would be safe there. Our religion says I tie it [referring here to a camel, included in the sayings of the Prophet Muhammad] first then rely on it.*

The lack of security also leaves women vulnerable to sexual violence. Although I was unable to secure much in the way of direct accounts of gendered violence from women in the Homestead, it has garnered the attention of celebrities and media figures, part of what Jumbert and Lanz call "globalized rebellion."[33] Human rights organizations have also produced voluminous reports pivoting around these facts: women are victims no matter where they go, are unable to avoid being raped, suffer stigma within their families and communities for being raped, and have to choose between starving or doing without basic necessities and the possibility of rape. Furthermore, reporting rape to authorities does not bring rapists to justice and sometimes has adverse consequences for the victim. The reports also come to similar conclusions: first, rape is understood as the lesser of two evils: women risk getting raped but men risk getting killed; second, repercussions of rape are widespread, both in the community and across time; third, towns are described as having "relative protection" compared to the camps; and fourth, the work women do that puts them at risk is nonetheless defined as unavoidable, "necessary," "essential," and linked to traditional gender roles.[34] A man from Mukjar gave an example of how women's traditional forms of labor, coupled with features of camps' layout, can expose women to danger: *"Many women get raped when they leave the camp to get firewood or water."* He stated that in March 2013, his brother's widow went to collect firewood and was attacked by three armed Janjaweed on horseback. She managed to flee by running to the woods and eventually made it back to the camp but with some of her clothes torn.

People in the Homestead also had numerous stories about hustling and the widespread, relentless competition over resources that plagues camp residents, both characteristic of a war economy. As I heard from a group of displaced people whom I spoke with in a local park:

> There is a lot of competition for aid. Some people say that the displaced people who come from the same tribe as government officials receive more. The aid workers don't know, but their guides instruct them, "Oh, give these people, and don't give these people." When Saudi people sent blankets in the winter, the cold was bone-chilling, but only some people were able to receive; others were just cold, their children shivered all night and were sick with bad cold. Again, the rumor was confirmed, only the relatives of the politicians got help. See, this is life in the camp. True, people suffer in it. But we don't all suffer in the same way. There is fighting, fighting all day, fighting all night! Some people who came last week to join us here mentioned to us that not all of the camp people were displaced because of real reasons like us.

A Sudanese journalist from Darfur who had visited camps corroborated their comments, telling me:

> In the camps, I was told that some incoming residents had rented their houses in order to move to an IDP camp and make extra income. This, I was told by disgruntled residents, was unfair. They did not need to compete with others who have real and desperate need for assistance because they had lost everything. These people, they added, are benefitting from the misfortunes in the region simply to make extra money at the expense of others. They consciously support the status quo, especially the conflict. Of course, they are aware that the camps are there to stay for many years. They are in a great hurry to make money and are not afraid to share their positive experience in the camp with any visitor who arrives here from different organizations.

Another aspect of the competition over resources emerged in a conversation with a Sudanese humanitarian worker who expressed her frustration with another woman "with means," as she puts it.

> I have been working so hard to help in my own small way. I reached out to many people in Khartoum to donate clothing and food items. My donations started to amass. I talked to my friends about delivering these items to women in one of the camps near Nyala. Soon we were confronted with the real problem of bringing the stuff. My friend knows this woman whose name I cannot say. But if you put

this story in your book, maybe she will read it, and she will know right away that I referred to her. I called her in good faith to ask if she could help. This woman owns a Land Cruiser and has a driver. She is a woman with means, unlike us. So I said to myself, we have nothing to lose, the bewildered has to open the cow's mouth for answers. I called her mobile phone and asked. She agreed right away. She came to pick us up.

Up to this point all was good, right? We got to the camp after an hour or so. My friends and I sat in the back and she in the front. Her car was like an airplane; this woman is in a very good situation. When we got there, she ordered us to stay put. She opened the door and asked her driver to unload the boxes. We didn't expect that she would block us like this. Her driver obeyed her. What else was he supposed to do? She started to call on some women who were outside already, "Come, come quickly!" Then she asked the driver to take her photo next to the women, and she pretended to take out the clothes as if she was the one who worked hard to collect them.

My friends and I still could not believe our eyes. She was very firm with us. We started to get very worried because if we got out of the car, she wouldn't have hesitated to leave us there. We were happy that the people managed to get the donations, but we were very disgusted. After she took the photos, she was smiling, showing us her entire teeth. We were just paralyzed. Later on when she got in the car, we could not even open our mouths. The woman was dangerous. But we wanted to get back home. In my heart I was cursing her, and until now when I remember the episode, I just say I left her to Allah to punish her. When we talked about this problem when we got back, people said this woman although Fur is a government affiliate and a member of the National Congress. That explained it to us. The woman was so comfortable.

The presence of strangers in the camp was also of concern to the people I interviewed. They viewed them with suspicion and were averse to living among them. As one research participant said to me:

After the war started and we went to the camp, we were stressed out. Now we were living with thousands of people, we didn't know who they were, and they also didn't know who we were. Yes, we knew they were forced just like we were forced. But people are not the same. The fingers in one palm of the hand are not the same. We didn't trust them, and they felt the same way about us.

Fear of strangers contributes to the consolidation of ethnic identity in the camp, as people seek familiarity to overcome their own loneliness and estrangement. The situation is further complicated by the fact that Chadians sometimes find their way to the camps, stirring up suspicions among Darfuris about their motives for doing so. Thus, anxiety over the omnipresence of strangers can be explained not by any inherent xenophobia but rather by the pervasive sense of insecurity these strangers arouse. Also mitigating any charge of intolerance is widespread banditry in the camps, suggesting that insecurity is rooted both in and outside of the immediate frontier of conflict. Disorderliness and a conspicuous absence of law enforcement also contribute to fears within IDP camps.

One woman I spoke with described the conditions that give rise to this pervasive distrust, citing it as a reason for her family's move from a camp to the city:

> When we came to the Homestead five years ago with my sisters and our children, we knew that we could not carry on living in Tawila [Northern Darfur] like that. In our village everyone knew the neighbors. Now thousands live in Tawila camps like Argo and Dali, not knowing how long they will be there. A lot of stress and attacks from in and outside of the camps. Robberies are very common. That happens when you bring so many strangers and put them together and think that things are going to work out. Long ago, our life was simple in spite of the struggle with lack of money. But I have to say that our life was very nice. Money is not everything. Contentment is.

Some individuals, aware of camp conditions and averse to living among total strangers, decided to journey directly to the capital city rather than reside in a refugee camp in Chad or elsewhere. I quote from two such individuals whose stories, echoed in broad outlines by many others, speak to conditions that made a decision to migrate there both rational and warranted. First:

> When the trouble arrived at our village, it did not come as a surprise. We heard the fighting erupt around 4:00 a.m., continuing all day. For some time, Darfur has been filled with fighting [but these were low level, local quarrels adjudicated in Judia courts]. Only this time it became very ugly because the fighters don't want us to live in peace as we had before. People were in shock. Some fainted when their homes were invaded. We had to run away, each trying to escape for their lives as if it were doomsday. For me and my other family members and neighbors, this was our situation, run away, escape. We didn't even have time to ask ourselves, what are we going to do now in Darfur? We know of so many people who ran to Chad. But Chad is not a safe place to hide in. It has a lot of problems too, and its people who were in Darfur were also troublesome. We have seen a lot and suffered enough from the troublemakers. Always armed and always ready to fight just like the Janjaweed, some of them are Janjaweed themselves. They are very strong because of the weapons that don't leave them. All we could do was keep our mouths shut. We could not resist any of their bad deeds [when they came into our villages]. What will they do if we go to them in their own place?

We started to run so fast with children in tow. We reached the neighboring village, and we were on our feet for hours. I didn't know anything at that time about the fate of my children's father. We remained in Shoak village until the lorry arrived to take people to El Fashir. We remained there for the next ten days to wait for transportation to the Homestead. Another lorry took us there, and the journey lasted for four days under very difficult and crowded conditions. We contacted some people from our village who lived there for a long time, and they helped us to find a chance.

We received word about my children's father, notifying us that he was fine and that he escaped unhurt. One week later, people told us about a vacant building in Karrary, in fact, a lot of abandoned buildings. We moved there and passed the information to others in our village to let them know our whereabouts. We settled there, and my husband joined us six months later. We heard from people about the suffering in the camps. Many women, we were told, were killed or raped. Large numbers of our relatives and neighbors live in camps to this day. We didn't want to stay in any camp. The problems there are big. The shenanigans told to us by those who stayed there are so dangerous. They too want to come here.

And the second:

Naturally, there was fear. Our neighbors and families did not even think twice. We had to run away; of course, we had to. The dogs ran away, let alone the son of Adam [i.e., a human being]. For us coming to Khartoum was easier as my sister here said just now. Why don't we escape to Chad? Since we were in El Geneina we knew the problems in Chad. A lot of people went there, but their situation was also bad. We have seen enough of what Chadians had done to us. Chadians were as bad as Janjaweed. They stole everything even from very poor people. If they found a bowl of porridge, they would take it away.

I didn't go to school that day. The fighting was intense, and of course we were so afraid. My mother owned a donkey. Luckily. So my brother and I rode with her to the next village. My father joined us later, and we boarded the lorry heading to Khartoum. We arrived at a big station. Then we were told that we can go to another place where we could find a lot of people from Darfur who find work there. It is Suq Libya; a lot of Zaghawa own shops there. The shopkeepers were very kind; they gave us food and water. We spent the night just sleeping by one of the shops. The next day we went to Dar es Salaam [another camp], and we also lived in a vacant room for two years. The municipality people came to the neighborhood, and they said we should not stay and asked us to leave. I got married and moved to Al-Thawra 102 District. My father took another wife whom he met after we moved. We were angry because even in the middle of a bad disaster, he wanted to be selfish. My brother then moved to Kosti. He is a street-food peddler. We heard about people going back to Darfur. We will never go back even if all our neighbors do.

ON GETTING BY AND GETTING ALONG:
AN URBAN EXPERIENCE

Following Gilbert and Gugler's refutation of the assumption that urban life is marked by a lack of meaningful personal relationships, forced migrants maintain strong ties with kin communities and establish "new communities . . . or do both."[35] An earlier group of migrants had preceded post-2003 IDPs to the Homestead, men and women who had been pushed out of their homes by environmental disasters in the 1990s. As an interviewee commented, "*We came to the Homestead to end the problems we faced because of the drought and the desertification that killed our farms and our animals.*" Comparing himself to the more recent migrants, he continued, "*We could not depend on the humanitarian aid at that time, when the only thing we got was a small ration of flour that we used to call George Bush Bread [referring to the forty-first US president, George H. W. Bush].*" It was this group then, in the heart of the Homestead, that came to host Darfuri kin and countrymen who arrived two decades later, providing them with material and moral support.

Nowhere is the instrumentalization of existing ties of both kin and community more evident than in women's work in the Homestead, particularly in the food service sector, where everyday life is a practical exercise in transforming challenges into opportunities in order for life to go on. As one woman explained:

> The fighting made our lives miserable, and our journey itself took a long time and it was hard. We arrived here, and we thought to go to Suq Libya to find work. The shop owners are Zaghawa from Darfur. They are very rich, and they know how to make money. But our search there did not work out. The market was already packed; and if our plans to sell food were to succeed, we needed a lot of money for the license. This was impossible. We did not have a pound on us. I found relatives in Ombbada, and they suggested that I start selling food nearby. I did with great help from them, thank Allah. I sold tea and donuts in the nearby suq in the morning, and in the evening I made falafel [tammia]. These sell very well, and in the course of a couple of hours I run out.

It is perhaps worth noting that contrary to what the interviewee above implied about aid, contemporary IDPs act on their own behalf and contribute to the economy in the absence of official state support, in violation of the UN's "Guiding Principles for Internally Displaced Persons," which mandates such state assistance.

In exploring the urban experience of women, we must take into account the overall structure of the Sudanese economy in a fragile state. Anthropologists dealing with the complexity of urbanization in what is now called the

Global South have focused critical attention on broader survival strategies within the context of marginality and rapid urbanization. Among these are participation in the so-called informal economy, ranging from petty commodity production to reciprocal, kin-based exchanges to service sector employment.[36] Homestead women's involvement in food service also brings to mind an important question, one Keith Hart asked over thirty years ago in the context of his work in Accra, Ghana: "Does the reserve army of urban unemployed really constitute a passive, exploited majority . . . or do their economic activities possess some autonomous capacity for generating growth in the incomes of the urban (and rural) poor?"[37] Based on the experiences of women in the Homestead, the latter is the case. As market women in the Zaghawa-dominated enclave, they are generating new microeconomies of exchange with skill and agility.

As women struggle to find an economic niche in the food sector, they face problems of extortion and exploitation by so-called popular committees and local police. Yet they cooperate in surmounting these and other dilemmas, developing new community ties as they do. As one woman described:

> These people want us to give them money. They leave you alone for two days, then new faces appear like devils to start again. We try to find out together about when to take our food out and when to hide. But these thieves are following us everywhere—police from popular committees they call themselves. They are from all over the country. Ethiopian, Nuba, and poor women from this neighborhood are all harassed. We live in great fear and stress because of these evil men. You cannot report to anyone. Probably they split the money with their superiors.
>
> My troubles started when people from the local committee came to ask for my license. These people have no hearts. "Where is your permission?" they asked me. I did not have one. The threats followed. If you bribe them, they take the money and leave you alone for a day or two. If not, they dump your food in front of you. I always set aside cash to pay off until Allah lifts the harm from our way and keeps the bastards out of our world. This problem also faces Ethiopian and poor Sudanese women who sell tea. They accuse them of selling prohibited drugs. Lies. We live in continuous fear of these devils. We are forced to come up with a plan every morning when we take our food out. But as they say, we escaped from under the shadow of the sword in Darfur. We can find our way here, inshallah.

Another suggested the informal sociability that develops among those sharing common circumstances:

> I now work in Suq Libya. I bring food there, I take the bus daily in the morning, and I return as soon as I sell all the food. I am not making big profits but enough to make do. I return home and all of my neighbors sit together to eat and drink tea. When visitors come, we talk about Darfur's news, about updates

about people going back from camps to the village. We chat about their hard conditions.

As they struggle to make do, women describe how their parochial views about residents from whom they differ in ethnicity, religion, and migratory experience have shifted. Urban poverty is seen as the great equalizer, a fact that exposed many Darfuris to the dark underbelly of the government's neglect of their Sudanese Arab compatriots. A Homestead resident originally from Zem Zem recounted an interesting story that I saw as akin to any informal interfaith dialogue:

> I have been working in the tea business for many years now. I don't sit in the neighborhood market by myself. I sit together with my other neighbors from Darfur and Ethiopia, who like me have lived here for a very long time. We go together to buy our sugar, tea, mint, and charcoal for the portable stove. If the people from the popular council come to ask for permission, we run away together. We talk about our problems with these people to find solutions together. We do a lot for each other. In Ramadan, when people are not allowed to sell food or drink, my Christian friend from Ethiopia told me about a church where nonfasting Muslims and Christians go to get their tea and food. They sit there to have their water, tea, coffee, food, and chewing tobacco [saʾout]. Probably they are sick or have other reasons preventing them from fasting, Allah only knows. When I fast during Ramadan, I only sell after dusk. During the day I give my friend my donuts to sell it for me. When she returns with my money, I thank her and ask Allah to bless her and to bless her children. Her help during Ramadan is important because I don't lose any income for thirty days. My income in this situation is important. It helps me of course, and it helps some of my people back home when they me ask for help.

Even as I listened to these stories of facing challenges with resourcefulness and faith, I remained under no illusion that arrival in the capital, though a welcome change, had ended women's daily battles for survival. Khartoum is a bedrock of dispossession, as many participants in this ethnography would confirm. According to Ahmad and Al-Battahani:

> Few Arab capitals, except those where wars have been waged, can compare with Khartoum in its sad, swift decline over the past dozen or so years. Symptoms of poverty have invaded the city both on an unprecedented scale and in new ways. This poverty affects the individual in two ways: through their own poverty, that is, their lack of adequate means to support themselves and their dependents; and through the poverty linked to the actions of the state, which has stripped them of many essential rights, commodities and services even if they were rich.[38]

These conditions were brought home to me especially by the fact that many residents found themselves unable to afford the exorbitant cost of an increasingly privatized education for their children. Instead, they had to surrender them to the cruelties of child labor. One woman explained:

> The boys usually go the market. They are usually hired on a day-to-day basis by shopkeepers. The shopkeepers give them water bottles, boxes of tissues, and sometimes glass to sell in the street. This is very hard because they have to cross the road and move from one car to the next to sell in exchange for a small tip they are given at the end of the day. Sometimes they work in the market to push wheelbarrows filled with vegetables and fruits. They sit under the sun and sometimes are chased also by security because of the license issue. But this is the only way for the family here. Everyone has to contribute. We cannot afford to send them to school. The schools charge a lot of money.

So, while children managed to get by without extending their hands to beg, they were forced to remain at the lowest echelons of urban life, deprived of their basic right to education. A janitor in a college not too far from the Homestead commented on her aversion to begging: "*What is the use in asking people? You wait to see whether they will give or deprive you.*"

From the many conversations I had with both women and men, I came to learn how significantly social relationships were being restructured in the urban environment. Participants who have become well acquainted with the fact that poverty has no ethnicity or race articulated newly tolerant views about poor "Arabs" in their neighborhood: "*These are our neighbors. They enter our houses and we enter theirs. They were not responsible for our problems. They are busy with their problems. Our relations with them are just as good as those of our neighbors in El Geneina [in Darfur].*" As Irigaray would have commented, this meta-commentary about social relations reveals a sophisticated political awareness about whom to blame for the mayhem. It also suggests a unique form of democratization based on shared class consciousness. In his futuristic novel *Two Years Eight Months and Twenty-Eight Nights*, Salman Rushdie describes denizens of a "peripatetic world" in terms that evoke the profound shift in consciousness present in the Homestead: "They splintered away from the authentic narratives of their life stories and spent the rest of their days trying to discover, or forge, new, synthetic narratives of their own."[39] With all its good and evil, the capital has afforded Darfuri refugees a measure of safety. To repeat the words of the Homestead resident quoted above: "*We escaped from underneath a shadow of a sword.*" This was a conversation stopper.

Return to Darfur?

In 2018, the *Sudan Tribune* reported the intention of the government of Northern Darfur to transform displaced persons camps into permanent residential areas.[40] In light of this plan, an official presented three options to the residents of El-Sereif, one of the largest camps in Darfur: integrate into existing towns, remain in the camp, or return to their home villages. Of these three options, the government promoted the last most aggressively because of the relative progress in establishing the security of the region since 2003—despite the fact that over two million people remained in long-term residence in the camps, apparently concerned for their safety or with no home to return to.

When queried about this plan, an interviewee in Khartoum responded with a skepticism that typified how the majority of people received it: "*Return of IDPs and repatriation of refugees are not within the realm of possibility. Accurate information about disarmament and demilitarization is lacking. People have every right to question the information about the improving security situation in a region awash with Kalashnikovs*." He explained further the reason for his skepticism, echoing so much of what I heard in my fieldwork about the violence in Darfur:

> *The deep concerns about return are legitimate on several fronts. Bloggers and contributions to online forums have sounded the alarm about the looming threats of dismantling the camps. NCP [National Congress Party] perceives IDPs as a site of resistance, a pawn for rebellion. They are represented as the bastion for supporters of the armed rebel movement. They are also a symbol for the failure of the state to restore normalcy.*
>
> *Everyone in Darfur, we can say, has always had access to knives, swords, daggers—what we know as "white weapons"—that are wrapped around the arm for protection. Amulets have also been worn so that if someone is stabbed the knife could not penetrate, pierce the body. Guns were very rare. The militarization of today is systematic, given the spillover wars and conflicts from our borders. The current violence in the region and the ease of buying arms have contributed to their wide use. Bandits own sophisticated weapons, sometimes surpassing those owned by the state police. Lack of faith in the government and its ability to provide protection and redress is a major factor in people owning guns.*
>
> *People buy them from arms merchants from Chad and Libya. Disarmament that people, officials talk about in conferences and in the press is impossible because of the supply and demand in an ongoing conflict. Without addressing the causes, we cannot collect arms and assume that peace would automatically be restored. Nimeiri created a power vacuum when he dismantled the native administration where chiefs had been able to exert tremendous influence in their community. No police today have the moral authority of a shartayi court.*

Thus official plans are at odds with what the most important stakeholders, the IDPs and refugees, deem desirable. Perhaps the refusal to return has something to do with the enormous problems still facing Darfur and the apparent unwillingness of the government to address them. As one research participant said to me:

> What peace means for Darfur is structural and not oversimplified quick remedies. The Janjaweed issue must be addressed and rooted out. Investigation of all the crimes they had committed along with their supervisors is a just demand. Right now, displaced people are reliant on humanitarian aid. But humanitarian workers are being robbed and assaulted. Do something to organize the process— these are commonsense and self-evident steps.
>
> But can we really talk about rehabilitation of the villages that burned, repatriation of the original inhabitants, providing security and health care, and providing effective measures to ensure repatriation, and all of the wonderful recommendations proposed at international conferences? These efforts are fantastic on paper, but in reality relief to the people of Darfur will not actualize under the conditions that our eyes are seeing now. The government is still severely restricting humanitarian aid in Darfur and appears unwilling to address the human rights crisis in the region. As a result, international attempts, including attempts by the United Nations, to resolve the human rights and humanitarian situation in Darfur are being delayed. Relief comes to the powerful, but the poor have to wait and suffer.

If media scholar and activist Marc Lamont Hill were asked to comment on this last sentence, he would argue that the state's failure to restore habitable conditions to Darfur is a manifestation of its views on what he terms the "invisible" people who "are rendered disposable through economic arrangements, public policy, and social practice. [The state's failures] spotlight the nagging presence of the exploited, the erased, the vulnerable, the dehumanized—those who are imagined, treated, and made to feel like Nobody."[41] The epic story of Darfur's destruction should be read in this light. Summoning David Harvey, I also read my interlocutor's plea in terms of Darfuri citizens' rights to the city: "[By] the astonishing pace and scale of urbanization . . . we have been re-made several times over without knowing why, how, or wherefore." In this rural-urban story that many commentators in the Sudan call the ruralization of the city—an inversion of Marx's notion of the urbanization of the countryside—I see the "right to the city" as a fundamental right of people to move freely and with dignity in the world.[42]

A Sorcerer's Justice

A forty-five-year-old driver originally from Gereida arrived in Khartoum in 2006. When I met him, he was in the process of migrating to a Gulf state for employment. His knowledge of Darfur's ethnology was extraordinary, as was his understanding of the dynamics of state and society. In spite of the difficulties he has encountered throughout his journey, he told me that the violence he's seen and experienced has neither broken his spirit nor weakened his resolve to seek a better fortune elsewhere in the world. He attributed his fortitude both to his faith and to magic. These were not mutually exclusive. He went on to explain:

> *People who endured the crimes of the Janjaweed when their villages were burnt, and children thrown in the flames did not recognize how powerful they were. Could anyone criticize them if they decide to retaliate? There is a lot of ignorance here about what our sorcery could do to harm and retaliate. We have both holy people and sorcerers in Darfur who could turn water into yogurt before our eyes.*

He paused for a minute before submitting his intimate knowledge about the sway of sorcery: "*Did you ever think about the amulets [hijbat] that fighters wear around their necks and tie around their arms?*" "Yes," I replied. "*These are powerful amulets against gunshots and knife stabs. They contain notes written by these powerful men who can inflict harm on anyone they want. The knives and the bullets cannot penetrate the fighter's flesh.*" Although I had a sense of the direction of this conversation, I did not wish to assume the absence of a deeper meaning to what seemed tangential:

> *If you want to harm someone, go to an old experienced person known by a lot of people for magical outcomes. Nobody told me about this, but I have seen it myself. I went once to a sorcerer. I sat on the floor with my legs crossed and my arms folded. He talked to me about my problems and promised to deliver speedy results. I said: "Ya al-Sheikh, I don't know why my situation is so bad, and every road I took leads to a dead end. I know that someone did something bad to me, and I need your help." Between you and me, I had two suspects. The first was a woman I was supposed to marry. But then I started to think about the future. What would I do with a big family? Why would I go out of my way to marry someone who is always suspicious of me: "Where did you go? Give me money." Constant demands. I said to myself, look at the situation around you. Is that suitable for bringing a woman on board? No. The other I was certain was the sorcerer she consulted for sure. I was not sure if he buried some evil concoction in the cemetery or in the mouth of a lizard to close doors in my face.*
>
> *I did not share my suspicions with my sorcerer. I wanted him to confirm on his own. He was supposed to be among the best; he was recommended by friends. He sat there to listen and listen, only interrupting me by "aha aha oho oho," just like that. He was concentrating. He asked me to go out and fetch a tree branch from outside. I went outside and came back with a long branch. I was afraid in the beginning as though he was going to beat me. When he held it in his hand, I*

asked him: "Ya al-Sheikh, tell me about the person who is harming me and mak-
ing my life hell!" He said: "Be patient. Sit." He started to murmur words, very
strange words I have never heard before in my life, almost in a language that
did not resemble anything I have heard in my life. This sheikh, mind you, never
went to school, so I couldn't say maybe he is speaking English! He moved then
so swiftly to slice the branch. Human blood came out of it and sprayed all over
me. I am not a person who can come up with this story. My brain is okay. My
heart started to beat like a drum. He said "From now on, don't look back. I com-
municated with my jinn servants, and the blood you saw belongs to the people
who tried to hurt you and make you miserable. Inshallah, now their sorcery
is undone. Inshallah, no harm will touch you!" "But who were they?" I asked.
"I need to know." He said it wasn't important: "The important thing [is] that I
stuffed them in their cans [meaning they were reined in]."

We went back to our initial conversation about how to resolve the tragedy
in Darfur. "*Well, maybe the sorcerer will find a solution for Darfur, but these*
people who my eyes are seeing are useless. They want to fill their bellies and
enjoy their lives." This participant did not speak sarcastically. His meaning became clearer as he continued: "*There are certain people who are known to have*
caused the fighting in Darfur. People should go to their holy man or sorcerer to
take them down one by one."

Could this be read in light of a region's cry for an impossible justice? As
I listened to this man's invocation of a powerful mechanism for retaliation
against the perpetrators of violence, I wondered what A. J. Arkell's response
would have been. For hadn't he been told by a Zaghawa from Mirra and Geni-
gargera that "many of their people were [more] afraid of an oath on Mani
magic than one on the Koran"?[43] And didn't al-Tūnisī record accounts of Fur
hiring the *damazouqqa jinn* to protect belongings and herd their animals?[44]
Within hierarchies of beliefs, it is no wonder that many have given up on human resolution of the Darfur crisis and found more hope in the "gaze of the
wild."[45] Furthermore, these invocations of the sorcerer's uncanny powers are
examples of the desperate quest for relative calm. The sorcerer's abode within
this social and political imaginary is a bona fide court of last resort.

Qatar Notes

The state of Qatar has been a fascinating locale from which to explore both formal and informal forms of engagement with Darfur. As soon as I arrived in 2009, I realized that the Gulf state is host to one of the largest groups of Sudanese overseas. Sudanese migrant communities in Qatar include thousands from various ethnic affiliations and occupational backgrounds, including citizens from Darfur. Here, I was presented with valuable opportunities to pursue my ethnographic interest in Sudanese migration, both voluntary and forced. This chapter describes various encounters and interactions I have had for more than a decade exploring diverse perspectives on the politics of mediation in Qatar. I first describe my initial experiences with the Sons of Greater Darfur League, a social group of expatriate Darfuri men in Qatar (henceforth, the Sons). Second, I turn to a unique mediation initiative called Rakoobat Ajaweed Darfur (hereafter, RAD) in which I participated as reporter. This forum opened opportunities for reflecting on fieldwork's fluidities and contingencies. Finally, I share my introduction to a Sufi leader who arrived in Doha from Darfur. Sheikh Musa Abdullah Al-Husseini's voice amplifies our understanding of potentialities for mediating the spectacular violence that has bedeviled Darfur.

The Sons

It is one o'clock a.m. I am determined to stay awake to write this entry about my first meeting with the Sons of the Greater Darfur League several hours ago. I drove to the Sudanese Cultural Center in Doha's posh West Bay to meet up with Yassin, who arranged to introduce me to members of this group. Yassin told me that this center, an ornate building, hosts numerous gatherings of Sudanese migrants ranging from social events to religious holiday celebrations. As I entered, he introduced me to nine men who have worked in Doha for many years, including lawyers, teachers, veterinarians, and engineers. They came from different provinces in Darfur; some were Fur, others Zaghawa, Reizeigat, or Bani Halba. That is why they called their league Sons of Greater Darfur, to celebrate both the diversity of the members and the inclusion of all as Darfur's sons. These men are also part of the larger Sudanese community in Qatar. The fact that they have their own league was born of the desire to help those in need back home. Invariably, all of them mentioned that they have extended family members who still live there. Their presence in Doha as I understood it is important not only for the remittances, but also for being able to take part in conversations within the city about how to restore normalcy in the region. The Sons' generosity and openness to my idea of meeting once a month was heartening. Ali, who volunteered to take charge, had arranged the logistics.

Three weeks following our West Bay gathering, we met at one of the Sons' houses. This time more than fifteen people joined in the meeting. The conversation focused mainly on the need for greater appreciation of the root causes of the conflict in Darfur, without which sustainable and viable solutions would not be possible. As one interjected, "*We need to go back to the destruction of Darfur by politics and by the environment, and these two are interdependent.*" He went on to elaborate: "*The policies taken up by [Sudanese president Gaffar] Nimeiri, such as the dismantling of native administration, chipped away at our communities' ability to solve conflicts over water and grazing land peacefully. The wars next door in South Sudan and Chad had also a ripple effect. The flows of weapons changed people's lives forever.*" Comments like these were of paramount importance for my understanding of the perspectives of those who were born and raised in Darfur and were thus able to articulate how its precarious border politics and geography caused the fateful transformations that swept through the region. Here I also came to understand intercommunal violence as a phenomenon deeply rooted in people's refusal to respect conventional notions of borders. There is the national border that has always been crossed by neighboring Chadians who have used Darfur as a military base for their insurgency against their government; and then another border emerging between the nomadic and farming communities whose lives in the past were both intertwined and complementary. As competition over water and land became weaponized and politicized, so too was nomads' amenability to recruitment and mobilization by political opportunists in Khartoum. The combustible mix of weapons, scarcity, drought, desertification, border politics, and political Islamism in a region under duress was structural rather than natural.

Having imparted their perspectives on Darfur, the Sons continued our discussions on the past, present, and future of Darfur over the next several months in an atmosphere bursting with energy. The Sons invited me to a wave of events, gatherings, and receptions focusing on the Darfur question; these included frequent appearances of important stakeholders in the conflict who were visiting Qatar. A conference call with the slain leader of the antigovernment Justice and Equality Movement (JEM), Khalil Ibrahim (prior to his death), and a lunch in honor of a delegation from opposition rebel groups during which a Southern Sudanese lawyer confronted them about JEM's involvement in the so-called jihad against his people are two examples of migrants going toe-to-toe with rebels on numerous subjects. Additionally, I moderated a town hall with opposition leader El-Tigani Sese, who later headed the Darfur Regional Authority, an interim governing body for Darfur following the 2006 Darfur Peace Agreement;[1] and a meeting with Eisa Maru, a French diplomat invited to explain the role France's former colony of Chad has played in the Darfur crisis. Fundraisers to benefit Darfur were also among numerous events offering wonderful occasions for participatory observations.

Among the most extraordinary conversations held at the Sons meetings was that with Bahr Idriss Abu Garda, at the time the leader of the United Resistance Front and a JEM commander fighting against the government in Darfur. Like President Al Bashir, Abu Garda had been a defendant in a case before the International Criminal Court (ICC-02/05-02/09-2) involving war crimes. Unlike Al Bashir, however, he agreed to appear before the court. Charges against Abu Garda included an "attack [that] was carried out on 29 September 2007, against the African Union [peacekeeping] Mission in Sudan [AMIS]" stationed at the Haskanita Military Group Site (MGS). In the words of the ICC prosecutor:

> The attack on the MGS Haskanita was allegedly carried out by splinter forces of JEM, under the command of Abu Garda, jointly with the troops belonging to another armed group. The attackers, approximately 1,000 persons armed with anti-aircraft guns, artillery guns and rocket-propelled grenade launchers, allegedly killed twelve and severely wounded eight AMIS soldiers. They allegedly destroyed communication, installations, dormitories, vehicles and other materials and appropriated property belonging to AMIS, including 17 vehicles, refrigerators, computers, cellular phones, military boots and uniforms, fuel, ammunition and money during and after the attack.[2]

However, three years later, on February 8, 2010, the pretrial chamber prosecutor stated, "I decided not to confirm the charges of 3 war crimes against Mr. Abu Garda."[3] This statement heralded Abu Garda's exoneration. "*I had my day in Court*," he told us. When one of the Sons asked about this experience, he responded in a tone exuding a deep sense of pride and triumph: "*I accepted to go to the ICC's prosecutor because I was not guilty of the accusations leveled at me. The fact that I am a free man now is a testament to my innocence. I urge the president to follow suit.*" Among the political paradoxes in the Sudan is that this former fighter against the Sudanese government has subsequently aligned himself with the Islamist regime in the Sudan, becoming the federal minister of health under Al Bashir. The entire episode is yet another example of the instability of the African/Arab binary, as individuals jockey for power and shift alliances. However, he remains in the crosshairs of the court of public opinion.

My participation with the Sons along with parallel efforts with the Qatari Red Crescent, a relief organization, and the Sudanese Women's League and the Higher Popular Group for Darfur's Peace, two community-based aid and advocacy groups, were all important in my continuing effort to understand the complex strands and the urgency of Darfur's humanitarian crisis. Collectively, these groups functioned within the context of the Qatari state's commitment to adopting the Darfur crisis as a formal foreign policy portfolio.[4] The support lent by Qatar to various Darfuri rebel leaders, refugees, IDPs, and civil society activists was thus critical for broadening the scope of my ethnographic work in various capacities and occasions, as we shall see below.

Throughout this work, Darfuri migrants, delegates, and rebels frequently invoked Qatari involvement in the crisis, especially the paramount role embraced by His Excellency Ahmed bin Abdullah al-Mahmoud, Qatari minister of foreign affairs. His regular visits to Darfur and his interactions with displaced people stood as testimony and affirmation that his government has taken seriously the suffering of the Darfuri people.

Of particular interest to me was the Qatari government's invitation in 2009 to displaced people and those from less privileged groups in Darfuri society to participate in discussions preliminary to formal Doha Darfur peace talks between the Sudanese government and its opponents, scheduled to begin weeks later.[5] Its motives for doing so were numerous; according to the author of *Desert Kingdoms to Global Powers*, Rory Miller:

> Qatar's adoption of Darfur as a foreign policy portfolio cannot be understood in isolation of several considerations. Qatar's mediation role is an attempt to distinguish itself from other local competitors, emphasize its strategic value as a regional actor and increase its profile as a way to gain security shelter. In a sense, the actual mediation is secondary to achieving these three objectives. It also has the opportunity through its energy revenues to achieve these goals through financial diplomacy and the expenditure of serious amounts of funds in supporting its mediatory efforts. Finally, its meditation role is characterized

by two other interrelated important factors—it is very pragmatic and will talk to anyone anytime regardless of ideology or political concerns. This is a very valuable approach for meditators to conflict.[6]

These efforts at promoting the state's branding on the global stage notwithstanding, I was particularly drawn to the anthropological elements of Qatar's mediation efforts, most notably the views of Darfuri stakeholders themselves vis-à-vis these efforts. For example, Qatari efforts fit into what Carol Greenhouse calls "inclusive mediation," which "involves a third party whose neutrality is based on involvement with both sides of the dispute, and whose normative references are implicit, i.e., adduced from factual constructions of the dispute relationship."[7] Throughout my encounters in Doha, I heard statements reiterating Qatar's investment in Darfur's peace and its manifest neutrality, as evidenced by its invitation to all factions in the dispute to participate in discussions. Many added that the fact that not every armed group agreed to join the Doha forum did not reflect any insincerity in the state's attempts to ease the pain of Darfuri people.

This invitation represented an extraordinary form of "conspicuous redistribution"[8] offered by an affluent state, and various state and nonstate Darfuri actors availed themselves of a unique opportunity for dialogue. IDPs and refugees, among others who arrived in Doha, were accommodated in the fanciest, most glamorous hotels, where they remained for months as peace talks were under way. They received daily allowances similar to more official representatives and were assigned drivers with BMWs and Range Rovers to move about the Gulf city. As a Sudanese migrant commented to me: "*Since these displaced people arrived here, I have been running into them all the times in money transfer offices here. They send money home from the daily allowance they receive. The problem though is when their visit ends and they go back, now that they are used to receiving these daily gifts.*" Notwithstanding the condescension lurking in this comment, it is clear that IDPs were making an effort to ease the hardships of those back home, even if for a short while.[9]

Beyond Glamour: Darfur in the Corridors of the Millennium

The lines below are from my field notes. They refer to my meeting with delegates from Darfur who arrived in Doha as part of RAD, a civil society initiative for peace, convened in Doha in April 2009.

It has never crossed my mind that one day I would encounter Sudanese displaced people in a hotel. Nevertheless, anything is possible. I attribute my shortsightedness to the fact that shantytowns, slums, and camps have been the primary sites of my work for many years. To listen to these fellow citizens articulate their visions earlier today in the spectacularly exquisite Millennium of Doha is an experience apart. The opulent hall was carpeted wall-to-wall, softening steps and conveying a sense of absolute comfort and warmth. On round tables stylishly covered with white cloth, waiters laid large bottles of Evian water and crystal cups and candy dishes, which mirrored the lights shining from the mammoth Murano chandeliers above. The glare was at once symbolic and real, not only telling of the owners' wealth but also in stark contrast to sites more typical of my work with the displaced and of their own daily lives. It gave me pause, as I was sure it did for my new friends and fellow citizens. When one delegate after another stood up to preface their remarks by expressing utter gratitude to the Emir of Qatar, the pioneering first lady, Sheikha Moza bint Nasser Al-Mesand, and the people of Qatar, without whose support their stay in this venue and their conversations would have never been possible, they spoke from the heart, exuding deep appreciation for a rare opportunity to talk peace. This experience has certainly heightened my convictions about the unpredictability and nomadism of the "field" and imparted to me and hopefully to a new generation of anthropologists an opportunity to ponder the "deceptive transparency" of our discipline's cardinal method of fieldwork.[10] *I am equally convinced that the grace of this place, where these Sudanese delegates were to live for some time, has also sharpened their own understanding of war and peace. I pondered too the accident of birth that had converted so many of these people into IDPs and refugees, while giving a few the opportunity to accumulate incredible wealth, seize power, and destroy everything in their path. Politics makes all the difference in the world, as it has since the invention of the idea of ownership of resources, over which human have entered pitched wars.*[11]

But the Millennium Hotel was by no means the only place I encountered Darfuris. This metamorphosis of Doha into a theater of Darfuri mediations opened doors for me to rethink what constitutes "the field" and where "the field" is located as contingent, not enclosed by a territorially bound space. I contend that the field changed dramatically when Doha witnessed the steady arrival of Darfuri native chiefs, leaders and spokespersons for major armed movements, and activists, as well as displaced people and refugees. Here, the field has been located in concerts, town hall meetings, charity dinners, the Four Seasons, the Ritz Carlton, the Sheraton, and the Mövenpick. Rarely do IDPs find opportunities to venture away from the camps and the slums they inhabit. That they were afforded this rare opportunity to make their viewpoints known in Qatar was itself significant, heralding a unique kind of a "dialogic imagination" and "multivocality."[12] These gatherings assembled an orchestra of voices and thus offered an excellent opportunity to hear local perspectives on the conflict as well as epistemologies of remediation and community-crafted solutions from people who have borne the brunt of the violence. This scenario has led me to concede the nomadism of the field, its impressive mobility as an idea and method within the larger ethnographic project, as will become apparent below in my discussion of RAD.

It was my great honor to accept the invitation of the Arab Democracy Foundation (ADF), an independent Arab civil society organization promoting democratic values, to participate in the RAD forum, which took place in Doha March 30 through April 3, 2009, under the ADF's auspices. The forum was the largest of several RAD events that, although independent of the formal peace talks, nonetheless informed them. Attended by more than fifty delegates from diverse sections of the Darfuri community, it occurred at a time when Darfur's torment was at its peak.[13] In both general sessions and workshops throughout the forum, presentations and discussions addressed the issues of transitional justice around the world and the significance of its applications in Darfur, with particular reference to the model of Morocco's Equity and Reconciliation Commission (IER), a body similar to truth commissions established in postconflict countries.[14] Discussions also dealt in depth with the prerequisites and prospects for peace as the foundation for instating transitional justice in Darfur. These comprehensive discussions resulted in both general and detailed recommendations and crucial procedural guidelines for establishing a truth and reconciliation commission in Darfur. The meetings also resulted in establishing procedures for following up on many of the recommended actions.

As a participant in the entire event and chair of a couple of working groups, I had an exceptional opportunity to expand my thinking about the crisis and its possible mediation by listening to many deeply thoughtful views from Darfuri men and women with firsthand knowledge of the lethal violence in the region. I received permission from the conveners to include in the proceedings a childhood friend of mine, Azza Al-Zain Alnayal, a Sudanese who shares my concerns about Darfur. Alnayal and I took extensive notes over the five days of RAD and compared them at the end of the forum, thereby ensuring a level of completeness that I alone might not achieve. Our notes spared no detail as we aimed to include all the ideas put forward.

What is in the name RAD? From the outset, RAD's status as the first event of its kind was as interesting as its objective. Created with ordinary Darfuri people in mind, it recognized their authority and the value of their views about possible strategies for mitigation of violence. The forum drew its vision from two interwoven concepts that have regulated social relations in Darfuri society, Rakooba and Ajaweed, both deeply symbolic terms with cultural and legal resonances. "Rakooba" is a Sudanese term referring to a shaded shed-like structure where people sit to work, socialize, and reflect on the happenings of everyday life. In this outdoor space in Darfur, wise community elders and mediators known in the local lexicon as the Ajaweed used to convene regularly to resolve disputes, adjudicate transgressions of communal norms, and enforce law and order and good conduct. The dispensation of justice by people with accumulated wisdom exemplifies the core ethos of mediation. In their study *Traditional Authorities' Peacemaking Role in Darfur*, Tubiana, Tanner, and Abdul-Jalil explain the concept: "The Ajaweed are elders or notables. They usually come from a family clan, or 'tribe' not involved in the dispute. . . . The Ajaweed will swear on the Quran to be neutral."[15] Central to the inner workings of this exceptional mechanism of justice is the notion of *uruf*, i.e., the customary ethos by which people regulated both their public and private lives. Crossing the boundaries of uruf has serious implications for every member of society. Here lies the ultimate allegory of Darfur as a series of transgressions by perpetrators who violated norms well respected in the past. In other words, the impunity with which the political, sexual, and symbolic violence has taken place in Darfur could happen precisely because of the perpetrators' audacity in trespassing an important ethical frontier to which people had adhered since the Law of the venerable Sultan Dali in the seventeenth century. The voices and visions for mediation expressed under RAD's aegis thus draw their power from the memory of venerated community members with enormous moral authority deliberating under the shade of the reconciliatory shed. Under Ajaweed, these adroit mediators served justice expeditiously and much to the satisfaction of the plaintiff, as one chief told me.

The day before the meeting began, I headed to the Millennium to meet with the delegates. Upon entering the atrium, I was drawn immediately to an area where recognizably Sudanese men and women attired in their national dress were sitting. I introduced myself and told them that I would be chronicling their deliberations over the next few days. At that point, a chief from Jebel Marra commented: "*We are very happy to hear this. We are also very pleased that Darfur has come to you here in this place. However, we promise, once our situation settles, we will take you with us to Jebel Marra. Say Amen.*" "*Amen,*" I said.

On the inaugural day of the forum, Mohsen Marzouk, the secretary general of the ADF and the main convener of this event, delivered a powerful and inspiring opening address highlighting RAD's central purpose. As Marzouk described it, the forum was one of a series of pilot projects ADF had undertaken to discuss the possibility of reclaiming social peace for the citizens of Darfur through the mechanism of transitional justice, understood to be a powerful apparatus for resolving political crises when deployed appropriately. In addition, Marzouk emphasized the important role social activists and civil society had played historically in reconciliation processes in ways that go beyond political bargains between governments and armed rivals. He added: *"Today is one of these moments that enable individuals and communities to make history for themselves and for those who come after them. This moment alone is capable of aiding us in circumventing crises otherwise irresolvable by weaponry or delusions of grandeur."* Continuing in the same vein, he emphasized that the ultimate goal of the ADF, as the main mediator in the case of Darfur, was to reduce dependency on foreign expertise in crisis management and develop local capacities for managing Darfur's political business based on its own historical and cultural referents.

This point was well taken by the delegates, who conceded that experts frequently lack precise knowledge of local concerns, especially given their reliance on translators. Recognizing the significance of local knowledge necessarily puts great emphasis on the religious, social, and cultural frames necessary to reinvigorate dialogue; and the hybrid Arab-African identity of the Darfuri community needs acknowledgment and respect to bolster people's uruf. In turn, the notion of uruf, when used adroitly, can support efforts at effecting a measure of transitional justice.[16] Furthermore, as a community leader pointed out, the political undercurrents of the present situation need to be understood in context to enable the principles and mechanisms of social and transitional peace. At this point, a native chief from Southern Darfur noted:

> Notable obstacles to peace have been created on an international front. National and international communities and civil society organizations have miscarried missions [intended] to secure material and financial resources and facilities essential for the implementation of any reconciliation program. The presence and the continued deterioration of refugee and displaced persons camps and their humanitarian situations have also aggravated the local conditions in Darfur. Beyond the Darfuri state, the conflict in neighboring Chad has resulted in social, political, and economic problems that have spilled over into Darfur. We cannot talk about human rights without realizing the problems that live next door to us.

Throughout RAD's conversations, the relationship between political, economic, humanitarian, and social dimensions of the conflict indeed came to the fore. As stakeholders raised hands to shape the agenda for the next few days, they identified some of the nodal dilemmas and offered recommendations. Discussion circled around the following topics: political conditions in the region, *hakoura* (a traditional Darfuri system of bestowing land) and the use of land resources, security and local governance, voluntary return and reconstruction, female victims of human rights violations, and reparations and redress of grievances. Delegates then broke into smaller focus groups to consider a single theme in depth. Subsequently, the delegates came together as a group to marry genealogies of conflict to visions for the future. I had the opportunity to report on the discussions of female victims and reparations and redress. Other groups shared their reports with me prior to ADF's preparation of the final document intended to guide further discussions. This forum was quite unlike others I have attended in the United Kingdom and the United States, where such a plethora of voices was absent. I summarize the groups' discussions in the following paragraphs, providing ethnographic and historical contextualization where needed and including each group's recommendations for carrying the discussion forward.

However, in addition to the content of these discussions, their significance lay in the fact that people whose voices have not been heard in deliberations about the crisis in Darfur—IDPs, refugees, and native chiefs—were able to convey their understanding of the causes and consequences of the devastation of their communities. Although it is important to recognize the structural difficulties that militate against the materialization of their recommendations on the ground, delegates nevertheless felt it important to contribute solutions as people who were bearing the brunt of the devastation in Darfur. RAD was thus a field of local knowledge, a kind of ad hoc hakoura that demonstrated to me the value of listening to a diversity of lived realities in Darfur. That these discussions occurred in the Millennium Hotel made them no less legitimate than if they had taken place in the delegates' home communities, in the midst of war. Throughout the five days, I was struck by the way the discussions focused on the predicaments of everyday life in Darfur, interweaving a host of past and present political and economic concerns. Darfuri delegates also brought a particular sense of urgency to the existential concerns voiced here; one could hear their longing to be heard. Indeed, doing ethnography at the RAD forum challenges the authority people try to accrue when they physically enter war sites. While I don't discount the dangers faced by those who do so, I also aver that the very contrast between RAD's luxurious surroundings and conditions in Darfur—and the relief RAD allowed from those conditions—nurtured both thoughtful reflection and a sense of urgency among delegates.

DELIBERATING POLITICS

A few months before RAD took place in Doha, Darfur's suffering was reaching epidemic proportions. Entering the fifth year of the crisis, Human Rights

Watch was reporting attacks along the Darfur-Chad border in Abu Suruj, Silea, and Sibra; sexual violence, pillaging, and assault of aid workers abounded.[17] At the same time, the arrival the combined United Nations–African Union peacekeeping mission, due to start operations at the beginning of 2009, raised expectations for the mitigation of security concerns.

Against this backdrop, it was no wonder that prevailing political conditions were on everyone's mind. In the minds of participants in RAD's Political Conditions Group efforts at mitigating the region's tragedy must derive from a fundamental understanding of the multilateral nature of the conflict. In a situation in which a host of social, cultural, economic, and political factors are at play, it would be nearly impossible to envisage a permanent and just settlement that depended entirely upon political bargains between the government and the armed rivals or those with very specific political interests. Group participants also understood that the intercession of social activists and civil society organizations would be crucial to a successful outcome. In the past two decades, no major quest for peace and reconciliation or transition to democratic governance has been successful without their involvement.

Members had no doubt that addressing structural issues, including a democratic transformation capable of respecting human rights, was a self-evident and necessary cornerstone of peace. But group members also spoke movingly about the cost of war and of the human dimensions of peacekeeping. One member noted the humiliation that violence has brought to Darfur: "*Something needs to happen for the perpetrators to know that [without] restoring the dignity of our people, peace in Darfur would not be fulfilled a hundred years from now. We need to acknowledge that our deliberations must place trust front and center in our discussion about political conditions in the country.*" Another delegate noted, "*With years of undergoing savage turmoil, we must stress the importance of paying attention to the topics of political will, courage, and genuine intent to reach a peace. Trust and credibility will be restored only if there are good intentions.*" Others concurred unreservedly that cultivating trust and embracing transparent and accountable procedures were necessary to show respect for the human beings in Darfur.

The group alternated between the local and the international as complementary approaches to peace without agreeing on top-down solutions. It was obvious that members understood that valuing the universal language of respect for human beings in Darfur does not mean consenting to imported concepts or borrowed power that has no relevance to people's lives. A woman spoke to emphasize ways that United Nations Security Council [UNSC] Resolution 1325 on women, peace, and security as explained by community activists nonetheless has direct relevance to Darfuris' conditions of existence.[18] She repeated key points in this resolution to make the case for the inclusion of women as fundamental to political approaches to peacemaking: "*As per the prior UN Resolution 1325, ensuring female participation of at least 25 percent is crucial if women are not to be overlooked and underrepresented in peace processes.*" Unlike some feminists worldwide who criticized the resolution as inadequate, this woman and others in the group recognized that "half a loaf is better than none," in a manner of speaking, seeing the resolution as having great potential for their inclusion.

Also apparent was consensus about the urgent need for the comprehensive engagement of all stakeholder voices and collective perspectives to consolidate the otherwise scattered and compartmentalized peace process. A female community activist added the following:

> *Local governments would need to be reactivated, their previous position and powers reinstated, and their administrative capabilities strengthened by bringing in qualified personnel to enable them to support the peace effort. In parallel, hostilities would need to cease through agreements involving all parties that would need monitoring for compliance to avoid jeopardizing our efforts.*

Unlike the other groups' discussions, which resulted in several specific recommendations, what this group expressed was a yearning to make their voices heard. The group did agree to convene a meeting with Djibril Bassolé, the joint African Union–United Nations chief mediator for Darfur, to review and hopefully facilitate broad dissemination of its ideas. As it happened, I had a brief chat with Mr. Bassolé in Qatar, where he had an office at the Retaj Hotel since the start of the Doha Darfur negotiations. Counterposed to his years of observing Sudanese peace negotiations, his optimism about this particular gathering was extraordinary: "*I have never been in a situation where so many factions of rebel movements and government officials at war have sat together for meals and socialized with each other, even if they didn't see eye-to-eye politically. I see this all the time with the Sudanese delegations here. I am very hopeful.*" Of course, Bassolé's optimism must be weighed against the enormous challenges of overcoming the segmentation of Darfuri opposition movements.

HAKOURA DILEMMAS

RAD's Land Tenure and Resources Group took up debate over ways in which the invisible political economy governing resource allocation has produced enmity and competition over the distribution of land and water. Discussions

related to land use were anchored in the concept of hakoura, a system of bestowing land that had been observed by the people of Darfur for centuries.
As with other RAD groups, an in-depth examination of historical contexts
and current conflicts allowed discussants to understand that land disputes
could not be isolated from the larger Darfur crisis and that they needed to
design recommendations based on cultural precedents adapted to present
realities.

To accommodate some non-Sudanese participants, delegates explained
that traditionally in Darfur, as in most African regions, land was initially understood to be owned communally. Various principles had historically regulated the management of these lands, including an understanding of the role
of the local government as the administrative authority acting on behalf of
the community. It would distribute land leases directly to members of the
community or indirectly through the mediation of counselors, i.e., the Ajaweed; collect prescribed taxes, such as *zakat* or fines due the government; and
ensure that farmers, nomads, and the community observed the traditional
norms and regulations. Settling disputes was traditionally the responsibility of the Ajaweed, which would not involve individuals with a stake in the
dispute, including both plaintiffs and defendants, their kin, and friends, to
avoid a conflict of interest. Each party was obliged to comply with the decision reached by the Ajaweed. If it failed to reach a settlement, then the local
government court intervened. The judgment of this court was final; it could
not be appealed in civil or criminal courts of the central government. Relying
on his sharp institutional memory, a chief recalled principles of land management within the hakoura:

> If a piece of land was left fallow or unused for a fixed period of time [for ex-
> ample, between three and five years], the land was expropriated and returned
> to communal ownership to be reallocated according to customary procedures or
> preserved by the administrative authority on behalf of the sultan for the use of
> future generations. In addition, according to traditional norms and regulations,
> land tenure would not exclude persons from outside the local community. People
> of diverse tribal origins inhabited most villages. In other words, land tenure was
> a clear manifestation of citizenship in Darfur across its multitudinous tribes.

RAD emphasized grazing pastures as arenas of intercommunal violence.
Accordingly, it expounded on the logic of pasture rights, access, especially to
grazing pastures, and the impact of government neglect of this fundamental
source of livelihood. Among participants there was a consensus that local
government authorities had effectively overseen the fair use of pastures by
farmers and animal grazers according to traditional practices, as stipulated

in the 1989 tribal reconciliation agreement between the Fur (settled villagers) and multiple nomadic tribes of Arabic origin.

When the discussion turned to the present, discussants conceded that land use issues had become increasingly complex for more than a decade, due primarily to the gradual corrosion of governing systems and officials' failure to perform their duties.[19] Governments had repeatedly neglected to address questions of land tenure and land registration for purposes of residence, farming, horticulture, and grazing. Instead, both federal and state authorities showed greater interest in planning, organizing, and registering lands in and around major cities and towns. Here, they noted, we observe firsthand the urban bias that continues to plague African governments' stance vis-à-vis rural areas in general and the Sudan in particular. Yet participants also noted how recent and current neglect is rooted in a long history of, as a community activist put it, *"disregard for local land norms and traditions"* that organized relationships between farmers and grazers.[20] A chief commented on government failures this way:

> *Successive governments had debilitated traditional local government institutions in Sudan in general, and in Darfur in particular, in order to replace them with bodies composed of politically appointed local government leaders. In a haphazard progression of replacing traditional institutions that played positive roles in local regulation with modern administrative systems, the authorities created a vacuum for settling land disputes and maintaining law and order within Darfuri communities. Central governments had also perpetuated their own failures by failing to abide by the resolutions of previous settlement and reconciliation conferences for the Darfur crisis.*

Finally, the government's failure to manage significant ecological factors and to develop environmental resources, including especially resources of water and land, had exacerbated conflicts between farmers and pastoralists. To add further pressure, the waves of drought that had hit the region since the 1970s forced large numbers of people to move south and west with their herds, encroaching upon lands traditionally owned by other tribes.[21]

Informed by a deep knowledge of history and politics, this group concluded with an urgent call to address issues of land use and resources. Regarding land tenure, the central task as the group understood it would be the restoration of the hakoura system governing rights to own, use, and organize lands as it was applied before national independence. It agreed that immediately after the conclusion of a new peace agreement, the group would need to organize a pan-Darfur conference for all the peoples of the region, with the aim of clarifying the hakoura system and addressing dynamic developments related to land usage. An authorized body within the regional government would need to be granted suitable judicial and administrative powers to regulate the system wisely across all three states of Darfur. With a designated regulator in place, the local authority would then need to mitigate current tensions and land disputes by drawing upon traditional norms and customs. Lands occupied by foreigners or newcomers since the outbreak of hostilities would need to be returned to the original owners, including the villages' traditional inhabitants who had been evacuated. The government would also need to address the fate of Sudanese occupants of previously deserted villages and lands. In parallel, the group also agreed that tensions over grazing pastures would need regulation, with particular attention to previous reconciliation conferences, notably the tribal reconciliation agreement of 1989 between the Fur and the Arab tribes regarding grazing routes for camels and cattle. Finally, delegates addressed the need to encourage enforcement of more proactive measures, such as developing Darfur's natural resources, including subsoil (i.e., mineral and oil) and underground water resources, while maintaining the right of the central government to use subsoil resources pursuant to the relevant provisions in the 2006 Darfur Peace Agreement.[22] Associated actions would include reclaiming land and regulating its development for farming and grazing; settling nomadic tribal groups far from farming lands;[23] and revising procedures for land allocation to large privately owned investment corporations for mechanized agriculture.

As important as their specific recommendations was this group's observation about the elitism that inhibited substantial land reform and the need for grassroots activism. As one delegate noted cogently:

> The people of Darfur themselves needed to play a more active role in making the issue of land a priority concern. We have to speak about these concerns and about the lack of interest shown by Darfuri elites and intellectuals towards the conflict in the state. There has seemed to be a distinct lack of connection between these parties and the grassroots players to consolidate any peacemaking efforts.

WHY SECURITY?

RAD's Security and Local Governance Group was formed primarily to address the thorny topic of security, a broad concept that includes public security, comprising both public peace and public order, as well as the security of national borders, economic security, and personal security. Accordingly, it focused on reinstating the role and authority of local governments within a framework of good governance, rebuilding conditions for peace, and maintaining law and order. To produce a realistic set of recommendations, discussants first identified factors that had eroded the framework of security in Darfur, resulting in a rampant lawlessness that challenged efforts to reinstate peace. Key among them were government actions (or inactions) at both local and higher levels. As wars and disturbances in neighboring countries spilled into Darfur, political relations with neighboring countries significantly deteriorated. Meanwhile, various tiers of government fueled conflicts by distributing arms to the so-called tribal militias and by failing to prevent rebel groups from smuggling weapons and drugs across national borders. Local government bodies ignored rising tensions between Darfuri tribes resulting from limited resources and disputes over hakoura, thereby failing to perform their traditional role as mediator and peacemaker. The situation was compounded by the lack of interest among Darfuri elites and intellectuals in the deteriorating state. The neglect of community development, the lack of national development projects and the collapse of existing ones, and the abandonment of athletic, cultural, and religious pursuits that would typically engage youth in constructive activity were further evidence of the state's discounting the people of Darfur. Meanwhile, the state itself became implicated in random and indiscriminate killings, rape and other forms of sexual abuse, and mass destruction of property, houses, and sources of livelihood.

Bemoaning the corrosion of local security measures resulting from the marked absence of justice and judicial systems, a delegate noted:

> The looting, the attacks against people's property and honor, and the impunity with which they are carried out by criminals and Janjaweed are a direct result of past policies towards Darfur's established judicial tools. Today I can go on forever to give one example after the next: open displays and sales of contraband weapons, ammunition, and goods without fear of impoundment by local authorities, the proliferation of bandit attacks, et cetera, et cetera are horrible problems. The roads connecting Nyala and Zalengi today are minefields.

Homing in on some of the most difficult predicaments bedeviling their communities, group members developed a number of recommendations for maintaining law and order and reinstating Darfur's security framework. Especially urgent was the call for a special subgroup to discuss the problems of disarmament. There was general agreement about the need to prohibit carrying unlicensed weapons; develop and strictly enforce a ban on weapons sales in coordination with security agencies, specifically the police, security forces, and the local government; and create a regional mechanism to monitor the weapons trade across national borders. A reduction in factors fueling the violence would then allow dialogue and negotiations between the armed movements, the government, and other stakeholders in Darfur. In the words of a delegate: "*A mechanism would need to be established to monitor and follow up on the implementation of the recommendations as per the Darfur Peace Agreement.*" The group as a whole agreed that activating popular diplomacy was fundamental to strengthening community relations. The group also stressed the need for its inclusion in the conversation about the return of displaced persons and refugees to their home villages, a recommendation that overlaps with that of the group tackling the subject of voluntary return and reconstruction of the region. It envisioned a greater role for local governments in enforcing security measures pertaining to pastoral activities related to routes and seasonal movements. Given the political significance of intercommunal violence in disputes between pastoralists and farmers, this concern was also present in conversations about voluntary return and rehabilitation. In my view, these measures, although optimistic in the face of the political realities of the country, could result in significant breakthroughs in mitigating communal violence.

VOLUNTARY RETURN?

Discussions of return were animated by delegates' deeply personal experiences of displacement, that is, forced migration resulting from both natural disasters and man-made tragedies. As one delegate stated baldly, "*My village was totally burned by the Janjaweed. When we talk about return, I wonder what am I to return to.*" The discussants acknowledged that return to homelands would be viable only under certain conditions, including assurances that returnees will enjoy personal safety; the provision of basic necessities supporting resettlement such as housing, education, health care, and food; and the availability of opportunities to sustain everyday life, such as farming inputs and income-generating development projects. This group agreed that before any recommendations could be implemented, potential beneficiaries of a repatriation program would need to be identified, primarily by government-designated, internationally monitored committees. Members also urged that announcements of the repatriation project should be actively disseminated; and that for the implementation phase, Arab Democracy Foundation's support be availed. It was noted that, based on an estimate of 4,820 pillaged settlements and burned villages, the number of targeted persons could be as high as 1.6 million presently located in thirty-seven refugee camps.[24] Participants also accurately identified displacement as a gendered phenomenon; existing studies show that 90 percent of the population in refugee camps are women and children.

This group also agreed that the most afflicted villages needed to be prioritized for reconstruction projects so that returnees would have habitable accommodation; and that sufficient financial resources would need to be provided to avoid discouraging potential returnees from returning. Finally, the group recognized the need to establish an on-going working group including NGOs, OCHA, and donors to supervise the process of voluntary return through all its phases.[25] The discussion cascaded into a debate about two distinctive and interlaced problems—of the female victim and of reparations and redress of grievances—taken up by the two groups to which I now turn.

UNSPEAKABLE ATROCITIES:
FEMALE VICTIMS OR SURVIVORS?

To be noted at the outset is the group's preference for the term "female victim" rather than "survivor," the latter being the label frequently used in NGO narratives. "Victim," they averred, communicates more fully the particular traumas war has inflicted on women and girls; "survivor" implies an infrastructure of moral, medical, and material support for those so violated that is absent in Darfur. The Female Victims of the Darfur Crisis Group thus addressed possible remedies for the atrocities and injustices women have experienced.

By way of background, it was first noted that women had once occupied stable and secure roles in their communities, participating in every aspect of domestic life and engaging in a wide range of economic activities, including farming and trading. They moved around the village with freedom to fetch water and collect firewood. From a life of relative security, women in Darfur were plunged into a nightmare of torment as they witnessed their parents, husbands, children, and other family members being killed. They also experienced a particular form of violence reserved for women. As a woman community activist explained:

> Women experienced rape and other forms of sexual abuse. They witnessed the same of their daughters—which was a newly introduced element into the culture of war in Darfur. Some underwent circumcision at very young ages for fear of rape or were married off while still underage. Young girls were deprived of education under the pretext of protecting them. Some endured domestic violence stemming from men's devastating awareness of their inability to protect female members of the household against imminent rape. Others holding jobs in certain industries or in informal economies faced high probabilities of sexual harassment and abuse. Those at home witnessed the devastation and pillaging of their

*homes and villages, displacement, and the consequent search for asylum and
security.*

The subjection of women and children to such heinous crimes has deeply
marked them and led to severe trauma. A counselor in the group described
the results of these forms of physical and emotional suffering based on her
interactions with victims:

> *The consequent psychological conditions have manifested in many ways includ-
> ing depression, schizophrenia, and anxiety disorders; uncontrolled emotions of
> hatred and revenge, loss of self-esteem and self-confidence, nightmares and un-
> bidden recollections of their experiences, and other indications of posttraumatic
> stress disorder; irregular menstrual cycles and recurrent abortions; either the
> lack of desire to have children or a craving to give birth to many children to
> compensate for their losses; estrangement from community norms and values;
> and other manifestations of trauma.*

Compounding the problem is the deafening silence surrounding gender-
based crimes, rooted in a deep-seated taboo against talking about sexuality
and a patriarchal culture that blames women for their own violation.

To secure support for their concerns, the group agreed that it would be
necessary to monitor the occurrence of violence against women and prepare
fact-based, balanced, and unbiased reports for international organizations. It
concurred that there was an urgent need to establish activist institutions to
support women, provide training programs, and specifically address gender-
based issues, grievances, and concerns. Likewise, national awareness cam-
paigns would need to be designed and disseminated to give voice to women's
issues, emphasize the need to prioritize their traumas, negate incriminating
perceptions of female victims of sexual abuse, and empower women to com-
bat the traditional attitudes that assume they are powerless. Concomitantly,
social-psychological studies of gender-based violence would have to be carried out in order to develop appropriate ways to integrate victims into society economically, psychologically, and socially.

Apart from the sheer burden of addressing women's plight, restoring wom-
en's dignity, and supporting their empowerment, the delegates emphasized the
importance of embracing the gender dimension of peacekeeping and peace
building, particularly the engagement of women in the peace process to ensure that both the government and armed movements recognize the plight of
women, issue apologies to them, redress their grievances, and secure financial
compensation for their suffering and losses. A member of the group reminded
it of a potential ally, noting, "*Of course we need to appeal to the United Nations'
good offices at least to monitor these efforts.*" While many of these initiatives

would take place on the local level, the group also agreed on the need to establish a nationwide truth and reconciliation commission, a recommendation that other groups made also, although in this case one that would explicitly include women's concerns within the scope of its work. The country would also need to guarantee its commitment to implementing agreements resulting from this commission in order to build stepping-stones to civic trust and avoid another futile peace effort. Whether or not implementing these recommendations would bring about relative calm, a term I prefer to peace, simply speaking the recommendations drove home the power of voicing experiences that have long been unspoken.

ON RECOMPENSE

Finally, the Reparations and Redress of Grievances Group tackled the rampant human rights violations and the devastating physical destruction that have occurred throughout the state since 2003. The grievances addressed are understood to be violations of the rights of the individual and the community, as defined by international law. The discussants agreed upon categories of victimhood based upon the nature of harm inflicted, including harm affecting one's body, mind, or honor; loss of property, livelihood, stability, education, and other means for self-sufficiency and advancement; damage to one's community and environment; and harm resulting from the absence of appropriate systems of justice. A community activist offered a way to conceptualize reparations as both individual and collective: individual reparations would be offered against material claims, including blood money for the dead and injured and monetary compensation for stolen assets, properties, and livelihoods; and against nonmaterial claims, such as provisions for psychological rehabilitation and healthcare services. Collective reparations could be made to rebuild villages, provide government-supported production inputs and construction material, build roads and other necessary infrastructure in Darfur, establish a comprehensive database of neglected development projects—such as the Jebel Marra, West Savanna, and Ghazala Jawazat projects, among others—and proceed to resume these initiatives, as well as seek the expertise of both national and foreign experts to integrate these solutions at a regional level.

As we have seen with other groups, the reparations and redress group articulated specific goals related to its particular areas of concern. It defined as the top priority the establishment of an appropriate framework and set of strategic guidelines for reparations, drawing upon historical precedent for compensation. With the aim of guaranteeing fulfillment of the 2006 Darfur

Peace Agreement, the group also agreed that such guidelines should establish mechanisms for enforcing accountability, preventing impunity, offering reparations, and redressing grievances; and further, that that these mechanisms should include a clearly defined policy for identifying the programs to be implemented and rules and regulations for implementation, an eligibility registry specifying the victims who will receive reparation measures, and modes for delivering compensation through official channels and procedures. The proven, positive aspects of the Darfur Peace Agreement, the members agreed, are an appropriate basis for the stipulation of compensation, the settlement of disputes, the reform of security and judicial institutions, and the prevention of a recurrence of human rights violations. Accordingly, the Reparations and Redress of Grievances Group formed under the provisions of the 2006 agreement needs to be reactivated to facilitate payments.

A further critical component, the group agreed, is the creation of a commission for truth, charged with disclosing the truth about violations, abuses, and injustices carried out in Darfur by all parties of the armed conflict and educating communities about the historical context of the conflict since the independence of the Sudan. The group strongly advised applying the principle of continuous consultation with victims in any implementation of a program for reparations and redress of grievances; that such a program be appropriately respectful of those who have suffered harm; and that the commission follow transparent, impartial, and objective procedures and produce comprehensive reports. Additionally, a mechanism would need to be created to protect witnesses and victims appearing before said commission, especially victims of rape and other forms of sexual or violent abuse. For more general grievances, the group emphasized the urgent need to implement a program of redress based on indicators of positive discrimination, with priority given to short-term infrastructure projects to be completed in a specific period. The aim of such initiatives and any future projects would be to restore the dignity and confidence of the people of Darfur so that they may enjoy a sense of continuity in their lives and entertain the possibility of a future.

In the interstices of plentitude in Qatar and despite seeming powerlessness and poverty at home, RAD delegates put together the pieces of the Darfur conflict in a manner that defies facile summary. I cannot overstate the depth of their deliberations. My pleasure was boundless as I basked in delegates' vibrant and intelligent company and listened to voices subverting the interventionist notion that Darfuris are dependent upon the power of others to define their concerns. Bringing together people across ethnic, linguistic, and gender differences, RAD's appeal for the conditions of peace was both cognitively and emotionally persuasive. Recognizing the risk of seeming to romanticize or idealize RAD, I remain convinced that this risk is worth taking. Such was the cumulative power of the gathering, a power no doubt heightened by the glamourous, otherworldly setting, where one might succumb to the illusion that anything is possible.

Of course, total consensus is unimaginable in any human interaction, and the RAD delegates certainly had their divergences. The yearning for fruitful debate, however, largely superseded dissonance and discord over the course of these extensive conversations. RAD as metaphor for traditional Darfuri modes of reconciliation, drawn from the delegates' deep historical, social, and political consciousness, helped reclaim the possibility that collegial dialogue can abate conditions that have been undoing their homes. I remained won over by RAD's focus on the voices of ordinary people otherwise excluded from formal debates about Darfur in the world. That these voices must be heard if there is to be a viable peace is the most important lesson of the entire exercise.[26]

A Sufi Mystic's Whirling Trance for Peace

Beyond the deliberations of RAD, which presented me with the well-considered outlooks of delegates who have borne the brunt of the war, I had the rare opportunity to expand my ethnographic observations when I met Sheikh Musa Abdullah Al-Husseini, a pillar of the Tijania Sufi sect (trariqa), who was also a participant in this forum. His interventions in the dialogue intrigued me, as did his personal trajectory as an ardent educator and peacemaker. His personal philosophy vis-à-vis reconciliation and cultural diplomacy in Darfur has proven valuable to the peace process over the years. A man with a commanding personality, Sheikh Musa has drawn from the spiritual ethos of Sufism to play a paramount role in bolstering strong ties among divergent groups within communities ravaged by political violence.

Sheikh Musa was born in Qeiraida in Darfur sometime in the 1930s, and as a youngster he accompanied his father to Nyala, where he has lived since the 1940s. A disciple of the Grand Mufti of Nigeria, where Tijani Sufism is the dominant spiritual worldview, he learned the Quran, its jurisprudential core, the prophet's life history (sira), and the Arabic language. His mastery of these subjects enabled him later in life to establish Quranic schools (khalawi) in communities where government support for education was conspicuously lacking, a fact that itself is telling of Darfur's marginalization. No substitute for formal education, Sheikh Musa's khalawi nonetheless provided an opportunity for pupils at least to learn to read and write. Through his unique merger of Sufism and activism, he has knit together threads of consciousness about the

sanctity and wholeness of the self, ethical principles regulating the self's dialectical relationship to society, and the Sufi belief in the inviolability of the
human. According to the sheikh, boundaries between the self and society are
manifestly blurred; self and society are but one entity, at once cohesive and
inseparable. The affliction of the self is a privation for society, irrevocable and
injurious to the vigor and healthiness of the whole. It is on these beliefs that
Sheikh Musa has focused his undivided attention for more than forty years,
animating his convictions about human rights, peace, and the regulation of
one's aversion to difference.

On February 18, 2007, Sheikh Musa received the blessing of his Sufi guide,
the Sheikh of Islam Al-Sharif Ibrahim Salih Al-Husseini, the Grand Mufti of
Nigeria, to combine his spiritual teachings with social activism and spread
his mission of mediation more widely. Subsequently, he launched the People
of Allah Call for Peace in Darfur, referring to both a group of his own disciples and a charter that guides their work. The group's mission has been
twofold: to invoke memories of peacetime in the region when communities
lived shoulder-by-shoulder and the Ajaweed, drawing from the deep well of
local knowledge, defused intercommunal tensions and reached amicable settlements; and to call for the consolidation of the much-venerated ethic of tolerance. These are the core spiritual and epistemological givens in Sufi cosmology. This conceptual context may help the reader appreciate the ways in which
this Sufi leader shaped the People of Allah Call for Peace in Darfur. The idea of
communities of grace married to an anthropological version of consciousness
has produced within the Call for Peace an emotional tone at once less hostile
and more amenable to reconciliation. With these goals in mind, Sheikh Musa
shared his ideas in 2007 in El Fashir, El Geneina, and Nyala, sites featured
prominently in the massive political violence perpetrated by both insurgents
and counterinsurgents that left the communities utterly devastated. By distributing over ten thousand cassette tapes of his Call for Peace document among
the people in these besieged communities, he spread the word not only about
Sufism but also about a uniquely reconciliatory ethos derived from Darfur's
own past. As we have seen, reconciliation, dispensed through Ajaweed mechanisms of justice, lies at the base of the strong bonds that existed across Darfuri
ethnic communities for centuries.

In the course of his wanderings across Darfur, Sheikh Musa attracted
large numbers of disciples from the entire range of ethnicities eager to hear
his message of peace in the face of an insidious catastrophe. Women and men,
old and young all listened and absorbed the spirit of a Sufi message that acted
to calm inflamed passions. As we came to learn from the sheikh, the cassettes
he distributed communicated an inspirational message of a *scientia sacra*,[27]

one that attempted to assuage a fixation on vengeance and anger in the face of massive atrocities and instead stressed forgiveness, which he saw as a necessary step for healing. Forgiveness is not surrender to the will of the perpetrator, Sheikh Musa avers. Rather, bestowing it is a way to reclaim one's power, thereby breaking the shackles of a perpetrator's hold on its victim. This is the same argument Martha Minow makes in her powerful book *Between Vengeance and Forgiveness*:[28] to forgive the unforgivable is the ultimate power a victim can recover for himself or herself. At the same time, the sheikh's Call makes clear that forgiveness does not mean laxity in the pursuit of accountability. Nor does it mean that Darfur's tragedy is reducible to communal violence, which is understood as the state's exploitation of ethnic difference. Rather, it recognizes that the path to peace must resist hierarchies that silence the voices of those whose lives are gripped by war. Indeed, Sheik Musa believes that intellectuals, political elites, and experts, as well as IDPs and native leaders in and outside of the camps, must come together if peace is to occur. For him, all who embrace the Call are welcome.

Although I did not consider predicaments of consciousness in any depth, the sheikh's teachings turned my attention to the connection between consciousness and the topic of mediation. I wanted to understand the philosophical basis of his approach toward social healing. From Nigel Rapport's carefully crafted anthropological analysis of consciousness I learned about the relationship of individual consciousness to larger notions of collective consciousness, as well as interpretations of the cultural dynamics that create our specific self-understanding vis-à-vis the cosmos.[29] Within this framework, it is not surprising that the sheikh's message, rooted in the Sufi consciousness of the indivisibility and holism of the self and linked to processes of mediation and arbitration once held in high esteem in Darfur, achieved veritable consensus among communities that have heard it. Its spirit and ethos hold relevance for those experiencing daily troubles in this temporal world. It also belies binary notions that split societies into neatly defined social formations. In the context of Sheikh Musa's work, such a collective consciousness has been cemented through numerous public ceremonies, speeches, and dialogues. His message, embodied in the Call, has found popular resonance within IDP camps, where the sheikh himself has recognized the prevalence of khalawi and Sufi circles and the continuation of celebratory ritual practices of the Mawlid of the Prophet, Eid al-Fitr, and Eid al-Adha.

How are the words of the Call translated into action? At the level of political institutions, where decisions about peace are linked to a people's very right to exist on earth, the eloquent Sufist call is presented in a straightforward manner, so those who hear it may grasp how it is linked to an ontology of the inalienability and indivisibility of human rights. Sheikh Musa argues that notwithstanding the transnational interest that Darfur has garnered, it is Darfur's people who hold the key to unlocking the power of mediation much as they did in years past. He understands that trust among numerous factions in the region cannot be restored easily, and one must abandon naiveté when strategies of rehabilitation and reintegration are discussed. Trust building is an acquired organizational skill. Furthermore, if the Call for Peace in Darfur is to succeed even partially, it cannot do so by itself. Working closely with native leaders who wield considerable moral authority has helped Sheikh Musa communicate the spiritual underpinnings of the declaration, "The Call of Allah's People for Remedying the Self," in which he explicates his efforts at furthering equanimity in the Sudan.

At times, it must be said, Sheikh Musa has been overly optimistic in his attempt to revitalize forms of native governance abolished by the military in the early 1970s. Within and beyond RAD, its abolition has been understood as a primary reason for the security breaches in the region. Nonetheless, hearing a leader call for its return, regardless of the impossibility of that happening and of critics' skepticism, has been a source of hope for people. If Sheikh Musa's vision for peace does not—cannot—exist, real healing also will not exist, nor will an understanding of "native" answers to local problems. I read the man and his mission in this context despite my own uncertainties that without a dedicated constituency in the country at large, loose ends will never be tied as easily as the preceding lines suggest. Still, this vision is significant for its holism: the sheikh understands the Darfur crisis as an embodiment of a larger predicament, one that mirrors the postcolonial state's fragility. This Sufi mystic whirled in a trance for peace during a time when many thought it impossible.

My encounters in the corridors and halls of RAD culminated in a concert by the talented Darfuri musician Omar Ihsas singing one of his greatest hits, "Darfur, My Mother," as delegates repeatedly and with rising voices chanted its powerful lyrics in unison. It was a spectacular moment of convergence and consensus. As I conclude this chapter, I wish to reiterate the lessons that I learned, regardless of the outcomes or implementations of the insight of the Sufi or the deliberations of the RAD delegation. As a Sudanese anthropologist who comes from the North, not the West, encountering Darfur in Qatar palpably demonstrated the fluidity of the notion of anthropological fieldwork. While many have pointed out that its unboundedness has been dictated by global transformations and mobilities, I experienced it in Qatar. Participating in RAD also afforded me a rare opportunity to expand the field of knowledge by advancing the notion of mutuality as among anthropology's changing terms of engagement.[30] No longer are we as anthropologists bound to depart for far-away territories inhabited by our "subjects" to impose ourselves on them and report to the world what we have come to learn about their societies and cultures. Rather, when Doha metamorphosed into a site of Darfur mediations, I learned that in the face of the massive global circulation of people and ideas, "the field" is everywhere. Beyond any doubt, RAD made a double move, first by listening to the delegates' explanations of the root causes of the crisis; and second, by exploring the potential for healing a raw political wound. Both RAD and Sheikh Musa's call are imaginative, dialogical, and most importantly, conducive to imagining new geographies and possibilities of peace, ontologies of remediation, and philosophies of democratization. Of course, this optimism assumes that an amenable environment for implementing the delegates' recommendations is ever possible.

5

"All Dust and Panic":[1] Sinai Desertscape

Listen to a symphony: a symphony has a beginning, has a middle, it has an end, but nevertheless I would not understand anything of the symphony and I would not get any musical pleasure out of it if I were not able, at each moment, to muster what I have listened to before and what I am listening to now, and to remain conscious of the totality of the music.

CLAUDE LÉVI-STRAUSS, *Myth and Meaning*[2]

Taj Haroun was born in Darfur and escaped the genocide there by fleeing first to Egypt and then to Israel. When I was in touch with him in 2016, he was residing in Tel Aviv as an asylum seeker and studying for his master's degree in political science and communication at Tel Aviv University. While in Israel he had completed undergraduate study at the Interdisciplinary Center Herzliya (IDC), where he specialized in counterterrorism and conflict resolution. He was actively involved in the Darfuri refugee community in Israel, including serving on the board of B'nai Darfur and working with human rights organizations.

Prior to the start of the war in 2003, Haroun had lived with his family in a village he said was beautiful. As he tells it, the region was intentionally neglected by the government, and the rebel groups were fighting for what they believed the region deserved. The government supported the Arab Janjaweed militias in the conflict, authorizing them to attack villages of ethnic Africans and engage in systematic killing. Haroun's family had been warned that their village would be attacked the day before the Janjaweed arrived. They were unable to protect the village and fled to a refugee camp. Haroun's stepmother was badly burned by the Janjaweed. Because of widespread fear that the Janjaweed would kidnap and enslave young men from the camp, at his stepmother's urging Haroun fled to Khartoum to stay with his aunt in late 2004. At that time he and his family hoped that the war would be over in a few months and he could return to his family. They had no idea that thirteen years later the war would still be going on.

In Khartoum, Haroun worked with a group of Darfuri students to raise international awareness about the dire situation in Darfur. He was arrested and detained overnight for questioning about rebel activities. During this first detention, he was brutally tortured. After his second arrest, he decided to leave Khartoum, and in 2007 he fled to Cairo. His dream was to return to school, but when his Egyptian visa was about to expire, he was afraid that if he tried to renew it, he would be sent back to the Sudan. After hearing Israel was a safe haven for refugees, he decided to go there. In winter 2008, he was taken to the Israeli border by Bedouin smugglers. He managed to make it across the border without getting shot and was met by the Israeli army, who provided him and those with whom he had traveled with apples and water before dropping them off in the Be'er Sheva detention center the next day.

Haroun is living in Israel as a guest; because of the conflict, he cannot return to Darfur. However, he prays that he will be able to go home. His family still lives in a refugee camp and is eager for his return. Although Haroun has been physically safe in Israel, he

has faced many challenges. The greatest of these is his precarious status because the Is-
raeli government purposefully has no clear policy regarding the Sudanese refugees. Like
individuals whose stories are included in this chapter, he has to renew his visa every two
months and lives with the constant fear of being unable to renew it. Furthermore, it is
unclear if his temporary visa permits him to work.

The lack of certainty about his future has been an enormous psychological strain.
Although Haroun is enrolled in a master's program, he reports that only four among the
ten thousand refugees in Israel are pursuing a graduate degree. Haroun emphasizes that
anyone who sees war as a positive has never suffered from it. He does not expect the UN
or the superpowers to do anything to solve the conflict in the Sudan, as it is not in their
interest to do so. Asked what Israelis can do to support Darfuris, Haroun responds that
the status issue is the most difficult, and most helpful would be to encourage the Israeli
government to grant refugees asylum status.[3]

"The Boasian Circle" Online

Taj Haroun's life story, recounted in the epigraph above, vividly exemplifies a
resistance to the circumstances into which he had been thrust. This chapter
presents an analogous story about life lived at dangerous crossroads. It marks
a shifting consciousness within a community that has come to embody the
liminality and ambivalence characteristic of a diaspora. From this story, we
come to know how refugees disarticulated and masked their identity as citizens of the Arab North and simultaneously denaturalized attachments and
sentiments vis-à-vis their Islamic faith. The individuals in this chapter, refugees from Darfur in Israel, have found it necessary to adjust to a precarious
situation in which the future seems to hang in balance. Their extraordinary,
often harrowing migratory experience raised many questions in my mind,
among them: What does migration to Israel mean to refugees? To what extent
does this migration represent an ultimate break with their country, which
identifies itself as Arab, Islamic, and pro-Palestine? How have Black and Muslim asylum seekers been received in Israel? How do refugees navigate laws in
Israel that define them as infiltrators and citizens of an enemy state and that
grant citizenship only to those who can prove Jewish ancestry? I contend that
this migration is ultimately about border crossings—a movement not only
across geographic locations, but also across an imaginative space, altering
consciousness and notions of self.

Because Darfuri refugees are citizens of a country that has no diplomatic
relations with Israel, they are legally prohibited from traveling to that country, as evidenced by a statement on the first page of the Sudanese passport
that it is valid for "ALL COUNTRIES EXCEPT ISRAEL." Unlike their compatriots who entered the United States legally as refugees, the subject of chapter 6,

the individuals discussed in this chapter are unable to enjoy such a privilege. Hence, once they make it to the Israeli border, entrance into the country is fraught with difficulty. Because Israel is a signatory to the 1951 Refugee Convention, the country must initially accept all those seeking asylum. Border security then sends them to a detention facility, where immigration officials determine the legitimacy of their request to enter. Assuming legitimacy is established, refugees are issued a temporary visa, which they then must renew every two months. Many have stated that issuance and renewal of a visa hinge on where and when they entered, the mood of the presiding immigration officers, and the geopolitics of the moment. As we shall see, obtaining permanent legal status in Israel is the objective Darfuri refugees seek and for which they are willing to risk much—and to date has been largely unobtainable.

My work with Darfuris in Israel was precipitated by a conversation with an anthropologist colleague at an Israeli university about my ongoing interest in exiled Darfuri communities. I was thrilled to learn that he knew of a Darfuri student at his institution who might assist with my research. He immediately put me in touch with the then graduate student in African studies, who subsequently identified interviewees for me and administered a short questionnaire to those who preferred the anonymity of this method. In the summer of 2017, I communicated directly with fifteen individuals and gathered other materials for the story of Darfuris in Israel.

Unlike ethnographic interviews I have collected previously, the narratives included in this chapter were secured through Skype conversations, email exchanges, and structured questionnaires administered in person by my research assistant. From the outset, Darfuris in Tel Aviv evinced interest in these platforms as both practical and preferred means of communication. Given their uncertain status in Israel and anxieties over immigration and asylum seeking, their circumspection and preference for online communication made sense. I managed to rein in my curiosity about those elements of their lives they chose not to share. This largely online ethnography, therefore, emphasizes the contingencies, variabilities, and fluidities of fieldwork in the digital age.[4] While I was aware that I was missing "the ethnographic magic" of in-person conversations, I still valued this virtual contact as an exercise in ethnographic mutuality, a recognition that these refugees own their stories and have the right to determine the means of telling them, using their own tired bodies as damning evidence against the prevailing violence at home. Despite the formulaic nature of the accounts produced, I understand our engagement to be an experimental "Boasian circle" online. Franz Boas had unqualified faith in his interlocutors, and I too aver that however imperfect the mode of communication, the accounts I gathered signified indispensable insider knowledge. In the end, the digital platform has demonstrated interesting possibilities for access across space and time, even as questions about the ethics of emerging e-ethnographies remain vitally present.[5]

These narratives communicated significant lessons about a particular kind of migratory experience and helped piece together a tapestry whose "colored pieces can form a variety of patterns: the pieces are the same but the pattern can change dramatically depending on the severity of the knot."[6] Other sources, such as YouTube videos, news programs, and Israeli newspapers, supplemented the e-ethnographic accounts. Adam Ahmed's *The Nightmare of the Exile*, the first published autobiography of a Darfuri in Israel to appear in Hebrew, also proved exceptionally useful in understanding the experience of his community's lived reality.[7] Ahmed's evocative, painstakingly detailed account of the tearing apart of his village, his subsequent sense of displacement, and the challenges he faced borne out of fear of difference all provide a window onto the refugee experience. A good part of his account presented the stories of African asylum seekers in Israel's ghettoized areas, including some who had been detained in a facility in the Negev Desert. He describes the refugees' abject poverty, compounded for a time by the strict residential policy imposed upon them.[8] He also describes in moving detail the aggravating circumstances refugees encountered on daily basis.

THE QUEST FOR ASYLUM AND
SELF-REFASHIONING

The narratives I gathered pivot around three thematic axes: the trajectory from refugee to asylum seeker, the instantiation of a Sudanic Black identity as distinct from a Sudanese Arab identity, and the uncoupling from religious practice. I had considered as a fourth theme the ways gender inflects the migratory experience, but given that young men make up the vast majority in this particular refugee flow and that I was able to correspond with only two women, I had little in the way of specific ethnographic data focused on gender. Most interviewees did remark that the number of Darfuri families in Israel is small, pointing to the exertions of crossing Sinai as families with children in tow. Additionally, the threat of sexual violence against women who crossed the Sinai Desert, along with fewer opportunities than men for work in Egypt. constrained many from making the journey; those who did generally accompanied men in their lives. As Mrs. H, one of the two women I was able to communicate with through my research assistant, explained, her marriage to a man who worked in Khartoum enabled her to leave the IDP camp where they had been living. Although the trip to Israel had its dangers, she felt secure in her husband's company.[9] Once in Israel, if a woman finds herself alone, she feels acutely the absence of communal support structures present in Darfur. The other woman I communicated with, Mrs. G, who is divorced, stated that with no family to help her, she has had to deal with her children by herself. Her life is a daily round of child care and work. She worries that if she falls ill, no one will come forward to help care for her and her children. Tasked with the responsibility for children, Darfuri women are more likely to flee to Chad, where NGOs assist their resettlement to places other than Israel. Freedom from such family responsibilities, coupled with a deep-seated culture of masculine risk taking and adventure seeking, also helps explain the preponderance of men in Israel. Clearly, the fact that I communicated with far fewer Darfuri women than men in Israel is powerful evidence of a broader gendered experience.

To address the aforementioned themes, I have incorporated material from the narratives as recorded in my field notes. I both communicated with research participants and recorded those communications in Arabic, and I have translated them here into English. With their approval—as with Mrs. H and Mrs. G above—I have used a letter rather than a pseudonym to identify each narrator, not to efface their individuality but rather out of respect for their precarity. The absence of any name renders a profound anonymity, a less personal presence and hence a greater degree of protection than a pseudonym. All interlocutors made clear that their quest for asylum in Israel was born out of deep desperation, and I ask the reader to understand their experiences as situated within the confluence of political violence and the perpetual pain of displacement they have felt at home, during their sojourn in Cairo, then in Sinai, and finally in Tel Aviv. To give a sense of the full scope of the refugee trajectory, I begin with a single complete account, that of Mr. A; I have edited my fieldnotes in the third person to create a coherent narrative.

Mr. A, in his thirties and single, started his journey soon after the war began in Darfur in 2003, when Janjaweed militia burned his entire village to the ground. His family fled for their lives, settling initially in El Geneina, the capital city of the Sudanese state of Western Darfur, where he thought he would be able to blend in and not attract unwanted trouble. Instead, Mr. A found the setting frustrating. He found it difficult to remain silent about the abrogation of the rights of his people, the sordid actions legitimized by the Sudanese government, the massacre effected on the so-called African people of Darfur, and ethnic cleansing as a means of Arabizing the nation. In 2011 Mr. A decided to leave the Sudan altogether. Considering alternatives, he chose the precarious journey through Egypt to Tel Aviv. He paid Bedouin nomads to include him in a group of refugees crossing through the Sinai Desert to the Egypt-Israel border and into Israel. Constant dread of being arrested by the Egyptian army, which killed many who made the same expedition into Israel, accompanied the journey. However, the safety that Israel represented served as impetus to endure. When Mr. A reached the Egypt-Israel border, he felt welcomed by the Israeli army, who assured the arrivals they were safe. According to protocols determined by the Geneva Conventions, the army escorted them to a temporary detention center for registration as Darfuri refugees; once registration was complete, they were allowed to leave for Tel Aviv. Mr. A says he was amazed at his reception in Tel Aviv, where there is an established community of Darfuris and it is easy to accommodate newcomers' entry and settlement.

As of 2017, Mr. A remained categorized as an asylum seeker and was waiting in hopes of eventually being granted residency. Sometimes he encounters people who hate the mere idea of Darfuri asylum seekers settling in Israel and rage at them to go back to their own country. However, he claims that many Israelis he encounters also stand up for Darfuris and show care and assistance, which he finds uplifting. He adds that in Israel he is more secure and treated more humanely than in his own country. Yet his life there is also significantly more difficult and complex than in Darfur. The setting is different and new; he lacks the support of a family; everyday life is a struggle; worry is constant. As an asylum seeker, Mr. A experiences the despair of losing his dreams (*"dreams of education, dreams of the future, and dreams of being someone successful"*), and he recognizes that in Israel strenuous physical labor is the only work available to him. The absence of his family, alongside the sheer uncertainty of ever being able to go back home and resume a normal life, compounds his distress. A very small part of him seeks a glimmer of hope of returning.

For now, Mr. A makes the most of his life in Israel. He closely follows the news of his home country, most of which torments him as he hears of its continuing deterioration. To maintain his connections to Darfuri culture, he is a part of the visible Darfuri community in Israel. Members uphold their traditions, their songs, their cuisine, and other manifestations of their culture. Community centers that preserve and promote Darfuri culture and restaurants that serve Darfuri cuisine enrich their lives. Community members keep their language alive by speaking it with each other; they commemorate historical events and celebrate personal events together and promote Darfuri tribal music. There is a definite Darfuri vibe in Israel. Mr. A himself is a keen enthusiast of his heritage and participates in many endeavors and events that spread awareness of it. Like many in his situation, his heritage brings him relief from the strain of living in a foreign country. Furthermore, he feels that in Israel, Darfuris are able to organize public gatherings for both political and social purposes more freely than in the Sudan. He admits that in Tel Aviv, many Darfuris do not practice their religion as seriously as they did in the Sudan, where peer influence encourages religious practice. Himself a Muslim, Mr. A has chosen not to practice since Israel offers that freedom of choice. In his view, the government of the Sudan considers itself omnipotent, enforcing the practice of religion and robbing people of choice. He recalls how young people learn to read and write in religious schools or khalawi, which teach only the Quran and personal hygiene according to sharia law.

Mr. A emphasizes the importance of understanding the local culture in order to connect to the host country and recognizes its stark differences from Darfuri culture. A lack of understanding, he feels, results in the mistrust evident in interactions between certain Israelis and asylum seekers. Media coverage tends to exacerbate misunderstandings as well. Mr. A explains that many NGOs have failed to address the problem because they do not understand the culture of the asylum seekers. The Israeli community itself is also ignorant of the Darfuri ethnic identity. Often it assumes that all Sudanese are Arab and Muslim. Mr. A does consider himself Muslim, but not Arab; he claims an African identity, with its own culture, language, and traditions—a concept that tends to surprise the average Israeli. Although Mr. A states, "*I am not a politician,*" he also notes that "*the situation made me become involved in politics.*" He is a member of the B'nai Darfur (Hebrew for Sons of Darfur), an organization that aims to unite the dispersed Darfuri tribes within Israel. He is also a member of the Fur Center, a subsidiary of B'nai Darfur, where he is actively involved in developing awareness of Darfur's culture and language.

Despite yearning for his home, Mr. A has come to respect and admire his host country. He appeals to his friends to visit Israel, a country only four hours away but, he claims, many decades ahead of the Sudan in the freedom and protection it affords its inhabitants. In his view, the Sudanese government has misrepresented Israel as an enemy of all Arab states, banning travel there and criticizing the regime publicly. Still, he ends his story by stating that should Israel grant him asylum status, his love for his home will not diminish. Although for now his prime interest is establishing himself someplace safe, his dream is to return to a Sudan that is secure, democratic, and stable.

ARRIVALS AND DEPARTURES

Mr. A and his fellow Darfuris have made clear that to fully understand their journey to Israel, it is necessary to understand the challenging circumstances they had to reckon with prior to undertaking it. Fleeing violence at home, these young people initiated and executed transit to Israel on their own, without official support for the journey, i.e., without certification from the United Nations High Commission for Refugees. Initially they sought safety in Cairo. The Egyptian landscape is familiar, and the country is Arab speaking. It is also relatively easy to get to Cairo from the Sudan by train and boat; and the city includes an established network of Darfuri refugees. Most important, however, Sudanese passports are honored at the border. The refugees have stressed that when they fled to Egypt, they did so with great expectations for improving their life circumstances. However, things did not turn out as they had hoped. When interviewed for the Egyptian newspaper *Al-Ahram Weekly*, they had only tales of destitution to offer. They spoke of miserable living conditions in small apartments shared by twenty people: "If one of us gets a cold or the flu, everybody gets it, because we are cramped in these small places," reported one refugee. "We don't even have money to buy medicine. We look at our brothers lying there sick, without being able to do anything to help them because the little money we have barely covers food and rent."[10] Arriving in Cairo with few resources, unable to secure employment in an already tired economy, and unwilling to return to the killing fields of Darfur, they feel desperate and alone. These difficulties, coupled with threats of deportation back to the Sudan, have pushed them to seek the assistance of the Bedouin of Sinai, who have mastered the art of smuggling African refugees across borders into Israel, exacting exorbitant sums in a lucrative war economy.[11] Thus they crossed the harsh Sinai Desert in a frantic plea for the future.

Invariably, participants in this ethnography described the journey to Israel in chilling terms. Mr. C's was particularly terrifying. In Cairo, he found a Sudanese agent who connected him to a Bedouin nomad who would take him to Israel. To seal the agreement, he paid the agent $100 and the nomad $300. Initially, he and the five others with whom he was traveling stopped at a farm in the outskirts of the city, where they remained for ten days. They had inadequate food and barely enough water, but the fear of being caught by the police kept them in their hiding place. The group finally demanded that the Bedouin nomad either take them back to Cairo or move forward to the border. The nomad agreed to head for the border under cover of night. He obtained a large truck filled with sand with a small gap in the middle in which he fit his six passengers. The ride through the Sinai Desert was difficult, especially crossing checkpoints manned by the Egyptian army. After passing through them successfully, the group switched to a pickup truck and sped through the desert for two days, during which they spotted others also heading for the border.[12] At that point, two of his party were captured by smugglers and the remaining members trapped and rounded up. Their hands and legs were bound together, and when they were unable to respond to the smugglers' demand for money, pleading that they had none to give, they were repeatedly beaten with sticks. The beatings continued for four days before the captors realized that there was no money to be had and finally released them. The nomad warned that from this point on, they could die because of the dangers as they closed in on the border. Now was the time to decide whether to continue or turn back. It had been sixteen days since the group left Cairo. All six decided to proceed to cross the border under cover of darkness. They got off the truck and ran through the last leg of the journey. Even after crossing into Israel, they continued running into the early morning. At 6 a.m., an Israeli army car spotted their group. The absconders rushed towards the car. The officials stopped them and asked if anyone was injured or shot. All said they were fine because now they were finally in Israel. The officials took them to the closest military base where they spent a night; the next morning a bus took them to a detention center. They were kept in detention for twenty-one days, where they were provided with necessities and treated well enough, after which they were released to go to the nearest city. From there, Mr. C, like thousands of other refugees in Israel, took a bus to a park in Tel Aviv, where he disembarked to face the uncertainties of a new life.

And so begins a new chapter in the refugees' struggle for recognition and acceptance in a country reluctant to receive them. As we shall see, these refugees had to strategically construct their own multipronged system for adapting to their new circumstances and negotiating the vine-like sociocultural entanglements before them. So, can we claim that Darfuri refugees are successful in their adaptations? The brute fact of the matter is that there is no "one and done" approach to the process of adjustment. Distinctions between success and failure are hard to make, insofar as Darfuris' adaptive strategies are very much context dependent, including especially prevailing views about their presence in Israel and uncertainty over their ever achieving the security of asylum status. If these were to change, would their approach to life in Israel change? Interlocutors also assess their situation in relative terms. Perhaps the comments of Mr. K offer some insight into the complexity of a response. He, like many Sudanese, welcomes the opportunity to live in Tel Aviv. He feels safe there, more secure than in the Sudan, where he had been imprisoned, risked the death penalty, and generally felt hunted. He would tell anyone that life is hard, but one should simply face it head-on. He also feels the excitement of living in a place so foreign to his previous experiences, where he learns something new every day. Still, Mr. K admits that his future is unclear, a reality that fills many Sudanese with sadness and uncertainty as they wonder if they will ever be able to return home. If conditions do ever get better, Mr. K will not think twice about returning, for his greatest dream is to be able to live in a peaceful home and be reunited with his family in the Sudan.

ANOTHER LAYER

Given the importance of context in shaping Darfuris' experiences in Israel, I turn now to a discussion of the ways in which they have been received in the country. My intent is to provide "the reader with concrete, sometimes vivid if fragmentary, vicarious experience of the social world in question," to which I would add the political world as well.[13] It must be said first that there is no single Israeli response to Darfuri refugees. Responses vary in the extreme, from marked resistance to remarkable support, and are related to perceptions of the sociopolitical valences of their presence. Still, it is accurate to state that since its inception, migration to Israel has occasioned an enormous emotional response and hatched contentious debates in both the Sudan and Israel. Fixing our sight on reaction in the Sudan, we note first the attacks waged by Islamists against the Sudanese Liberation Movement leader Abdel Wahid Nor, a Fur, when in 2008 he opened an office in Tel Aviv to serve as a base for his international activism and praised the Israeli government for protecting Darfuri youth from genocide. Sudanese Islamist officials decried Nor's action, treating it as inconvertible proof of Israel's incitement of violence in Darfur and claiming Nor himself was intent on converting people to Judaism. According to a news brief appearing in the *Sudan Tribune*:

> Sudanese Presidential Assistant and government top negotiator for Darfur peace talks said that Abdel Wahid Nor wanted to establish direct relations with Israel, instead of dealing with the Israeli lobby in America. He also accused Abdel Wahid of placing Sudanese in Israel "to convert them to Judaism." He considered this step as a provocative action to Sudanese people and particularly to the Fur tribe. The Sudanese state minister of information, Kamal Obeid, said that Abdel Wahid [*sic*] move targets Sudan in its unity and faith predicting strong reaction from Darfur people. . . . "The revolution that started in Darfur intends to change some of the norms in Sudan, including the taboo regarding the relations with Israel" Nor had told *Sudan Tribune* this week.[14]

Within Israel, indignation towards the surge of Black people entering the country has been cast as concern about threats they pose to public safety. Vague fears of contagion, pollution, and criminality arising in the body politic surfaced in public debate, one driven by anxieties over the refugees' gender, race, complexion, religion, social status, and national origin. According to the mayor of the city of Hadera, "When I was told that people saw them, four or five men standing near the shopping mall and drinking beer, all my body shook. Because these are single men without women . . . and if, Allah forbid, there is a rape, I don't want to think what people will say about me as the City's Mayor." In January 2011, Eilat mayor Meir Yitzhak Halevy launched Safeguarding Our Home, a campaign that involved hanging fifteen hundred red flags throughout the city accompanied by a call for townsfolk not to rent apartments to asylum seekers.[15]

These and similar challenges are the result, at least in part, of Israel's Prevention of Infiltration Law, according to which, as Holly Buchanan has explained, "a person who is either a national of an enemy country . . . or has passed through one of these countries before entering Israel may legally be detained."[16] In place since Israel's statehood in 1948, the law reflects the view expressed by the late Israeli foreign minister Moshe Dayan: "No state is as vulnerable as Israel in the configuration of its frontier."[17] The discourse on infiltration permeates discussion of the Darfuri presence, conjuring up images of an invasive force wreaking havoc as it sweeps across the land.

Caught in the quagmire of "infiltration" in a society in which security concerns are always at the forefront of public culture, provocations are expected. Some interlocutors in this ethnography expressed dismay at those who shout at them in the streets to go back to their own country. Mrs. H, for example, hates witnessing local demonstrations demanding that the Sudanese go back home. Sometimes she feels that the Israeli people do not like her. Other times, people may treat her cordially, but the government shows clear resentment, and that makes even sympathizers dislike her community and its share of the job market. If it were not for the war, Mrs. H would not stay in Israel a day longer. Tel Aviv to her is just a transit station—somewhere to wait until the chaos at home subsides. She also believes that life is not easy anywhere and almost wishes her fellow Sudanese would remain in the Sudan. Members of her own family still reside in the IDP camp they fled to in Mornay in Western Darfur. She hopes they will all still be alive when she is able to go back home.

Such an environment prompts a keen awareness among the refugees of the extent to which Israelis remain unaware of the ethnic struggles encompassed by the Sudanese war, a reality that accompanies them constantly as they consider where they have been, why they are in Israel, and what their prospects might be. Persistent suspicion and ignorance of the reason why they are present in Israel, accompanied by the government's purposeful lack of a clear policy towards the refugees, render the experience all the more difficult to bear. And so they live in a precarious state, renewing their visas every two months, living with the fear of being unable to renew it next time, and bearing the psychological strain of uncertainty about the future.

Some Israelis, it must be affirmed, are distressed at the xenophobia directed at Darfuri asylum seekers, if not their downright criminalization. Writing in opposition to government efforts to deport them, scholar Sheldon Gellar has stated:

> Asylum seekers in Israel are not criminals. They are more like Israelis racing through a red light on the way to a hospital to save a human life than infiltrators clandestinely sneaking into a country to do harm to the people there. They should not be imprisoned or put in detention camps for not being willing to leave Israel to go to an unnamed African country like Rwanda and Uganda where they have no guarantees for protection and freedom.[18]

In the same vein, Israeli human rights activists have lauded discussions of awarding Israeli citizenship to Darfuris and have appealed to the government to issue thousands of work permits to them. According to a 2007 article in *Ynetnews*, for example, more than three hundred Darfuris have been absorbed in the tourist economy in Eilat, where "they have become a part of the town's environment." The vice president of human resources at an Israeli hotel chain has stated, "We hire the refugees to work in our hotels at the Dead Sea and provide them with housing.... We feel that helping, especially in areas that the authorities neglect, is of the utmost importance."[19] Ordinary citizens have also expressed support: They have established a hotline to receive calls from distressed refugees and invited refugees to share a Passover meal. Thousands have suggested revising existing laws aimed at preventing infiltration and protested the treatment of refugees.

Some Jews both in and outside of Israel have invoked the collective memory of extermination in Germany's Third Reich as a way of framing their sympathy for the Darfuris' plight. Jewish museums and such notable civil society organizations as the Anti-Defamation League and Rabbis for Human Rights have drawn analogies between Darfur and sites of Nazi pogroms and concentration camps in Drancy, Warsaw, Auschwitz-Birkenau, Krakow, and Rivesaltes. In the words of Ruth Messinger, president and executive director of the American Jewish World Service:

> As Jews, we have an increased moral obligation to respond, to speak out and take action against ethnic cleansing regardless of the ethnicity, race or religion of the people being victimized. Such lessons we learned only too well from the Holocaust, when six million suffered the consequences of silence from the international community. The world looked the other way then and did again 10 years ago in Rwanda when 800,000 people of the Tutsi minority were slaughtered in 100 days by their government. The phrase "never again" must

not be reserved for Jews alone, but in fact, Jews must be the guardians of this epithet, highly sensitive and responsive to all attempts by any people to annihilate another people because they are somehow perceived as different. . . . I went to Darfur in August to bear witness, to assess humanitarian needs, and to ensure that funds provided by the American Jewish community are being and will be used effectively. I met many of the displaced farmers and listened to their chilling and all-too-similar stories. The government bombed their villages, and then men on camels or horses rode in, often yelling ethnic slurs and shooting wildly. They plundered the farm animals that were the lifeblood of these communities. They stole, they raped, and they killed. They stuffed wells with dead bodies or carcasses and burned villages to the ground.[20]

Similarly invoking historical memory, in 2007 then–US Representative Rahm Emanuel wrote Israel's ambassador to the US to protest the country's efforts to refuse entrance to Darfuris: "I am writing today to express my disappointment that Israel would turn away any person fleeing from persecution. . . . If any country should understand the special needs of those affected by the genocide in Darfur, it should be Israel."[21] Emanuel's family history gives particular force to his support for Darfuris: his father was at one time connected to a militant Zionist group that sought Israeli independence; and his family adopted the surname Emanuel as a tribute to an uncle, Emanuel Auerbach, who was slain in a skirmish with Arabs in Jerusalem in the 1930s.

Meanwhile, Darfuris do not hold their breath waiting for favorable decisions about their petitions for asylum and permanent resident status. Rather, they join with their activist supporters to affirm their right to be in Israel and challenge restrictions imposed on them, often within the public space of Levinsky Park in southern Tel Aviv. Here Darfuri asylum seekers come together to pass the time, chat, smoke, and exchange news from home. Here too they and their allies come together to protest immigration and detention practices. "We are not infiltrators, we are refugees," read a sign raised by Darfuris in a rally by the park organized by an Israeli nongovernmental organization. In a corner called the Garden Library, citizens read stories to young Darfuri and Eritrean children under the blossoming jacaranda trees. Similarly, international artists, musicians, poets, storytellers, and embroiders, in collaboration with Darfuri residents in the neighborhood by the park, have used their talents to address the quandaries of the refugees. Darfuris along with Eritrean asylum seekers participated in the development of an exhibition titled *The Infiltrators*, designed to destigmatize them and address the common misperception of Darfuris as a danger to national security. The consortium of artists who tackled this task wrote of the vision behind the project:

The exhibition *The Infiltrators* examines the local and global state of asylum seekers and refugees through works created with the participation of communities of asylum seekers in Israel and elsewhere in the world. In Israel, the term "infiltrators" is used to describe the transgression of the country's political borders in order to commit a terrorist act. At the same time this term is commonly used to refer to Africans who have crossed the border from Africa into Israel. Alongside additional terms such as "refugees," "asylum seekers," and "immigrant workers," it plays an important role in the discussion of their status and future. In this context, the term "infiltrators" fixes the status of border crossers as that of liminal subjects, who remain trapped between here and there, citizens of no place.

The exhibition title plays a double role, since it aspires to look at the included art projects as constituting an act of infiltration. The featured artists attempt to undermine existing stereotypes by enacting different forms of participation, thus questioning common perceptions of the complex state of asylum seekers or refugees. These artists infiltrate the communal or public sphere as outlaws or cunning spies and cross the thin line between reality and fiction in order to examine and destabilize the power relations that control and define this sphere. They search for the fissures within dichotomies, for the liminal spaces between points of contention, and linger within these borderline spheres.[22]

In programming related to the exhibit, the artistic team Documentary Embroidery employed embroidery as a documentary medium unfolding in real time. Spending many hours in Levinsky Park, they spoke with nearby residents and passersby and then embroidered a work based on the stories they heard, sometimes incorporating participants' drawings or writings. Whether by singing or drawing or embroidering, these art activists express sympathy for refugees and challenge the public to rethink conventional views. Through such actions, Darfuris and their Israeli supporters have propelled the Darfur crisis into public consciousness, after more than a decade of inconclusive discussion in the High Court, the Knesset, and the Israeli media.

SWIDDEN IN TEL AVIV:
B'NAI DARFUR: IN MEDIAS RES!

I wish my life and decisions to depend on myself, not on external forces of whatever kind. I wish to be the instrument of my own, not of other men's acts of will. I wish to be a subject, not an object, to be moved by reasons, by conscious purposes, which are my own, not by causes which affect me, as it were, from outside. I wish to be somebody, not nobody, a doer deciding, not being decided for, self-directed and not acted upon by external nature or by other men as if it were a thing.

ISAIAH BERLIN, "Two Concepts of Liberty"[23]

Darfuris also expressed the "wish to be a subject" by refashioning their identity, affirming their African—as opposed to Arab—origin and distancing themselves from their Muslim faith. The Fur forefathers of the young refugees employed the swidden method of farming, a practice whereby vegetation is slashed and burned to prepare the land for new cultivation. I invoke this technique as a metaphor for Darfuris' destruction of one form of identity in order to cultivate a new. Identities are situational and permeable, a fact illustrated here by the case of B'nai Darfur, a Fur organization in Tel Aviv. As I reflected on the name B'nai Darfur instead of Abnaa Darfur, with strikingly similar Hebrew and Arabic words for "sons," I came to recognize that the resistance to adopting the Arabic *abnaa* is rooted in Darfuris' growing rejection of all things Arab, an identity deeply at variance with their "structures of feelings."[24] In great haste, they changed Arabic personal names to their English equivalents (e.g., Yagoub became Jacob, Noh became Noah, Zachariah became Zachary, Isshaaq became Isaac, Ismail became Ishmael), all the while keeping their eyes on the road to permanent legal status in Israel.

So, what's in a name? B'nai Darfur, much like the traditional Israeli organizations B'nai Tzedek, B'nai Shalom, B'nai Darom, and the like, refers to sons or brotherhood, in this case of Darfur. The symbolism of using the Hebrew "B'nai" to title their service organization is made explicit in the group's mission statement: to "unite all the dispersed tribes within Israel." Quite simply, the Darfuris claim that they, like the Ethiopian Jews who migrated to Israel before them, are an Israelite tribe. Although at an advantage because they were Jews, Ethiopians too had to negotiate their incorporation amongst their coreligionists as Black Jews. This stratagem, with its patent philosophical tilt, involved a double move, simultaneously discursive and practical. The first involved nomenclature; the second, their desire to prove themselves as non-Arab even if they speak Arabic. They proclaim Blackness and Africanness as distinct from the Arabs, whom they see as responsible for their suffering. B'nai Darfur, born out of pragmatic engagement with new realities, thus registers a new consciousness, as evidenced in an interviewee's remark that "*yes, we are Black and African . . . , and we are not Arabs even if we speak it as the lingua franca.*"

Mrs. G's comments on the matter are typical. She reported that despite the presence of so many Darfuris in Tel Aviv, many Israelis around her grossly misunderstand the Darfur war. Israelis assume she is an Arab because she speaks Arabic. She tells them she speaks Arabic like she speaks Hebrew—a language not her own—and reminds them that she is African with her own language and culture. Sometimes people struggle to understand the implications of this, and it shocks her how little they know of the asylum seekers in the city. Mrs. G also does not follow closely what is going on back home. She will sometimes listen to Radio Dabanga, an independent Sudanese news station, and watches Sudan TV only for its entertainment, never its news, which she feels is filled with lies. Mr. L echoes her sentiments, explaining how some Israelis have only begun to understand that those who have fled the Sudan are not Arabs, despite speaking Arabic and coming from a self-identified Arab nation. Others, including some in the government, remain ignorant of who Sudanese are and why they are in Israel. And Mr. B spoke poignantly of this ignorance as he described his struggles to assert his identity as an African. When asked where he is from, his simple answer is usually the Sudan. When he specifies that he is from Darfur, Israelis look at him with pity. If he instead states that he is from Khartoum or another Central Sudan city of his childhood, he is looked at censoriously—the assumption being that he is an Arab. If he is asked if he speaks Arabic, he says yes, but it confuses the local questioner when Mr. B states that he is not an Arab but an African from a country that presents itself as an Arab, Muslim country. We see too in Mr. B's comment an awareness of the prevailing cognitive conflation of Arabism with Islam, a point taken up below.

For some, like Mr. E, the assertion of an African identity leads to a determined effort to promote and practice Sudanese culture. He speaks favorably of the Fur Center, which teaches those who know only the spoken form of the Fur language how to read and write in that language. The center also promotes Fur music and other forms of cultural expression. He himself listens to Fur and other Sudanese music and mostly dines on food from various regions of the Sudan. For him, maintaining Sudanese culture has taken precedence over religious practices. Mr. F is among those who avail themselves of the opportunity to gain literacy skills in the Fur language. Like many, his formal language instruction in Darfur was in Arabic, and learning to read and write Fur is part of reclaiming an African identity. He and his peers then use this learning to develop songs in their own tongue. Nonetheless, emphasizing one's African identity does nothing to stave off Darfuris' longing for their home, a longing only intensified by the uncertainty of their status in Israel. It is this longing that drives a young refugee to Neve Sha'anan, a century-old district in Tel Aviv where most of the Sudanese have settled. Here, the value he ascribes to his African heritage has increased, as it has for his peers in the same city. It allows him to connect to others who share the same culture, to feel even mildly as if he belongs.[25] And perhaps it is the very uncertainty of his situation that leads him to say that *"by belonging to B'nai Darfur I belong even more."*

B'nai Darfur then can be understood as a "minor cue" in a manner identified by Erving Goffman: "It has been suggested that the performer can rely upon his audience to accept minor cues as a sign of something about his performance . . . [And] performers commonly attempt to exert a kind of synecdochic responsibility, making sure that as many as possible of the minor events in the performance, however instrumentally inconsequential these events may be, will occur in such a way as to convey either no impression or an impression that is compatible and consistent with the over-all definition of the situation that is being fostered."[26] In other words, Darfuris perform Blackness as an indigenous identity targeted for extermination by Arabs, a move that relies on existing constructs of what Arabs are capable of in a climate where, as anthropologist Mahmood Mamdani has argued, they are the target in a war on terror.[27] We are reminded of Charles Piot's observation: "We are . . . dealing here with persons constantly involved in, and defined through relations. But if one's relations are always with others or between oneself and others, then so too is one's interest."[28] Such is the performance, the cultivation, the paradigm shift. There is no iron rule when it comes to identity.

"FAITH IN FLUX"[29]

Along with a disavowal of Arab identity, refugees with whom I have communicated, like Mr. B, frequently stated that they were no longer adhering to Islamic beliefs or practices. Although I am reluctant to generalize about the entire universe of Darfuri refugees' relationship to religion based on a small number of individual experiences, I nonetheless found them noteworthy for two reasons: First, in the Sudan, Arabism and Islam are closely intertwined; the government perceives Islamist ideology as a civilizing force within its militant Arabism, implicitly disavowing the prophet's deracializing claim that "whoever speaks Arabic is an Arab." But given the violence wreaked against them by government forces, Darfuris relate to this notion neither emotionally nor cognitively. Second, I understood their statements as an effort by refugees to distance themselves from popular notions of Muslim-Arab infiltrators, thereby making themselves more acceptable to their Israeli hosts and increasing their chances of remaining in Israel. Like the assertion of African identity, this too is a discursive move laced with pragmatism.

Apart from any utilitarian purpose, it must be said that these young Darfuris are free to reject Muslim identity without fear of reprisal. In the Sudan, under sharia law such a disavowal would be equated with blasphemy and could be punishable by death. A police raid on a church in Darfur in 2018, for example, led to the arrest of the vicar and worshippers, who had been newly converted to Christianity.[30] Whether or not such actions actually result in executions, they contribute to a culture of religious intolerance.

While pragmatic concerns and Israel's relative religious freedom may support the refugees' rejection of their faith, their disassociation from a Muslim identity has roots in their experience in Darfur. As Mr. C explained, he saw Israel as a savior from the Islamist government that had killed his family and shattered his life. He has stopped praying and fasting during Ramadan, practices he had strictly adhered to at home. Mr. C explained that even if he is invited by friends to join in an Eid meal, he goes to socialize rather than because of any genuine attachment to Islam. Islam and Islamists to this young Fur are one and the same, and Mr. C's rhetorical contestation of the seemingly shared identity with perpetrators has come from a place of hard and long thinking.

Such sentiments are widespread. Utter outrage at Islam is evident in words of a man whose video that has gone viral on WhatsApp: "They [Arabs] brainwashed you by repeating 'Oh, Darfur is the land of Islam. Oh, Darfur is the land of piety. Darfur is religious by nature, this, that, and the other.' Where was Islam when they bombed you? Ha! Where was Islam when they drove you out of your hay abodes? Throw Islam in the dustbin. Darfur is called Darfur because it is the home of the Fur, the Masalit. It is not Dar-Arab. Anyone who says to you he is an Arab in Darfur, beat the religion out of him. Show him he does not belong. Fuck them all. Fuck their mothers' cunts." The metacognition of the political association of religion and Arab nationalism is unmistakable, hence the reckoning.

Can we imagine how Mr. D, who had been in Tel Aviv for eight years at the time of our communications, would feel about this advice? Violent war and targeted genocide had engulfed Darfur. His mother, brother, and two uncles were killed. His village was burned to the ground, and he lost his home. He, like so many others, has simultaneously distanced himself from the practice of Islam and stressed his Blackness. Dislodging himself from a state that sees itself as primarily Arab also becomes an expression of the desire to be part of an "existentia Africana,"[31] an African cosmos in Israel.

If we take the comment "Darfur is religious by nature" at face value, these Darfuri refugees have grown adept at denaturalizing religious sentiments. Their disavowal of Islam is unlike the experience of African Christians in Israel, who have found in their religious congregations an indispensable emotional support for circumventing otherness. It is also unlike the experience of Darfuris in the United States, where religion remains salient in asylum seekers' lives. That Darfuris in Israel spoke repeatedly about *not* practicing their religion also suggests that it is constantly on their mind, perhaps most poignantly setting them apart from family and friends at home, where religion is seen as key to surviving hard times. If we take these disavowals of the Muslim faith as protest against political Islam, then it is fair to evaluate their distancing from religion as another form of resistance to a state that has thrust them into a condition of unyielding ambivalence and indeterminacy. By rewriting their own social history, one in which the most fundamental organizing principle of their society is a liability, this "difficult diaspora"[32] tries to repudiate its fate.

Is it deep play, these changes? Is the image of B'nai Darfur with which we began this section an attempt to make visible to everyone in Israel that Darfuris are achieving a new identity? By making this image public are they reminding people of the material damages incurred at home? Is it public testimony against the government? An attempt by Darfuris to present themselves as totally separate from the Sudan? There are more questions than answers. For now, we are left with the thought that B'nai Darfur signifies the ultimate reckoning in an exilic experience that warrants a profound metamorphosis.

Darfur's Jam for Justice in America

Prelude

Earlier today, two of my friends and I went to Baltimore to meet another friend who took us to interview Darfuris. He suggested picking us up at the arrival gate at Baltimore-Washington International Airport. He pulled up in a Land Rover Discovery 2017, exuding the lovely smell of a new car, which belonged to another Sudanese friend of his from Darfur, "a tax accountant," he noted. Both of them had lived in the United States for some time. My friend works as translator for Darfuris. Like so many Darfuris, he shared searing stories about compatriots coming from the region to Baltimore. As soon as we got in the car, one of my friends congratulated him for winning his asylum case. He sighed deeply, adding, "I can't tell you how relieved I am." We arrived at the house he shared with two other people; its light lavender interiors, new furnishings, and large eat-in kitchen conveyed an air of stability. We had a nice lunch and a fantastic conversation on the back deck overlooking a lush backyard. He rested a bit before driving us to meet the families I was going to interview. It took about half an hour to get to the big two-story apartment complex where they lived. Teenage Darfuri boys were playing soccer outside.

Our hosts lived on the second floor, in a two-bedroom apartment with a smallish, wall-to-wall-carpeted living room with a large-screen TV mounted on the wall. The table underneath was covered with guidebooks about becoming an American citizen and other materials. Six older women wearing colorful Sudanese robes were sitting comfortably on the floor and chatting in their Masalit language. Now finally at rest from their lengthy journey from Darfur, much of it on foot, they sat close to each other in one corner. Their body language gave the impression that they wanted to hold on to each other tightly and never let go. They greeted us with great warmth. A child of ten months was asleep on a couch. We sat down to chat and drink sweet tea and mango juice.

During this visit, I learned about experiences of war, flight, and arrival in America. I learned about the circulation of objects, herbal medicine, and people from Africa to America, from Darfur to Baltimore. As we were about to leave, word reached the community that one of the friends who accompanied me is going to the Sudan. People started to arrive in droves, bringing money, letters, medicine, toys, and other items for my friend to bring to their families in Nyala. After we left and after long silences during our ride back to DC, he asked, "Do you happen to know whether the airplane luggage allowance is thirty or forty kilos?" "Only thirty?" "Prepare yourself to pay for extra luggage," someone said. "Oh Allah! Been there!" I told him. We all burst into knowing laughter. So memorable was my visit to the family, I felt as if I had known these women forever. With every comment uttered, they gave life to their experiences prior to coming to the United States, illuminating what is important to them going forward.[1]

Orientation

This chapter is a reckoning with the circumstances that have produced a uniquely Darfuri political and cultural identity in the United States. Tackling the subject of Darfuri communities' subjectivity necessitated that I carry out an "ethnography in today's world."[2] In so doing, I have depended on extensive interviews, life histories, and participant observation at concerts, conferences, and rallies. As rapporteur or panelist in Darfur-focused town halls and as a speaker on college campuses before both American and non-American audiences, I engaged in fruitful interactions with Darfuri people. Other forums in the United States in which I took part also afforded important opportunities for a sustained discussion of the catastrophic conflict. Additionally, statements, testimonies, videos, and blogs accessed on the internet have all been useful in advancing my understanding of Darfuris' new visions of who they are and who are they becoming.

My chronicles of Sudanese migrations to the United States first appeared in 2002, in *Wanderings: Sudanese Migrants and Exiles in North America*.[3] Despite differences among these Sudanese, I underscored the emotional and cognitive ties that bound them to the Sudan as an idea. These ties personified what Tönnies called *Gemeinschaft*, that is, "place [land] and mind, with their sociological consequents of kinship, neighborhood and friendship. Together, they were the home of all virtue and morality."[4] The bonds described then were unequivocally "thicker than blood."[5] I concluded that regardless of one's ethnic affiliation or religious faith, Sudanese life in exile reflected a will to be Sudanese. Operating from multiple locales across the contemporary

globalized world, the Sudanese Darfuris channeled their efforts through os-
tensibly *pax Sudani* associations and causes,[6] evident in the charters, bylaws,
and mission statements of their various associations.[7] At the time, I imagined
these diverse communities as the Sudan in miniature, a nation in absentia.
My optimism and youth led me to believe in the potentialities of a progressive and wholesome view of Sudanese self and society. Such was the picture
inscribed in *Wanderings*.

Two momentous events transformed the Sudan's polity and therefore im-
pelled a pivot in my thinking. The eruption of war in Darfur in 2003 and the
secession of the South in 2011 shook the Sudan's Afro-Arab identity to its
core, as they did to its migrant communities in America. Sudanese citizens
from Darfur are now becoming Darfuris rather than Sudanese, an ethnonym
bestowed by outsiders but accepted by Sudanese from Darfur. Southerners
turned into citizens of the Republic of South Sudan. Insofar as detecting and
documenting change is a fundamental anthropological activity, time is a critical element of our work. "Change is a process in time. And time can be a crucial factor in a determination of what is changing, and to what degree, as well
as how rapidly this change is taking place," writes anthropologist Robert Bee
in his analysis of the anthropological strategies for the study of sociocultural
change.[8] Comparison of a statement about identity from a Darfuri acquain-
tance who identified himself as Arab in my previous work with one uttered
after 2003 inspired me to look into the discursive shifts in identity accompanying political change in the Sudan. In 1999 he told me, "*In this country there
is no Arab or African or Northerner or Southerner. We are Sudanese primarily.*"
Juxtapose this with his words in 2008: "*Our very existence on earth is doubtful
as Black people in the Sudan. Arab tribes did not experience the ethnic cleansing
that took place and is still occurring in our communities.*" Views such as these
became very common after 2003, highlighting Darfuri Blackness and indigeneity as opposed to an Arab identity. I was observing a migrant community
in the process of change. I had to cast a fresh look at my heretofore sanguine
conclusions about unity in diversity in exile.

Thus, in this chapter I seek to broaden the scope of my earlier work, incorporating the voices of Darfuri refugees and exiles to consider ways their
various subjectivities and transnational identities have changed in the US
context. In particular, many a refugee articulates Darfur's difficult dilemma
as one of both racial and gender injustice. As I circle back to reassess some of
my previous observations, I raise several new questions: How have post-2003
Darfuris been perceived by the predominantly white communities where they
have been relocated; and how do they perceive American activism, including celebrity activism, on behalf of Darfur? How has the prevailing narrative

about the Darfur conflict as one of Arabs against Black Africans transfigured a political problem into one of race relations? How has the preexisting racial configuration in the United States helped shape Darfuri subjectivity? Why and how are Darfuri women coming to speak about the use of sexual violence as a weapon of war? Uniting the disparate experiences detailed below is the notion of voice. As we shall see, these migrants spoke eloquently in their own voices about the US, their race, rape, and crimes against humanity.

I conducted interviews in Arabic, in which I am fluent. Some narrators spoke in Darfuri dialect, which I also understand. In those cases where I did not understand what a narrator was saying, I asked for and received an explanation. I did not record interviews electronically; to do so, I felt, would make speakers uncomfortable and perhaps hesitant. Rather, I took extensive field notes, also in Arabic, which I later translated into English. The accounts below are therefore reconstructed from my field notes. Also, it should be noted that all narrators typically present events out of chronological order and frequently conflate two or more events into a single incident. Survivors of traumatic experiences, which these narrators certainly are, sometimes speak in ways that appear to connect apparently dissimilar topics, leave gaps in logic, lack coherence, and otherwise indicate continuing psychological distress. At times I have retained their mode of speaking to reflect this distress; at other times I have slightly rearranged their accounts and added missing information in brackets to enhance reader comprehension.

The New Wave and Other Stories

The wave of Darfuris who arrived in the US after 2003 differ markedly from their earlier counterparts. Unlike the earlier Darfuri Sudanese, who were highly educated professionals, often students, diplomats, and government workers, the newcomers are neither educated nor upwardly mobile. In Darfur they were primarily rural, not urban dwellers, with a subsistence or near-subsistence standard of living. Also unlike the earlier arrivals, they have had sustained, firsthand experience of the brutalities of war, of flight and years of living as refugees, and of resettlement in the US with the assistance of NGOs. I begin with their stories, for their experiences have inevitably shaped their views about and identities in the United States, implicitly framing what follows. Although I present only a few narratives here, many spoke in the same vein, recounting similar experiences.

Post-2003 Darfuris arrived in the US from countries on the African continent, primarily from Chad and also Kenya and Ghana. They settled in Maine, Alaska, Nebraska, New York, Michigan, Iowa, the Washington, DC, metropolitan area, North Carolina, Indiana, Idaho, Minnesota, and Pennsylvania. Their arrival and settlement were covered extensively by national news media. Sewell Chan told *New York Times* readers that "Darfur refugees are scarred but free."[9] Stories about them also appeared regularly in countless daily newspapers of the states receiving them. Media representations, critical in shaping public opinion about the crisis, soon turned to exoticism and the Darfuris' purported inability to comprehend how to regulate their lives in accordance with American sensibilities. Several media essays drew attention to the presence of these new "exotics at home,"[10] depicting them as bearers of harmful traditional practices and thereby influencing how they were perceived in the communities in which they settled. Mounting worries consolidated around the plethora of traditional practices that clash with American moral and legal codes such as polygamy and female genital surgeries, a set of revered, age-old practices prevalent in Darfur but crimes in the United States.[11] Underlying these concerns was a reified notion of Darfuri tradition, unquestioned and perceived to be on collision course with American modernity. A miasma of fear arose at the possibility of importing grotesque mutilations masquerading as a traditional rite of passage. Yet normative and formulaic prescriptions assert rather than demonstrate the inevitability of an impending "clash of civilizations," à la Samuel Huntington.[12] In anthropological terms, reviving "cultural practices" after large-scale cultural disruption is not a straightforward process. As Mintz and Price argue:

> People ordinarily do not long for a lost "cultural heritage" in the abstract, but for immediately experienced personal relationships, developed in a specific cultural and institutional setting, that any trauma such as war or enslavement may destroy. A "culture," in these terms, becomes intimately linked to the social contexts within which affective ties are experienced and perceived. With the destruction of those ties, each individual's "cultural set" is transformed phenomenologically, until the creation of new institutional frameworks permits the refabrication of content, both based upon and much removed from the past.[13]

During the course of my own interviews with Darfuris in the United States, loss of "traditional practices" was not part of the discussion of "cultural bereavement."[14] Instead, they spoke in depth about their situation when the war started, their forced migration, and subsequent resettlement in the United States. Yet agency staff assisting with resettlement received "cultural orientation" briefs that, while sometimes helpful, also failed to recognize the complexity of the culture they were "resettling." Consider, for example, the cloud of confusion hovering over the heads of caseworkers encountering fictive kinship as an element of "traditional practices" that may collide with US customs: "Darfuris may often call a distant family member their son, daughter, brother, or sister, as the notion of family extends beyond biological ties. This wider use of biological terms has created confusion both for overseas processing and for establishing legal relationships in the United States."[15] Here it is important to note the ways in which Darfuris "invest social relationships with the symbolism of kinship to be transformed into kinship networks grounded in consanguinity."[16] This practice is important as a means of creating a surrogate family as a substitute for those who have perished in the war. The meaning of both kinship and fictive kinship terminologies as idioms of social ties has been completely lost within the context of a "cultural orientation" meant to explain the confusions of Darfuri ways of thinking.[17]

Engagement with Darfuris founded on the archaic trope of tradition frequently obscured the facts of their often masterful ways of navigating this American life. I came across admirable stories of courage and self-determination at every turn in my interviews. The following is an exceptionally complex migratory and asylum-seeking narrative. It was recounted by two Masalit women, Asha and Aziza, daughter and mother, whom I interviewed in Maryland. It speaks poignantly about flight from Darfur, life in a Chadian camp, the process of coming to America, and the painful separation from flight-mates upon connecting flights in France and Turkey.

My name is Asha. I was born and raised in Goz Baida municipality of El Geneina, Darfur. I want to start with the day when the war erupted. I was in the fields harvesting groundnuts. My six-month-old son was there with me on the farm. We heard bullets and then some people screaming, saying the Arabs arrived, run, run, run. This happened on the second day of the month of Ramadan 2004. People called "Asha, Asha, the Arabs are here. Take your child and run." We ran back to the village. We divided into three groups. We saw the Arabs proceeding on horses and camels coming so fast at us. They killed twelve people before our eyes. My stepbrothers died in the fighting. The Arabs injured the father of my child on the head with a blow from a sword. The Arabs saw him falling, and they thought that he was dead. Some people hid from the Arabs in the fields. Thank Allah, the fields were unharvested.

Now we had to flee on foot. I walked to the Chadian border and hid in the woods. Arriving at the border takes two hours if you walk and one hour if you run so fast. I had a donkey, but I was not able to get it. When I ran away, I did not know whether the people who were still in the village were alive or dead. During this crossing, my injured brother was also with us. I crossed the hot sand. I saw a girl there. "Did the Arabs hurt you too?" I asked her. She said yes. We went to Adday [in Chad] with the girl to find a doctor. He told us that the girl is suffering. My husband, who was critically injured, was also there. The doctors took him for treatment. They told me if he does not die in the next three days, he would never die. They stopped his hemorrhage. Later I learned the Arabs left to go on burning Haraza villages and killing people. I want to say that back in Goz Baida we owned cows, goats, and chickens. Some people had 350 heads of herd. At night, the Arabs entered their places to steal *[livestock]*. They killed a newlywed because he tried to stop the robbery.

We stayed *[in Chad]* for six months before we found an NGO. The staff gave us a place to live in Medina in Chad. The NGO gave us a monthly ration of sugar, a small bag of sorghum, two gallons of oil, and two soaps. Later on, this ration was cut down because the number of people increased. I stayed there for eleven years and gave birth to five of my children in the camp. Our camp had several sectors. Each sector had a sheikh to administer it. We were in sector one, where my children were all born. This sleeping baby here is the only who is an American; he was born here in a Baltimore hospital. I said we could not live like this. I started to work in other people's fields in Chad. We also got some seeds to plant okra (darrabba), sorghum, and sesame. I received five hundred Chad riyals *[for this work]*. This was okay during the rainy season. But I worked for others, too. I exchanged with them by asking them to pay me half in money and half in foodstuffs. Sometimes people shared food with us; whatever small amount they had, they gave. The situation was difficult.

But we had security in Chad. The Chadians protected us from the Arabs who tried to enter the country. They told them the people already fled; do not dare to lift your legs to cross the border. Some Chadians were good to us, but others were also bad. Thieves and soldiers used to share the goods stolen from people. Very bad. There was also a very big problem between the Chadian government and the opposition. When fights occurred, the rebels attacked refugees. The government people used to run away and leave them *[refugees]* alone. The NGOs used to visit after these attacks to see whether people were dead or alive. My grandfather Khater died from internal bleeding *[from a rebel attack]*. So many problems. Back home, we worked so hard and did not have anything, no schools and no medical treatment. The NGO staff came in a car. They said we want to help you, but you know that Arabs do not allow us. But it is okay here. They distributed tents. You can only get a tent if you have a large family, minimum of five. During the heavy rains, the tents did not hold. Things were tough. Now the NGO saw my husband's suffering. *[Because NGOs give priority to injured refugees,]* they took our information to process our papers to leave for America.

We had to wait for this for seven years. We went to Farshana to follow up. The people who talked to us about our paperwork asked us so many questions, questions, questions. If your answers are different from your husband's, both of you are finished. You have to tell the truth. So they told us go back and come again three months later. We went back; the same thing again—questions, questions, questions. Then go back and come again. Ahhhhhhaaaa. This lasted for

*years. When we finally got the approval [to immigrate], the NGO people told us
to go for medical checkups in N'Djamena. NGOs would announce the names
of people who were approved. They also ask you about your camp unit just to
double-check [that you are who you say you are]. When the day arrived, we left
for N'Djamena. We stayed there with 150 other people who were refugees in need
of immediate medical attention for injuries.*

*Then people started to come in droves to America like this. When we were
waiting for the plane, we had food, water, and milk too for the children. The NGO
staff came. They announced our names. We left Chad at 7 p.m. on October 15,
2015. We traveled by Air France. When we reached France, some staff representatives were waiting for us. They took us to the place from which we traveled to
New York. But something happened in France. When we arrived with all these
people from Chad, I thought we would all stay together. Then people came and
asked other refugees to follow them, to take them to other places in America like
Michigan and Utah. We never saw them again. Then we arrived at New York.
People met us to help us until we finished the airport business and left in the bus
to go to Baltimore.*

*When the people brought us to the apartment, we found mattresses, plates,
and lots of food. We received an apartment, a stipend, and food stamps for eight
months. My husband felt better and started to work. Then the assistance stopped.
His money was not enough for rent and other expenses. I started to work at a
warehouse. It takes me an hour to get to work. I work from 6 p.m. to 6 a.m. three
days a week since things started to be difficult. My work allows me to send one
hundred dollars to relatives back home. I am also able to buy clothes and shoes
for my kids. English is a very big issue because I never went to school. But my
work doesn't need it. Here, such talk as "a woman stays home to rest" is not possible. We are in the hands of Allah, and we have to depend on ourselves.*[18]

Asha's mother, Aziza, interjected every now and then to add to her daughter's story or to remind me that she is waiting to tell hers. As she spoke, everyone kept quiet, listening to Aziza's words echo the experience of her friends
in the room, interrupted only by the recording of the Muslim Azdan (call for
prayer) on her cell phone. With her legs that crossed the Sudan-Chad border
stretched straight on the floor, she described her process of adjustment to life
in the United States:

*When I arrived at the apartment [in Baltimore], I struggled. The [apartment]
staff came to show me how to turn on the stove. My friend came from German-
town, and she tried. Boog, boog, boog, the fire started. I screamed, "Turn it off.
Kill it." She said, "How you expect to eat, hey?" One time I took the bus. I got
lost. A man told me to sit down. I did not want to. I was lost for a very long time.
Then I repeated to the driver, "Police, police." She stopped. The police came. I
knew one word only, "refugee." So I said to them. "Refugee." They gestured to*

open my bag. They saw my ID. Then they figured out where I lived and brought
me back, when I told my daughter [laughing, laughing]. Now I became familiar.
I take the bus to the hospital by myself. I take English classes in the church. In the
beginning, after my story of being lost, I told myself to stay home all the time. I
changed my mind. America is a place that gave me peace. I had three surgeries
for my stomach pain, I now am good. For English lessons, I told myself what is
the use; it goes in one ear and comes out from the other. I changed my mind. Now
I know some things. I understand. America is good to me. I have many friends
here in Baltimore and in Silver Spring [Maryland]. We chat all the time. I am
not alone.[19]

The accounts of both mother and daughter are laced with pain. Asha's
invocation, echoed by her mother, of the sorrow she felt as she watched her
flight-mates vanish in the crowds in an international airport was an especially
moving moment. Their experiences were similar to a large swath of Darfuris
who offered their perspectives in this ethnography.

As I returned to interview other men and women, several problems became clear beyond the struggle of dealing with a new reality in America. Fatima, for example, expressed a deep homesickness, as she felt exiled yet again
by isolation and loneliness after her resettlement:

Once I arrived in Washington, I moved to Middle River, Maryland. There was
no one to talk to me. Then another Fur man, a translator, told me about the
friend I am living with right now. I moved with her and her two sons because
they are the only Fur I know here. . . . They [the sons] are also working hard,
but my friend does not work. I go with her three times a week to study English.
I am happy with being with them but not with being in America. I am very sad.
Although I hope to find a place to live like the rest of Allah's creatures, I want to
go home; I want to return to the Sudan.[20]

The son of Fatima's host, Yagoub, a young man in his twenties, highlights
his family's struggles, part of the bigger picture of hardship the more recent
group of Darfuris in the United States face:

I arrived in America with severe injuries incurred in the war. I never thought I
would be able to move, let alone work. I thought to myself that these injuries, if
I were lucky, would take five years at least [to heal]. I shared my worries with
my caseworker. She was very sympathetic and supportive of me and my family.
She used to drive me for my medical appointments and to school to ask about
enrollment. Unfortunately, she moved to another city. I could not work as ex-
pected of me after three months of arrival in America. My brother was under
eighteen years old, and he was going to high school. Life was turning against
us yet again. We received $500 a month from our resettlement agency. It was
not enough. When I discussed our troubles with the new caseworker, he was very

different from our previous one, who was very helpful. He told me I had to work. It was the policy, and it was not up to him to change it. I told him I am in a lot of pain, I am injured, and he replied to me, "You must work."

I started at that point to look for jobs. I found one as a cleaner in Silver Spring. The money was very little to pay our rent. We were fined and at risk of expulsion. Then some people advised me to contact social services to see if they could help. I went to see the staff to tell them about our financial struggle. I told them I was not paid enough to afford rent. They too could not help. I went back to say that our rent is overdue and our electric bill was increasing. I had hopes that this time they would help. But they too had their own problems. I had to settle in court all of these cases. Then in court I was told that I had to pay my debt. "Are you planning on living for free?" I was asked. I started to look for a second job.

All of these pressures were bottled up in my chest. I did not want to share with my younger brother, who liked high school and was getting excellent grades. I do not want to sound ungrateful. In the end, the Americans saved us from suffering and death. I reminded myself about my faith in Allah and that if he wanted me to succeed, I would, with help from me by working hard. In this situation if you do not have a strong faith, you get lost. Life continued. Thank Allah. I remember relatives in Darfur who would be happy to experience my life here. When I reminded myself about their tragedy, my problems paled. My hard work has now started to pay off. I can afford rent. I bought a used van, in good condition. Little by little, we are all finding our way.

Yagoub continued, describing his life in Darfur and Chad. Doing so, he inadvertently emphasized the vast difference between the experiences of the "millions" of which he speaks and those of earlier Darfuri immigrants in the US:

Our experience is not different from that of millions of people who suffered in Darfur and Chad. I am twenty-nine years old. I lived most of my adult life in a refugee camp since we left Zalengi [in Darfur]. Thank you so much for wanting to hear me and about my experience. The criminals violated me; it is very painful even to talk about it. For no reason other than hate and dehumanization. So many of my family members died brutally by the Janjaweed. They inflicted tremendous fear. This suffering turned me into a refugee. I went for days hungry and stressed. My injuries were so severe, and I do not know to this day how I survived them. Many young people in the camp used to sit together to figure out what to do next and how to improve our sad lot. We talked for hours and hours about the violent death in our village. At least we worked hard to manage our pain. Some of the youths could not handle the pain. They turned to drugs, such as the kind they refer to as Rapid Defense Force [this is the name of new organized counterinsurgency militias in the Sudan]. We approached the NGOs with our stories, and they were the best. They knew I was a victim, and they responded by offering assistance. I am here because of them.

As refugees in America, we got a great opportunity for education, health care, and security. I work and attend a community college. My time is divided between work and college. I arrived when Obama was president, as did so many people from Darfur. My mother found a large group of old people like her. They created their own village going and coming and coming and going from each other's homes. I am very content with our effort to cope with our life here. The problem is about our relatives back home. We are physically here, but our hearts are very far away with them. Sometimes, thinking keeps me up at night. If I fall asleep, the tape starts playing and replaying itself in persistent nightmares. The injuries on my arms and legs are also constant reminders. I have siblings who still live in refugee camps. We think about them every day whenever we eat a good meal. When we fled, the old man [his father] was ill. Therefore, I did not apply for him to come to America. The old man died in 2009. I applied for the pilgrim,[21] my younger brother, and myself. The Janjaweed beat this pilgrim severely. When they invaded her courtyard to steal her goats, she tried to confront them. They knocked her teeth out and caused her severe anxiety and headaches, but Allah kept her and gave her strength. Her piety saved her from being killed.

When we came to DC, we did not meet any Darfuri refugees but [did meet] some who lived here for a long time and are not refugees themselves. We saw many Ethiopians but not Fur refugees. Then a well-to-do Fur man approached us to say that we need to move to Baltimore because he knew of many refugees in the area. He also thought that my mother could work as a babysitter for his children. So we moved, and I stayed with some men in Baltimore because the money we got in the first three months was not enough [for me to live on my own]. In the meantime, my mother went to live with the well-to-do Fur man and his family to take care of his children. They paid her $300 for the entire length of her stay and then notified our social service agents that she was paid $300 a month. Then social services stopped paying.

The husband also did horrible things. When my mother and I met a Sudanese man in DC, he took my phone number to call and see how we are doing. Then he called me one day to ask me whether I received money that he had sent to us with the well-to-do Fur man. I didn't see a penny. I told him no, I didn't. He said, "That is so strange," for he had sent the money to help us when we moved to Baltimore to offset some of our expenses. This man was not Fur, just a Sudanese, but he was very kind. Two days later, a man came with money to say this is the money sent from so-and-so. At that point, the Sudanese man called and asked me why I said I hadn't received money! Apparently, he called the Fur to ask. The Fur realized that he was caught, so he sent the money to say, oh, they got it. He told the Sudanese these people got the money a long time ago. My mother and I were disappointed in the kind of treatment we faced. I confronted the man and called him out on his lies. I told him that he was the reason for our suffering. We then *knew that the Fur man wanted us to move so that the pilgrim can clean their house, do their laundry, and take care of their kids. He did not advise us to move because of concern for our well-being. I had to return to the resettlement agency to explain our situation.*

I got a job working in a hospital and got my GED. The next step is university. My mother is doing very well. She goes to English classes three times a week. Now she knows how to use the phone and get on the bus on her own. She has a lot of friends now. She is never alone. But her main psychological pain is coming from the fact that her children still live in the camp. She always asks about them and worries about what they are eating, drinking, or sleeping![22]

Yagoub's mother, Sakina, the friend with whom Fatima is living, added to his story. Her words are a poignant reminder of how the traumas of the war in Darfur, the pain of multiple losses, remain in the hearts and minds of the war's victims:

The war at home did not discriminate. Old or young, human or animal, man or woman, they were all victims. No one in Darfur was safe; they all lost dear ones. My son told you how the family cheated me in Baltimore. This is a very small problem compared to my losses at home. I lost my animals in the war. I lost my teeth fighting with the Janjaweed who wanted to steal my goats and my donkey. They beat me so hard. Just outside of Surei, my village, I could hear tootooooto-ooo, loud noise from gunfire all around us. Then silence for a few minutes, then tooootootooot, noise again. We were frightened as the war arrived in our village. I ran away with blood gushing from my mouth, and my head was about to fall off because of pain. All that is left for me is prayer. I pray for my son who is now taking care of his young brother and me. I pray for the other children back in the camp. Many years have passed, and every minute of my life I just think about them, day and night. Now the Chadians want the refugees to return; they tell them that peace has returned to Darfur. If peace returns, we will all return. It has not. I am afraid for their life in the camp. I lived there for eight years, and I know what life looked like there. . . . I hold my prayer beads to ask for Allah's mercy and for Him to answer my prayers to reunite with my children. I do not know if I would ever be able to see them again; but I do not wish to give up on Allah's mercy.[23]

Although Sakina, Yagoub, and others profiled here are fortunate to be living in the United States, where they are physically safe and rebuilding their lives day by day, they nonetheless remain in a state of liminality, an existence permeated with uncertainty. For some, like Sakina, this state is rooted in an uncertainty about the fate of family members; for others, in a lingering sense of loss of what can only be understood as "home." Indeed, one might say about these Darfuris, "once a refugee, always a refugee," as they remain trapped in a condition produced by political violence that has characterized their lives before, during, and after their arrival in the United States.

A Voice from Prince Georges County

Told movingly by a brilliant young Zaghawa woman living in Prince Georges County, Maryland, the following story pieces together a patchwork of experiences reflecting her subject positions as a woman, migrant, and asylum seeker. Although her education, skills, and urban orientation differentiate her from most recent migrants to the US, she shares with them the experience of war, loss, and degradation. Yet against all odds, Riya commands respect for her sharp intellect, strong determination, and quick wit. Our several hours of interviews—conducted over several days—were interspersed with the kind of laughter that Sudanese describe as cutting one's intestines, even as we were painfully aware of what exactly was funny ha-ha and funny unnerving. These emotions, oscillating between joy and sorrow, reflect the reality she has had to outsmart.

I am Riya from El Fashir, *where I was born and raised. My mother was born in Southern Darfur, my father in a border village called Taina near Chad. When the violence started in 2003, I was still in high school. My father had a business, which he ran from Taina. Unfortunately, our village fell prey to the two rebel groups, JEM [Justice and Equality Movement] and SLA [Sudanese Liberation Army]. Both of them attacked IDPs, as they usually did. The place was awash with weapons. We were an easy target. We heard the shelling and smelled the fine particles of gunpowder poisoning the air. The rebels ran towards our homes. They came to ask for shelter and civilian clothes. I was too young to understand the full extent of what they had asked. I ran home and brought some of my father's clothes. I told my grandmother about them. I said, "These men said they are running away from the fighting. They will be killed, they said." Some of them hid in my grandmother's home for days. Now in hindsight I realized that these were big generals in the rebellion. I remembered that they had many stars on their military uniforms.*

Things became dicey in El Fashir, so the family decided to move to Taina so that we could continue our schooling. Me, my siblings, mother, and aunts all left together. Things continued to turn from bad to worse. My high school exams were around the corner. We had to go back to El Fashir to sit for my college admissions, the Sudanese certificate exam. Very stressful. On our way back, we saw many Janjaweed. We also saw women burying their children's bodies except for their heads. It was freezing cold, and this was the only desperate way to keep them warm. We spent three days on the road. People rushed towards our car and tried to force themselves, but the car was packed with people as it was. Fifteen days later, there was another attack on El Fashir. Atrocities. Very sad all round. Many displaced people, thousands upon thousands. The uncertainty over the fate of relatives sickened my mother. She fell ill. She had typhoid and malaria. Mental stress worsened her situation. Despite her ill health, she was so supportive, so encouraging to me. Mother died shortly thereafter.

Eventually Riya obtained a job working for a radio service in Nairobi and from there migrated to the United States, where, despite her education, she faced the same challenges as others seeking asylum:

A friend said she would recommend me for a job at a radio station dedicated to Darfur and based in Nairobi. She heard that they wanted a trilingual Arabic, English, and Zaghawa [speaker]. I said to her, "Recommend me," but I had no media background. I prepared a good embellished CV [laughter]. When I looked at it, I asked myself whose CV is this? I applied. The editor, who was a white man, said to his committee, "Let her start under probation for three months. I want this girl ASAP!" He told the staff. Now the time had arrived to let my father know. I knew that for a young unmarried woman to travel alone was very challenging. I reached out to my brother to let him know about the excellent opportunity. He suggested that I tell my father about this work assignment since I needed notarized permission [from my father] to allow me to leave the country. I got a passport and prepared myself. I told him finally by saying I was going for training in Kenya for two weeks. He said two weeks was not that terrible. I never returned [laughs].

I bid my family farewell. With my knife confiscated in the airport, I entered the gate as if in a dream. It felt surreal. I said okay, maybe it was time to bid it farewell too. It was 4:00 a.m. when I left the Sudan with tears and mixed emotions at my bittersweet departure. Throughout this flight, my brain played games with me. I kept saying, Is this job for real? What is happening? Are the people there impostors or criminals who intended to harvest my organs? I have heard so many stories like this. Queries, bewilderment churning in my head! Ahhhhaaaa! This situation continued until I got to Nairobi. I expected people from the office to come there [to meet me]. No one showed up. All the passengers in the arrival [area] met their folks except me. I started to weep bitterly. Then I turned on my email to find out that someone was supposed to meet me with a sign bearing my name. "Do not fret, go ahead and take a taxi to the hotel," the sender said. I took a taxi, and the combination of men and the dark scared me to pieces. The poor taxi driver was interested in his fare; he was okay. I could not help these frightful thoughts.

In 2015, I received an Atlas Corps Fellowship for Young Leaders in the US. I left Kenya on December 26, 2015. My fellowship started three weeks later, but I wanted to come to settle in. I visited people from Darfur in so many places, Michigan, Ohio, Illinois, and Indiana, all of them had come recently. As part of my fellowship I met people who gave me an internship at Voice of America. I did well, and they extended my contract to work for one and a half years. Their program covered Sudan, South Sudan, and Darfur. I followed all the demonstrations and rallies in support of accountability for Darfur, all led by refugees and asylum seekers. A human rights NGO heard my story and helped me with my asylum case. Now my year and a half was up. I started to work up to five jobs, just unbelievable. I worked in a pizza place, left for another, and then to the next. I slept five hours or less a day, just exhausted. I had to look for a job that appreciates my skills. I got a job as an Arabic/English translator for some refugees from Zaghawa. It was not a regular job, only when needed in the airport. I filed five tax returns in one year. I do not know what is going to happen. I miss my family; now eight years have passed [since I last saw them]. I am happy to say from the few dollars I get, I fulfilled father's dream to help him go to pilgrimage. That is part of my story! Can I ask you a favor? [Riya asked if she could dedicate this narrative in honor of her mother's family, her father, her grandmother who moved in after her mother's passing, all her mother's co-wives who stood by her father in time of hardship, and to friends and strangers who opened doors. I of course agreed.][24]

In each of these stories, the pain Darfuri people feel is paramount. All stressed the need for action if more of their people are to survive. This concern led me to probe Darfuri consciousness of America as a potential ally of the Darfuri people. While many spoke of America's freedom and beauty, countless statements expressed high hopes for what their country of asylum could do to ameliorate the suffering at home.

Darfuri Consciousness of America

In numerous conversations Darfuris emphasized the dreamlike quality of their first impressions of America. *"This is exactly how I would imagine paradise to look like, lush greenery, placid ravines, and beautiful faces,"* says a man from Nyala with whom I spoke in New York City. Another Darfuri in Virginia spoke in glowing terms of the reception he has received:

America is the best place on earth. It was worth the long wait I experienced in N'Djamena. When I arrived, people welcomed me with warmth and understanding of the terrible life I led in Darfur because of the war. My host knew so much about the Janjaweed Arabs. He even read all the reports that NGOs wrote to bring attention to our condition. That is why I keep saying to myself every morning that coming here is a dream came true by the mercy of Allah and the Americans. I have no complaints whatsoever about any aspect of my life. I have already started to take English lessons. I work as a baggage handler in the airport. Things are going very well. America represents freedom to me and to many of the people who sought refuge here. I do not think I would have been able to find the level of support I found here had I stayed in Africa.[25]

Invariably, they valued the support of American celebrities for their asylum and resettlement in the United States. In this they adamantly disagreed with those like Mamdani who are critical of celebrities' efforts to raise awareness about the extremities of war in Darfur. Whatever the value of academic critiques, some believe they come from a position of privilege and those who promote them would rather see refugees die than get assistance from the humanitarian organizations they detest.[26] For those whose lives have been disrupted by war, living in camps where basic necessities like water and sanitation facilities are scant, the attention of prominent individuals brings hope and sometimes material improvement. Some attribute their opportunity to leave the IDP camps and settle in the US to the activism of Save Darfur. Further examples of such support abound. On April 30, 2006, along the National Mall in front of Capitol Hill, Darfuri refugees were among a crowd of fifteen thousand people who had boarded buses from every corner of the United States to attend a rally calling for an end to the genocide in the Sudan. The scale and scope of this rally was unprecedented; so was the cause for which so many had assembled. Especially notable was the presence of several high-profile participants, including senior politicians and Hollywood celebrities, whose attendance signified a consciousness about a distant region towards which they felt the force of "the responsibility to protect."[27] Actors George Clooney and Mia Farrow, genocide survivors and humanitarians Elie Wiesel and Paul Rusesabagina,[28] politicians Nancy Pelosi and Barack Obama, then-Cardinal Theodore McCarrick, Roman Catholic archbishop of Washington, DC, and hip-hop mogul Russell Simmons were all present.[29]

In the following field notes, I share Darfuris' views about celebrity alliances in the United States:

> *Sometime in the summer of 2007, I went to New York City's Central Park to attend a concert to benefit Darfur. Several Sudanese performing artists contributed their time to entertain thousands upon thousands who converged on the spectacular park to support Darfur. As I entered, a teenager dressed in a green T-Shirt bearing the phrase Save Darfur greeted me. He was one of numerous young volunteers passing out information. . . . Mostly those who attended were white Americans whose Save Darfur T-shirts and green plastic bracelets testified to their participation in the powerful knowledge network spawned by the media and by the star-studded rallies opposing Darfur genocide. There was no doubt in my mind that the sympathetic New Yorkers, who arrived in droves, were at least familiar with the* New York Times *columnist Nicholas Kristoff's opinion pieces on Darfur and of Angelina Jolie's and George Clooney's embrace of the cause.*

Sudanese migrants too came from every area in the United States and Canada to lend their support to Darfur, representing a large swath of ethnicities and religions. The atmosphere was overflowing with life.

When the concert ended, I accompanied several friends to dinner; two of them were Sudanese migrants from Darfur. One of them stated his appreciation of celebrities' involvement in Save Darfur, adding that the sympathy these celebrities directed towards refugees was severely lacking in their homeland. When we turned our attention to the topic of military intervention and its limits, both refugees agreed that any action taken by the international community toward Darfur was better than no action at all. Both of them were convinced that the Darfur question is one of racial injustice and that the genocide was a culmination of sustained racism by a Northern adversary intent on their extermination. As another stated: "I appreciate that everyone in America recognizes the horrible acts that the government of Sudan and its allies, the Arab Janjaweed, did to us."[30]

The racial dimension of Americans' support for Darfur was evident at a town hall meeting in Providence, Rhode Island, that I attended with some of my students, who were part of the Save Darfur youth campaign. Members of several Jewish associations in Providence were also in attendance, along with members of synagogues around New England. At the reception that preceded the event, I chatted with several members of a Jewish group who had arrived together. An elderly man from a local synagogue remarked that he and his friends would not have missed the town hall: "*To hear in this day and age that millions of Black people are either killed or at risk of extermination is unbearable, so much so because it brings back painful memories of our own lot. We are in touch with a lot of Darfuris and with organizations helping them. We feel that this is our responsibility to do whatever we can to prevent history from repeating itself.*" This was the not the first time I heard of such equivalence between the Sudan under Al-Bashir and Germany's Third Reich. At the event itself, Jerry Fowler, director of the United States Holocaust Museum, spoke of his encounter with a young girl in a refugee camp in Chad who asked him if he could help her find her mother. He too noted that this encounter had brought back the memory of the suffering of his own family members.

A Shifting Black Consciousness

Engagements with activists in America, both celebrities and concerned citizens, although important, as Darfuris affirm, are part of the landscape of new imperatives and shifting priorities within which they choose to redefine themselves, including a shifted frame of racial identity. Voluntary associations

formed after 2003 by different affinity groups within the US Darfuri diaspora
provide one example. Their names suggest their members' goal of discursive
engagement with their Darfuri origins and experiences of genocide, ethnic
cleansing, and crimes against humanity: Darfur Leaders Network, Darfur
Women Action Group, Darfur Diaspora Association, Darfur Peace & Development Organization, Fur Cultural Survival, Darfur People's Association
of New York, the Darfur Rehabilitation Project, and the Darfur Women Network. The blogosphere is yet another arena for solidarity and advocacy. What
is less obvious but equally significant is that insofar as these organizations and
forums claim a uniquely Darfuri identity as distinct from Sudanese, they are
also de facto about members' sense of racial identity as Black Darfuris.

Darfuris are also making clear their views about their Blackness vis-
à-vis white and Black Americans, views sometimes laced with contradictions.
Identity formation is always a complex process. Among exiles, it involves a
recalibration of experience in light of the context in which the exile finds
himself or herself. Cast in this framework, we can appreciate why Darfuris
stress their Black identity in one context and not in another. No single example illustrated this process more concretely than the story a forty-four-
year-old man from Kuttum told me when I interviewed him at a rally in
Washington, DC:

> I was in a very big hurry to get to an event. I got in a taxi with an African driver
> and told him that I was kind of late. He started chatting with me and asked
> where I was from. I told him from Darfur; he told me he was Nigerian. The
> conversation soon turned to the miserable living conditions in Africa and the
> corrupt politicians and dictators. Up to this point, we agreed. It turned into a
> bizarre exchange when I started to relate to him the disaster in my region, with
> which he appeared to be very familiar. He kept repeating, 'Yeah I heard.' It soon
> became clear to me that explaining our situation as Black people in Sudan to this
> person was almost impossible. However, I pressed on. When I told him about the
> killing of Black tribes in Darfur, he mocked me by saying, "Oh, are they being
> killed by white people?" I said, "No, by the Arab government of Al-Bashir." "So
> Al-Bashir is white all of a sudden. Are you talking about the Sudan in Africa
> or about some white country I have not heard about?" He burst into a derisive
> laughter—hahahha!—and expressed his disapproval of my story: "This is crazy.
> You guys are something else!"
>
> He then proceeded to say, "You know, my country has also experienced civil
> war. It was so brutal. Can you imagine if I went around telling people that our
> people were killed because they are Black? They will wonder what I had been
> on!" When he sucked in his teeth at my story, I knew for sure that he was unwill-
> ing to hear me. You know back home we call this "sucking sour tamarind [mas

al aradaib]"; *it's a sign of ridicule and disdain. Others like this crazy taxi driver will also challenge you because they say all Sudanese people are Black like me [implying that the oppression of Black people in a Black country is not about race but about something else]. I never had such a frustrating chat like this with an American. I told this story to tens of people in this country. I talk about it all the time. The Americans showed me a lot of support by understanding the reality of the situation. The rallies in this country do not only raise awareness about Darfur, but to me I feel that they are important occasions to be among people who don't wrestle with you and make you look like a total idiot. They want to protect us from all the atrocities Darfur is facing.*[31]

How can we read this apparently exasperating conversation? What does it tell us about both Africans' conceptualization of race/color and the narrator's self-concept as part of "global circuits of blackness"?[32] The Nigerian taxi driver's conception "of a society divided into two hermetically sealed sectors"[33] is nonsensical within his own comprehension of the politics of race and ethnicity in another African state such as the Sudan. The narrator of the story, who defined himself as a member of a Black "tribe," then had to decide whether or not to explain his categories to a fellow African or to question the binary of Black vs. white. Yet the narrator's perception of concerned Americans also suggests the ease with which he accepts the binary as a "Black tribesman" utterly distinct from an Arab Janjaweed. This apparent confusion makes sense, however, when we take into account the fact that skin color typically supersedes all other markers of ethno-cultural identity. Hence the narrator's visceral reaction to what appeared to him to be a cynical response from an unsympathetic African. This story provides a good frame for delving more deeply into how race is defined, negotiated, lived through, and commented upon by Sudanese exiles and refugees themselves. The ethnic targeting that many of them have experienced has occasioned recalibrations of who they are. As they came to inhabit a new space, they made a double move: on the one hand, embracing subject positions as witnesses and victims, and on the other, as indigenous tribal Black Africans.

Nonetheless, acquiring a Black identity (*zurqa*) among Darfuris in the American context is a process not bereft of paradox. An African American friend once referred to another who happened to be very conservative as "my color but not my kind." Given that Baltimore is a majority-Black city and that many of its residents live in poverty, I wanted to gain a better understanding of Darfuris' unfolding views of themselves vis-à-vis poor African Americans. I frequently heard statements such as "*Baltimore is one of the most dangerous cities in America*" and references to African Americans' involvement in drugs and crime:

Since we came to this neighborhood, we always run into suspicious persons. There are so many thugs and thieves here. When one of them approaches me to ask for a dollar or a cigarette, I do not open my mouth, I just shake my head. If I say anything, the thief recognizes my strange accent and my broken English [making me more vulnerable]. Now I imitate their clothes, baggy pants and hoodies, so that the person thinks twice before approaching me. He will definitely confuse me for a Black American because I look like one. That is it; I share nothing else with them.

He went on to provide examples of how Darfuris managed to ward off the "thugs and thieves" in their neighborhood:

Some Black burglars managed to break into our friend's house and held him at gunpoint. They had no idea what they were dealing with. With a quick martial arts stroke, he knocked the gun off and turned it towards them. They pleaded with him to let them go. He called 911 to turn in the gun. The police officers were very surprised about this unusual behavior. Had this been another [crime] victim, he would have proceeded to shoot. My friend fought against the Janjaweed back home. He arrived directly from a war zone. Did these thieves think they could overpower him?[34]

These anecdotes led me to ask about the paradoxes inherent in Darfuris' claims to a Black identity in America. The reply was swift and unequivocal: "*Darfuris are Black people but not Black Americans.*" Another added, "*All the organizations that help Darfuris in America know very well that we are not the same as Blacks.*" And another: "*We are not saying that we are Black Americans [African Americans]. We are different, and we value education and hard work.*" While it is important to recognize the variety of Black experiences in America, the myopic views Darfuris held vis-à-vis African Americans were cause for concern. I queried my research participants about the reasons for their views of African Americans in light of the racial injustices they have endured and continue to endure. After all, Baltimore's majority-Black population is a bona fide victim of structural inequalities; as Christopher Ingraham notes, the city includes neighborhoods where residents have a shorter life expectancy than North Koreans.[35] One also finds echoes of these responses in Elijah Anderson's *Streetwise*, an ethnography of race and urban poverty. He writes: "Though one may argue that the institutions of both the wider society and the local community have failed members of the Black underclass, local working-class and middle-class residents often hold the people themselves to blame."[36]

So I kept probing. "Why do you think you are better than African Americans? Was it not their struggles that made it possible for all of us to be here?" I asked. Responses were all some version of the same thing: "*Everything we know about them [African Americans] is negative. They don't like to work."* Or as one interviewee said, *"Yes, we are Black but not Black Black!"* It is indeed a matter of when (or if) these Darfuris would realign their views about African Americans in light of their own lived realities marked by liminality, refugeeness, and especially racial difference.

As I listened to these comments, I thought of South African anthropologist Bernard M. Magubane's caution: "[Blackness] . . . has a fluidity which evades analysis if we attempt to immobilize it in order to dissect its structure, and can be fully comprehended only as embodied in real people in real contexts."[37] Indeed, Magubane's point acquires particular meaning when we contrast Darfuris' differentiation from African Americans in Baltimore to their embrace of a Black African identity in Israel. In the former context, the move is a way to avoid racial stigmatization in a majority-Black, racially divided city; in the latter, a way to distinguish themselves from Arab citizens of an enemy state. It is the same move that underlies their distancing from their Islamic faith and their claim as participants in a Jewish brotherhood in Israel, where Muslim equals Arab in the popular mind and the immigration system is predicated on Jewish identity. In the US, however, it is not so crucial to shed either Arab or Muslim identity.

Gender Justice: "My Words Are Not Trash"

She was about thirty years old. When her village was attacked by the Janjaweed, she and her two daughters and son—the eldest was six years old—were held for a week. The mother was raped repeatedly. They released the mother and her children in the desert far from any villages. That was probably cheaper than using bullets on them, or else they wanted their seeds to grow inside her. She walked for five days in the desert carrying her children without food or water. When she couldn't carry them anymore, she sat under a tree that she found. There was nothing she could do except watch her children die. She took her shawl and tied it to a high branch in order to end her life. We found her that same day, a few hours too late.[38]

Government officials have vehemently denied the use of rape as a weapon of war, with some going so far as to argue that rape does not exist in Darfur. They have instead accused women of promiscuity, reflecting a common mythology about women's licentiousness and thereby shifting responsibility for gender violence to the victim. And yet rape has indeed become an important element in state-sanctioned violence perpetrated by both its proxy militia and its organized army.

When we speak of gender violence and gender justice, we confront one of the knottiest of anthropological, historical, legal, and philosophical conundrums.

Gender violence manifests ways in which religion, law, and citizenship have become constitutive elements of gender politics and asymmetrical social relations emanating from the social organization of difference. For those who have fallen prey to rape and its chilling threat have been harmed in ways that men have not. Here too we find the trope of Blackness, as transnational activists agitating for gender justice decry the specific forms of violence perpetrated by fair-skinned Janjaweed against Darfuri women and girls. And yet then-President Al-Bashir pushed back against such claims in a video conference with members of the Nation of Islam and reporters attending the 2007 Saviors' Day conference in Detroit, Michigan. When asked by African Americans about rape as a means of ethnic cleansing, he responded: "Talk of Arabs killing blacks is a lie. The government of Sudan is a government of blacks, with all different ethnic backgrounds. We are all Africans, we are all blacks."[39] On the one hand, claims of impregnating Black women with the intention of producing light-skinned babies seem ludicrous given the reality of the complexion of Sudanese Arabs as Black people themselves. On the other, this fact does not negate the prevalence of multiple testimonies corroborating systematic rape and the gender inequality it embodies. Indeed, there is little disagreement about the physical and psychological injuries emanating from the gendered practices of warfare in Darfur, despite the government's official denial of its occurrence.

Such injuries are painfully evident in the following narrative, which bears the markings of posttraumatic stress disorder, including flashbacks and insomnia. Of the countless women I interviewed all over the world about political violence in Darfur, Altoma appeared exceptionally melancholy. As she talked about her brutal rape, hospitalization, and subsequent flight to Chad, it was clear that she was still haunted by the memories of these events some sixteen years after her rape. Married in the camp at seventeen, she assumed the position of senior wife when her husband decided to marry an even younger woman. At the time of our conversation, she had been living with her five children in a one-bedroom apartment since their arrival in Maryland in August 2016. She, like other Fur women, had been displaced from her village near Surei by the Janjaweed. Their crime lives on in her chilling story:

> One day I went with some girls and my brother to the well to fetch water, as we all did in Surei, my village. Men in khaki clothing approached us quickly, along with men on horses. They hit me on the leg, and I fell down. My brother tried to protect me. They shot and killed him. He was fifteen, and I was twelve years old. Then they raped me. They stole the animals too. When I crept in pain back home to tell people what had happened, my family rushed me to Umm Dukhun, the closest village to us, for treatment. We stayed there until the doctor saw me and wrapped the wounds, and then we moved to Chad. I got married there when I was seventeen years old.

Because of my severe injuries, the NGO helped us [Altoma and her husband and children] get out of Chad. We traveled to France, then to New York before we finally came here. I left my mother, sisters, and brothers back home. They continue to live in the camp, suffering in hell. When we got here, we had food stamps and some assistance for rent for three months. After that we did not receive any assistance. We were expected to work, as we were told by the resettlement agency. Since we did not have education, we could not find a good job. I started cleaning bathrooms on a college campus in Baltimore. It was exhausting. After this experience, I found another job in a warehouse. It is far [from my home]. More than half of my income goes to transportation by the company's bus. Our city bus does not go there. I try also to find a bit of time to join others in school to study English.

The suffering here is also inescapable. My oldest daughter is a teenager now, and she is not well. She has psychological problems that led her to be easily angered and disrespectful. She is taking pills for her disorders. This happened to her after she had malaria. She has not been fine since. People say that the fever affected her brain. I also make sure not to miss my doctor's appointment. My leg swells so badly, but I force myself to work in spite of my pain. Then I talk also to doctors about my psychological troubles. I keep thinking about my troubles in Darfur, and a strange feeling that overwhelms me. I feel as if I had just been raped. I lose sleep over painful memories. This is happening although the doctors gave me medicine to take every day to help me forget.

I am also very sad about the realization that my mother and siblings are still suffering the humiliation of being refugees in Chad. This is my life every single day. Then there is another problem. I work at night. When I return in the morning, I take care of these little kids until they go to school. The little one, who is American, stays home. Then when I go to the hospital [to see the doctors] during the day, I end up staying awake for two days in a row. I am in so much pain and suffering. The financial problems put extra stress. My life is pure pain and nerve-wracking troubles. The only change happens on the weekend when I see other women from Darfur to get together to chat. Then we go home and we remember these troubles all over again. I pray for the return of peace in Darfur; I pray for health and success of my children; and I hope to see my mother again, especially if she gets to come here with me. Now I am worried about her because her health is deteriorating. I am here with no capacity to help her out of the misery in Chad.[40]

Altoma's story gets at the heart of what it means to be a rape victim and a refugee in both the literal and metaphorical sense, even as it illustrates the intertwined institutional arrangements that have caused her suffering. What makes rape an exceptionally alarming affront are widely held Sudanese cultural and religious beliefs about men, women, and sexuality. Again we hear from Riya, as she describes in detail the vulnerability of women within a misogynistic culture of male privilege as she sought employment after completing her education:

> When I started looking for work in Darfur, then I figured I had my hell cut out for me. One of our relatives had a friend who worked with a top Darfuri official. He told him to help me secure an interview. He did. At that time, I was young, very fashionable. I was proud of my body and myself. I dressed nicely top to bottom. Bad idea. The senior, I will call him that without naming him, started to give promises. One day, he told me to come back the next day and gave me money as help until my paperwork was finished. I kept asking when, when. Ohhhhhhh, silence. He then said that I could work with him as his personal assistant. I was very happy. He said what he was offering was an advance of fifteen dollars. My brother was injured; I believed him and accepted the fifteen dollars. The only thing I owned was a gold ring and a small pendant from my mother. These mementoes meant so much, but I had sold them to help my brother. I sold the only memory [I had. Because I had not heard back from him,] one day I returned to inquire from the senior about my job. He said, "Come in, Riya." He closed the door and came towards me with a savage look on his face. He wanted to rape me. I fought him so hard and ran away, my heart racing and my extremities just numb. I could not tell anyone. Society blames the girl. After several months, other girls told me that sexual harassment came with the job; you have to provide sex. Of course, that was a nonstarter.
>
> My stepbrother knew of a friend of his who worked in an NGO, also in Darfur. He called him on his mobile phone. He promised to help. I took my CV to his house, which he shared with his mother and sisters. He was not there, so I left my envelope with his sister and left. He came to see me to say that my CV was not that great, but he could help me rewrite it in a better form. I agreed. [Because he was] a family friend living with a large family, I did not expect another despicable rape attempt. "Oh, you have grown!" He was sleazy. I bit him, fought him before he ripped my shirt. I ran to my friend, shivering and traumatized. I stayed home for a long time, distressed and depressed. I lost hope. A friend of mine knew of another NGO. She took me to ask them for help with a ticket to Khartoum. The ticket cost at that time around fifty dollars. Exorbitant. They helped, and I left for Khartoum. I kept reminding myself that with all the news about sexual violence in Darfur, I never experienced it with rebels or militia. I experienced it while looking for a job.
>
> In Khartoum, men are professional harassers, especially in public transport. They do not attempt to rape, but the comments about body parts are just disgusting. I started to take a knife in my purse to defend myself. But in the crowded buses you couldn't move. Sometimes you're standing up for over an hour with men glued to you. I swear that one time I felt that someone who stood behind me thrust something as hard as a rock in my behind. With nowhere to turn, I screamed. I used my voice to ward him and his erect part off me. What kind of

hell is this? This situation ignited bad memories of attempted assaults. Then one time a very fat man sat next to me in the bus. Kept moving closer to me. I kept scooting away little by little. I was securing my headscarf with a pin. I pulled it slowly and pricked him until he screamed. Another man cried to him, "You deserve it." These were good people. We Zaghawa girls are not that vulnerable. I said to him, "I fled across the Chad border. Do you think I am going to allow you to assault me in Khartoum? You are delusional!"

I pulled my knife very often. Remember, I was wearing my hijab all along. It did not matter one bit. In Khartoum, I stayed at a hotel in the wretched Arabic suq. I endured for the sake of taking my bar to look for work in my field. One of my friends knew a firm of a famous lawyer who accepted trainees. I went to see him to make my own case as to my resourcefulness and intelligence. I was so smart, especially in criminal law. He was an old man in his fifties, with a wife and daughters my age. First, second, and third week, things were cordial. He gave me transportation to the court sessions, gave me exciting tasks. I was relieved. Soon enough this dirty old man started to tell me to be his girlfriend or even enter into secret marriage. He promised me my own apartment in which he was to meet me every day. I refused. He told me that would be better than going adrift in Khartoum. I said, "No. No means no, ya ustaz [sir]." He changed 360 degrees and cut my benefits and transportation. He sent me faraway like to Kalklatt [an hour and a half to two hours on public transportation]. Horrible character! I confronted him. I said El Fashir beckons. It is waiting for me; people are waiting for me. I do not have any intention to fornicate. My life turned into living hell. Luckily my friend Awatif, may she rest in peace, was a kind and supportive friend. I told her about the dirty old man. She said, "Riya, we do not have options, but good for you. You will find an honest job!" Words of moral support.[41]

As Riya made clear, open discussion of matters pertaining to sexuality is proscribed by the culture, an interdiction linked to how society views sexuality in the first place. Sexuality in women is linked to the ideology of honor, which is understood to reside in a woman's modesty, chastity, and virginity. She alone is expected to guard her virtue, for on it rests the honor of her entire lineage. If she does not, whatever the circumstances, she is blamed.

A young Zaghawa asylum seeker in Virginia made this point forcefully as she told me about the rape and beating of a fifteen-year-old disabled girl who sold peanuts and melon seeds in a market. When she crawled back to her family and told them what had happened, they scolded her and accused her of acquiescing and keeping quiet during the rape out of will. The patriarchs of the family were simply uncompromising in their blame. Coded speech referring to raped women as promiscuous and *sharmoota* (whores, sluts) further compels victims into silence. But an older woman in Baltimore made clear that young women should not be blamed for rape; it is the rapists who are at fault:

I am here now, but fear has not left my heart. We were terrorized by the Janja-weed. I am old. So all they did was to steal from me. But so many people talked all the time about their evil deeds. Whenever they found a beautiful young lady, they would rush to rape. Sometimes a lot of men force one woman or girl. They force their stinking bodies on the young one. They raped their way [through a village], frightened people, and forced them to run away. They attacked us on the ground, the government [attacked us] from the sky. They were acting as if possessed by Satan. They forgot about Islam and its advice to be good to oth-ers. They are not good Muslims, just bad people who lack in morality. What do they want from a young woman to rape her like this and end her peace of mind? They wanted to satisfy their lust. They took advantage of the community. Did they forget about judgment day? How are they going to face Allah when they die? They thought that they were so strong to do all of these horrible things to us. I am here now. I ask myself, was the war beneficial to anyone? The Janjaweed robbed women of their dignity, their animals, and their family members.[42]

Altoma, Riya, and others who spoke to me about sexual violence have undertaken the difficult task of breaking the prevailing silence on a matter that women in the Sudan are most reticent about. Yet our conversations were in private, to me and sometimes a small audience of trusted countrywomen. Not so Souad, a Masalit woman who had arrived in Omaha, Nebraska, from Goz Amir Camp in Chad, who spoke publicly about her rape in Darfur when she was five months pregnant. *"Listen to what I am saying. My words are not trash,"* she said at an open forum on genocide, pleading with the audience to understand the predicament of refugee women. Channeling her pain into speaking out, Souad began by setting the story of her rape within the context of life as a Darfuri refugee in Chad:

In the Name of Allah, the merciful, the benevolent, I want to salute America for rescuing me from my difficulties and helping me to talk about my cause. I salute my beloved Sudan and Darfur. I am a victim of rape in Darfur. It is shameful to say I am a rape victim. In the beginning [after it happened], I cried in silence. If I continue to keep silent, I will lose my cause. I decided to shine a light on it. I hope to speak to people. I also hope that people do not treat my words as trash. Many years have passed, and every day is still very difficult for me. How am I supposed to endure this pain? I wanted Al-Bashir to stand trial, to be handed to the ICC, and to be behind bars. Right now, I am not speaking about this because I am here in America, but because I am a refugee.

I ask the international community why it abandoned Darfur. Did it give up on us? People cannot live with rape. I am wondering about the inaction. People

are tired living with fire under their feet. Please fulfill our wish for justice. Fol-
low up on women's situation. Where are women's rights? I urge you to ask for
accountability. Speak to your leaders as soon as possible. I gave you information
on life in the camp, no food, no water, even no graves. When refugees die, they
are not buried in dignity. . . . Just fifteen days ago, my people in Goz Amir told me
about imprisonment, hunger, and death. Today, I suppress my tears and keep my
anger at bay. My heart aches still, but I will not forget the camp. I want to have a
voice and even take my evidence to the Congress. My cause is to talk about rape.
I would have rather been killed than raped. Allah willing, my wishes come true
for everyone in the Sudan to live in peace.[43]

Like Souad, testimonies from prominent Darfuri community members in
America before the United States Senate, the House of Representatives, the
United Nations Security Council, and other policymaking institutions are a
powerful antidote to the silence surrounding sexual violence in war. In speaking out, they are also challenging the taboo against talking publicly about
rape. At a hearing I attended on the Darfur crisis hosted by US Representative Eddie Bernice Johnson of the Congressional Black Caucus in 2007, the
wife of a rebel leader sobbed as she took to the podium to share her fear for
her eighty-year-old grandmother in Darfur: "*She is at risk of being raped because she is Black.*" The forceful testimony of Niemat Ahmadi, founder of the
Darfur Women Action Group (DWAG), before the Senate Foreign Relations
Committee in 2009 is yet another example of women speaking out about conditions young girls and women regularly face in Darfur. In her testimony,
Ahmadi linked sexual violence to broader structures of violence in Darfur
and urged US government action:

Sadly, in the current history and in the current crisis in Darfur, war is too often fought on women's bodies. . . . Countless women and girls continue to face
brutal rape, humiliation, beating, starvation, and disease on a daily basis. The
United Nations' Stop Rape Now campaign, a partnership of twelve UN agencies, reports that hundreds of women continue to be raped in Darfur every
day. In Darfur, rape is being used as weapon of war. It is a systematic tactic to
destroy the very fabric of our community. Rape and sexual violence in Darfur
are not the product of chaos or uncontrollable troops during the attacks. It is
not an after-effect of war. It is well planned and orchestrated in a calculation
to break apart families, tear down leadership structures, and leave long-term
social, emotional, and physical scars on an entire community.

Women are raped when their villages are attacked, when they flee their
homes seeking safe refuge, and while they are living in camps for the internally displaced. Abduction and sexual slavery are tactics used by the Sudanese government and its allied Janjaweed militia. This terrorizing of women,

families, and communities is not a nightmare—it is the reality of daily life in Darfur. Direct protection of women must become the first priority in response to the conflict in Darfur. The US must work to engender the make-up of the UNAMID [United Nations–African Mission in Darfur] force by providing the resources, training, and recruitment of more female police within the camps. We must strengthen the command structure to better protect women.

As Ahmadi reminds the committee, "Even when guns stop, rape does not stop at all." To emphasize the negative impact of sexual violence inflicted upon women, Ahmadi recounted the story of a woman who had to decide whether to abandon her daughter after she had been raped by seven men or carry her home for treatment. She decided to bring her daughter home for medical attention and afterwards to gain an education. The daughter herself was considered "spoiled" by the rape and therefore rejected by their community. She also told of young women who refuse to nurse infants conceived from rape.[44]

I end this chapter with Amani's story, a powerful indictment of cultural misogyny and gendered violence both emotional and physical. It is also a story of courage in the face of enormous suffering caused by the war in Darfur, determination to make a new life in the US, and generosity towards refugees remaining in Chad. Amani was one of several Darfuris in America whom I met while attending a forum on "Women and Genocide in the 21st Century: The Case of Darfur," held under the auspices of DWAG and hosted by Georgetown University Law Center in Washington, DC, in 2018. A warm and colorful personality, Amani agreed with great enthusiasm to speak with me about her experiences: *"I want as many people as possible to know about my experience not only in Darfur but also as a refugee in Chad, where we greatly suffered."* She continued:

> I am speaking in this forum to let folks know about the NGO I founded to help people back home. When the war started in Darfur, I was a young adult. My cousins were killed in the genocide, and I saw with my own eyes the murder of little kids, mostly boys.[45] In 2007, when I fled to Gaga Camp in Chad, I brought four kids in tow. Two boys and two girls. I dressed my boys in girls' clothing because I knew that the Janjaweed would kill them [if they knew they were boys]. When a gang stopped me, they pointed at my kids and ordered, "Take their clothes off." Luckily, one of them said, "No, they are little girls." One of my kids was forty-five days old; I carried him on my back. Can you imagine, at twenty-two I was walking with four children! My husband left us. He just disappeared. Life became even harder [with him gone].

The camp was packed with women and children, widows and orphans. We did not have food, water, or any nutrition for the kids. I could not breastfeed. One small meal a day for the entire family was just too little. My kids had no clothes, no shoes. One morning I took my child to a clinic for vaccination. The woman held his arm trying to vaccinate, but clearly she did not know how. I stopped her. I told her I would not stand there watching her. I took the syringe and vaccinated my own kid. Then all the women who were standing there asked me to vaccinate theirs. I did. The woman ran to the clinic's manager to tell on me. Just before I left, they stopped me. They asked me why I vaccinated the children, and I told them. They asked me to go to N'Djamena for further questioning with the help of a translator. "Do you know that if anything goes wrong you will be responsible?" they asked. I said, "Yes, I know, but I also know I knew how to vaccinate, and why did you put a woman who does not have any experience to do it? Were you prepared to blame her if things went wrong?" At that point, they asked me so many questions to make sure that I was honest about my nursing knowledge. They said, "Congratulations!" I asked, "What are you congratulating me for?" They replied, "You got yourself a job." They said that I need to return to make plans to go for short training and for French language too. They sent me to Abacha for two years, during which I learned French to communicate with Chadians.

In Abacha, I applied for resettlement to America. My estranged husband heard about it. Suddenly he showed up to say he wanted to go. After all the neglect, now he wanted to be with us. I told him this was impossible. One day I took my girls to a woman to braid their hair. When I came back, my boys were gone. Their father had kidnapped them to prevent me from traveling. At that time, so many people were circulating rumors about resettlement in America, that kids would be taken away [there], women [would be] enslaved, this and that, so many rumors, so many lies. The agency asked me if I still wanted to leave. I said yes, although I almost lost my mind after several failed attempts to get my boys back. I could not eat or sleep. I said yes, despite the pain, yes. I said I want a better life for my girls. With my paperwork completed, I had forty-eight hours to leave the camp for America in 2010. Life had been so bad in the camp. The Chadians were involved also in rape and violence against refugees, and their officials put many pressures [on us] to go back to Darfur.

In 2014, when I arrived in Nebraska before moving to Michigan, I received a call from Chad, "Amani, we located your boys." "How, when, where?" I was going crazy with excitement. It turned out that my husband had had kidney failure and died. The relatives he left them with brought them back to the camp [where we had been], and they were very lucky that a worker recognized them right away. In the meantime, I stopped going to school [where I was studying nursing]. My teachers called to check on me since I was always punctual. I told them that my kids are alive, and they will be with me. I could not focus on my studies. The

NGOs helped them to reunite with me. Just one day before their arrival, I felt that time had stopped. One day felt like ten years.

Once they arrived, I gained more strength to go on. I finished a nursing associate degree. I also started a foundation to help refugee women in the camps. Now I am able to travel to Chad. Last Ramadan, I collected clothes and shoes along with foodstuffs for them. I brought sugar, oil, and flour in big quantities. People were fasting in a very difficult situation, and the heat was oppressive. I registered my organization so that I can start helping even more. My kids are doing so well and prospering in school. I think that our resettlement was a solution, but it is also not a solution, no matter how many people leave. If all the residents managed to come to America, we are wondering if emptying the region from its people is an answer.[46]

For Ahmadi, Amani, and others like them, channeling grief, rage, and fear into action reminds us how "emotion seeks to transform the world," as Jean-Paul Sartre put it. "In emotion it is the body which, directed by consciousness, changes its relations with the world in order that the world may change its qualities."[47] By averring "my words are not trash," Souad demonstrated how her consciousness about the violation of her bodily integrity is precisely what propelled her to call for action.

If we can speak about the allegory of Darfur in these stories, it is this: Although those who are breaking the silence about rape as a weapon of war are removed physically from the location of this torment, they remain emotionally connected to fellow sufferers, speaking in hopes of alleviating their own and others' pain and that others will never experience it. Yet it is precisely because they are removed from war and are living in the United States that they can engage in this work. No longer do they need to fear retaliation from their rapist or rejection by their community for speaking out. Furthermore, the alliances they have forged with other victims and Darfuri and American allies offer moral support in a culture where the discourse about rape is more open and where the rapist, not the victim, is increasingly considered accountable. And so begins the process of healing because they are believed.

Darfur the Rhizome

Hi! Thank you for reading me. I should be happy to be here, though I can't help feeling confused.

ORHAN PAMUK, *Other Colors*[1]

The ethnographic materials that formed the basis for *Darfur Allegory* were gathered well before the onset of the Sudanese December Revolution of 2018 that resulted, in April 2019, in the ouster of Omar Al-Bashir, who had brutally ruled the Sudan for thirty years. I cannot, however, avoid touching upon the emotions that engulfed the Sudanese people and Darfuris in particular in the aftermath of these events. Undoubtedly, the Revolution was a cosmically powerful, seemingly miraculous event that no one thought possible in light of the regime's ongoing brutality. The fast-moving currents swirling through the country, which have direct bearing on Darfur, militate against a conventional conclusion. Indeed, I could settle the matter by saying Darfur as an idea is about multiple stories branching into thousands of others. At its heart are issues splitting into minute arteries, veins, and capillaries that can be viewed only with microscopic scrutiny. The most important of these veins is the noticeable Darfuri recalibration of self and identity in diverse contexts, as we have seen in the Homestead, Doha, Tel Aviv, and Baltimore and environs. Throughout, I have stressed that Darfuri people are not victims but agents of change, as evidenced in both the innermost and collective facets of their lives. An obvious conclusion, therefore, is one I simply borrow from Deleuze and Guattari, the notion of the rhizome and multiplicity that challenges overdetermined answers and representations.[2] Having described the complexity of the Darfur crisis throughout this ethnography, I can easily insist that a neat conclusion is an unwieldy if not altogether dizzying exercise. In short, I am confused.

But that does not quite satisfy. Despite my circumspection, I have also thought that touching on the Revolution can perhaps catch in a meaningful way what Richard Sorabji calls contractive and expansive emotions[3] prevailing among the Darfuri populace. At first, exultation at the victory of the Revolution was incontestably real, followed soon after by uncertainty and despair about the situation of IDPs and the fate of the ousted Al-Bashir and the ICC. I turn to joy first.

In this ethnography, interlocutors in and outside of the Sudan bewailed the invisibility of the Darfur crisis post-2003, caused in large part by diminishing media attention. As we have seen, when Darfur turned into a ground zero of devastation and terror in 2003, significant attention focused on the manifold causes of the conflict. However, subsequent media silence led to the belief that the region's plight would never attract international attention and hence anxiety that the prevailing environment of impunity would never end. Nevertheless, the Sudanese Revolution has caused hopes to soar as Darfur's predicament came to figure prominently in the political drama being enacted. In particular, high expectations were placed on the new government to effect the long-awaited surrender of Al-Bashir to the ICC.

Moved by a powerful revolutionary fervor, Darfuris had arrived at Khartoum in droves to join the months-long sit-ins in front of the Army Central Command. Scenes of protesters carrying slogans such as "You arrogant racists, the whole country is Darfur" were everywhere, and for those Darfuris who remained at home, seeing their fellow citizens involved in protest was of great significance. As I, a Sudanese, followed the daily coverage on Hadath TV, I too was heartened by these slogans. Exceptionally powerful was a video I viewed in which young Darfuri women in their colorful dresses headed a demonstration chanting, "Freedom, peace, and justice. No more Zurqa or Arab. We are all Sudanese. Revolution. Revolution. Revolution." The crowd of men behind them, waving a Sudanese flag, repeated rhythmically in unison, "Freedom, peace, and justice. Revolution is the people's choice." "Madania [civilian]," they chanted. "Madaniaaaaaaoooooo! Madaniaaaaaaoooo!" exaggerating the word, drawing it out for emphasis.[4] In their gleeful cheers, I heard conviction articulated with gusto and courage. In Tel Aviv, jubilation at the Revolution's victory swept through the Darfuri community. Simultaneously, Darfuris in exile in the US along with their fellow Sudanese people marched in front of the White House calling for the government to act in support of those back home in their resolve to overthrow Al-Bashir.

Repeated statements by the formidable Forces of Freedom and Change in the Sudan, a coalition of oppositional groups that organized the strikes and rallies, stressed that "the Sudanese cause remains a unified concern and its solution must be comprehensive and indivisible." This solidarity too was a source of celebration across the breadth and length of the Sudan. History tells us that the Sudanese people have time after time gallantly mastered the art of revolution-craft. Educated by harsh circumstances, they have emerged as what Grant Farred calls "vernacular intellectuals."[5] The sit-ins were a stage that bore witness to a ritual reenactment of solidarity and connection. The protesters sat down to both defy and define the political future.

Yet, in spite of the euphoria and the rising ululations, Sudanese people also learned an important lesson: to remain more vigilant and wary of the subtleties of power dynamics than usual during times of dramatic political change. Along with exultation, there was a sense of foreboding. A note from my journal illustrates this.

November 30, 2019

First thing yesterday morning and before getting out of bed I switched on my phone. A text message popped on the screen: "Are you alive?" To my great delight, it was from Professor Sultan Barakat, someone with an illustrious career in international politics at the University of York in the United Kingdom and director of the Center for Conflict and Humanitarian Studies in Doha. At his introduction, I had been invited to many events in his native Jordan. On three different occasions I had joined him at the Majilis [gathering] of Prince Al-Hassan Bin Talal of Jordan, founder of West Asia–North Africa Forum (WANA), to discuss issues of conflict and mediation in the region. Barakat's own interests in mediation encompass places ranging from Afghanistan to Somalia, Palestine to Lebanon, Rwanda to Darfur.

Assuring him that I was indeed alive, I then spoke with him by phone. During the conversation he said that he had included me in a panel on Sudan's Peace, to Where? I would join Faruq Abu Bakr, counsel to the president of the African Union, Ali Alhaj of the Sufi tariqa of Sheikh Abdel Baqi Azraq Tayba, and Alamin Daoud of the Popular Eastern Sudan Front. When I arrived at Retaj Al-Rayan Hotel, where the panel was to take place, I remembered the scores of IDPs, refugees, and community activists who had stayed there in 2009. Ten years later, I found myself in a conference room with over fifty people who had arrived from Darfur for the workshop along with a few others from Northern and Eastern Sudan. So familiar was the event I thought to myself "Déjà vu all over again." Ten years later and the topics remained the same. Time had stopped. Darfur was frozen in its pitiless fix. Then came a recounting of concerns that sounded tediously familiar: lack of security, rampant crime, militia attacks, etc. Once the chair opened the floor for discussion, a social worker from the Zamzam IDP stated, "When the officials were asked about the IDPs' return to their villages, they said, 'Let them return, no one is stopping them.' This attitude is irresponsible. There is no security or homes to which to return. Also, no one is talking about the new settlers, people who were encouraged by the overthrown government and its militia to seize land that belonged to the IDPs. They took this land since the start of the war. They will not leave peacefully. These are the problems we are dealing with."

When someone else raised his hand to say, "We want money; money is the answer," a man from the Farmers Union of Aljazeera and Managil Schemes yelled, "What have we become? Money, money, money, stop it now. Beggars, is that who we are now? The government should try to exploit our rich natural resources and find solutions. The Sudan has to come to terms with the idea that begging is not a solution." In attempt to change the subject and defuse the heightening tensions in the room, others talked over each other, uttering all different kinds of opinions: We have to thank Qatar for building the model villages, clinics, and for all the aid they bestowed. But the dignified farmer pressed on with his calls for self-sufficiency and pride in our abilities. Others chimed in to remind themselves and everyone else in the room that Darfuris were critical to the revolution that unseated the dictator as the revolutionary slogan Tasqut Bas *[Just Fall] thundered all over Darfur. Their sacrifices must be acknowledged, and the new government must find remedies as matter of great urgency. Otherwise, who is the Sudan for?*

All the while, I could not help thinking of the words of the great poet and novelist D. H. Lawrence: "We've got a change of government. If you know what I mean. Auntie Maud has come to keep house instead of Aunt Gwendoline."⁶ Or, as the Sudanese saying goes, "exchanging Ahmad for Haj Ahmad," meaning that nothing has changed.

Although it is important to acknowledge that Al-Bashir's witch's brew cannot be eliminated overnight by some magical libation, the interim government that Darfuri people participated in establishing after his overthrow should be responsible for providing a road map of how and when he will be held fully accountable for his crimes, if at all. Al-Bashir and his ilk should not be tried for corruption and suspicious enrichment, as is currently the case, but for the devastation of the entire country. "Don't be too complacent. Don't let the joy of revolutionary change blind you to the realities of politics." So warned long-time human rights activist Sidiq Yousif in an impromptu meeting with revolutionaries in a corner grocery store in Khartoum on the eve of Al-Bashir's fall. Indeed, the most urgent issue facing the Sudanese government today is acting on the ICC warrant against Al-Bashir. Prior to his overthrow, legal scholars took his continued travels as a sign that the court's decision to arrest him was unenforceable. In the meantime, Sudanese humor offered much needed catharsis with such slogans as "Time Will Tell" and "Destination, The Hague" creatively displayed on buses, lorries, and public transport vans. Exiled Sudanese satirist Mohammed Terwis placed a skit on YouTube that mocked Al-Bashir's narrow escape when a Pretoria court ordered his arrest and surrender to the ICC as he attended an African Union conference in South Africa. Playing an old lady called Auntie National Congress and totally garbed in hijab, Terwis pretended to be on a cell phone speaking with Al-Bashir's wife:

> Hi, Widad. Many, many, many congratulations on his safe return. Thank Allah, he brought him back to us safely. Today, Sudanese people ran to the airport. They came from Kosti, El Fashir, Kassala. They came from everywhere [ululations]. By Allah, I tried to advise him before he left. I said to him, "Omar, why are you going to South Africa? What are the Africans good for? What is Zuma good for? Omar, don't lift your leg from here to go." He said, "No, no, I am going. The ICC and Bensouda are under my shoe. I am the lion. I am Africa's lion. I am the lion that jumped, oh, leapt so high." . . . But Omar didn't listen to me! He was always stubborn since he was a boy when he used to jump from one neighbor's *courtyard* [hosh] to the next.[7]

Terwis ends his clip with a doctored photo showing Al-Bashir in a boxing ring holding the ICC prosecutor in a chokehold while the Almushah military band is playing "When the Battle Erupts You Will Find Us Standing Our Ground."

As I write the final lines of *Darfur Allegory*, events continue to unfold in the country. Contrary to his earlier refusal to surrender Al-Bashir to the ICC, Abdel Fattah al-Burhan, the head of the governing Transitional Sovereign Council, more recently acknowledged the right of Darfuri people to seek justice by means of the ICC. The *Sudan Tribune* reported:

> In a meeting held at the Sudanese presidency [seat of government] with a number of displaced people, al-Burhan voiced his support to demands for justice and accountability for the victims of the war in Darfur. "We have not yet taken [made] a decision on the International Criminal Court. But we support our people in any place they choose to try the [those] responsible for Darfur crimes. . . . If we are unable to achieve justice for our people here, they have the right to demand that justice be done wherever they choose. We are bound to achieve their demands," he further stressed. . . . The pro-democracy ruling coalition, Forces for Freedom and Change (FFC), said [it was] willing to hand al-Bashir over to The Hague court. Also, during a visit to Darfur camps last November, Prime Minister Abdallah Hamdok expressed his support for the demand of IDPs who received him with banners calling [on the government to] hand over al-Bashir to the ICC. Fatou Bensouda, Prosecutor of the International Criminal Court (ICC), voiced confidence that the political change in Sudan after the collapse of the former regime will facilitate al-Bashir handover to the war crimes court. "Today, emboldened by events over the last six months, I repeat those messages with greater confidence that

Sudan will honour its commitments to deliver justice for the victims in the Darfur situation," said Bensouda in a briefing to the UN Security Council on Wednesday.[8]

I am sure that this article reports a positive development. It marks a resurgence of hope and is a sign of a capacity to make a clean break with the complacency and impunity of the past. Nevertheless, some questions remain. Will calls for justice in The Hague turn into a material reality? Will local courts try Al-Bashir for his crimes against humanity, or will we stay stuck in the status quo, reflecting the words penned on the back of a public transport minivan, "Only time will tell"? In the meantime, from a region that has experienced an apocalypse of cyclical violence, we stand to learn just how enormous are its inescapable sorrows.

It is one of the many ironies of Sudanese politics that while violence in Darfur continues uninterrupted, Mohamad Hamdan Daglo (Hemeti), whom many Darfuris blame for Janjaweed atrocities, is currently a powerful member of the Transitional Sovereign Council and as such was among those who approved the appointment of Omer G. Ismail as the new minister of foreign affairs. Ismail, as it turns out, is a Darfuri who lived in exile in Washington, DC, for decades and whose voice dissenting to Darfur's genocide reverberated loudly in the chambers of the United States Congress, the United Nations Security Council, and the United States Holocaust Memorial Museum. The blustery wind of Sudanese politics pushes us to ponder if race alone can ever be sufficient to capture the story of the violent Janjaweed attack that IDPs in El Geneina endured in January 2020. Class matters.

Acknowledgments

This ethnography, more than a decade in the making, would have never seen the light without the unwavering support of numerous individuals and institutions. In the Sudan, Qatar, Israel, and the United States, I had been extremely fortunate to receive such support from Somaya Kardash, Isam Abdel Hafiz, Faisal Hadra, the Sons of Greater Darfur League in Doha, Taj Haroun of B'nai Darfur, Abdel Rahman Dosa, Fahima Hashim, Nadia Taha, Niemat Ahmadi, Sabika Shaaban, and Omer G. Ismail. It goes without saying that I owe my greatest debt to the women and men of Darfur, those displaced and in exile whose voices I have attempted to amplify in this ethnography. Their enthusiasm and hospitality propelled me forward in times when I most needed encouragement.

I have also received support and encouragement from numerous friends, including Abdel Rahman Dosa, Grant Farred, Salah Hassan, and Tukufu Zuberi. Research at RAD in Doha would not have been possible without the support of Mohsin Marzuq and Waffaa Bin Haj Omar at the Arab Democracy Foundation. In addition, for many years my mother, Fatima Mahgoub Osman, gathered relevant materials and clipped thousands of newspaper articles on Darfur for me, all of which proved to be valuable to this work.

Over the years of my research, I received generous support from Georgetown University. Grants from SFSQ allowed me to carry out several rounds of ethnographic work; Valbona Zenku provided invaluable administrative support for these grants. Funding from the university's Gender Justice Initiative was critical to the work I carried out in Baltimore; Lisa Krim and Melyssa Hafaf were instrumental in facilitating this aspect of my research. The Center for International and Regional Studies at Georgetown-Qatar offered me a fellowship that freed much-needed time to develop the manuscript. I also am grateful to Dartmouth College's anthropology department for granting me a senior fellowship. The exchanges and engagements I experienced there have been invaluable for both my research and teaching. I am grateful to Dartmouth professor Dale Eickelman for his mentorship and support during my time there and beyond.

A grant from the Doyle Diversity Initiative of Georgetown's Berkeley Center sponsored my seminar, Anthropology of War and Peacemaking in Darfur, and I am appreciative of my students' active participation and extraordinary energy. Luke Brown served ably as graduate assistant in this course. My thanks also to students at SFSQ, Georgetown University DC, and Dartmouth, including Saoud Alahmad, Sara Al-Mesnad, Aljohara Althani, Osman Camara, Olivia Evans, and Meredith Foryth. I also benefited from my excellent research assistants, Hazim Ali, Mohammed Alsoudairi, Mohammed K. Harb, Taj Haroun, and Lauren Johnson.

To Alex de Waal at Tufts University I owe a great debt for inviting me to speak about Darfur to his graduate seminar at the Fletcher School of Law and Diplomacy. Likewise, I wish to thank Doumani Beshara and Keisha Kahn Perry for including me in the Brown University International Advanced Research Institute (BIARI), where I was able to engage with colleagues working on issues of war and peace. Other colleagues invited me to give lectures and presentations at Addis Ababa University, University of Pennsylvania, Harvard University, Yale Law School, Georgetown University Law School, Brown University, and University of the West Indies, Cave Hill in Barbados.

I am appreciative of Ambassador Swanee Hunt for including me for many years in the Women Waging Peace Network of the Inclusive Security initiative. While I was a fellow at Harvard University's Kennedy School of Government, Ambassador Hunt invited my participation in several workshops on Darfur and facilitated our Sudanese delegation's meeting with Rep. Eddie Bernice Johnson (D. Texas) of the Congressional Black Caucus and other parties interested in the ongoing crisis. She also facilitated my presentations at the United Nations Commission for Women. Within Inclusive Security, Carla Koppell's sharp perspectives and those of our delegates expanded considerably my views on civil society efforts to address gender-based violence in conflict areas around the world. I am thankful for the excellent comments and questions I received at these events. For an invitation to a civil society forum in Cairo, I would like to thank Amira Kheir for giving me a rare opportunity to listen to firsthand accounts of activists and survivors. Last but not least, I am thankful to Professor Sultan Barakat and Prince Hassan Bin Talal for including me in the stimulating WANA: West Asia North African Forum in two consecutive years in Amman, Jordan, where I interacted with scores of scholars and activists working on political conflicts in these regions.

At the University of Chicago Press I had the honor of working with Priya Nelson, whose brilliance helped me through much of the publication process; and with Kyle Wagner, who brought this work to fruition. I must also acknowledge David Brent, who supported my book prospectus and continued his support through his retirement. Also at the University of Chicago Press, I am grateful to Tristan Bates, Dylan Joseph Montanari, and Michael Koplow for their careful work with my manuscript. I am thankful also for the close read and substantive comments offered by anonymous readers of both the proposal and the manuscript. Finally, I am forever grateful to Linda Shopes, whose superb editing of the manuscript prior to submission and discussions over the years about Darfur were the absolute best.

Part of the prelude previously appeared in "Cartographies of Mutuality: Lessons from Darfur," in *Mutuality: Anthropologies Changing Terms of Engagement*, edited by Roger Sanjek (Philadelphia: University of Pennsylvania Press, 2014), 130–151. Parts of chapter 2 previously appeared in "Circuits of Knowledge Production," in *Networks of Knowledge Production in Sudan: Identities, Mobilities, and Technologies*, edited by Sondra Hale and Gada Kadoda (Lanham, MD: Lexington, 2016), 79–97; and in "Humanitarianism," in *Critical Terms for the Study of Africa*, edited by Gaurav Desai and Adeline Masquelier (Chicago: University of Chicago Press, 2018), 179–188. Part of chapter 3 previously appeared in "Debating Darfur in the World," *Annals of the American Academy of Political and Social Science* 632, no. 1 (2010): 67–85. Parts of chapter 4 previously appeared in "A Darfur-Doha Encounter: A Sufi Mystic Whirling Trance for Peace," *Black Renaissance/Noire* 11, no. 1 (2011): 73–89. I thank the publishers for permission to use these materials.

Notes

Prelude

1. Michael T. Taussig, *Shamanism, Colonialism, and the Wild Man: A Study in Terror and Healing* (Chicago: University of Chicago Press, 1987), 4.

2. Rex Seán O'Fahey, "Umm Kwakiyya or the Damnation of Darfur," *African Affairs* 106, no. 425 (October 2007): 709.

3. Andrew Edgar and Peter Sedgwick, *Key Concepts in Cultural Theory* (London: Routledge, 2005), 10.

4. James Clifford, "On Ethnographic Allegory," in *Writing Culture: The Poetics and Politics of Ethnography*, ed. James Clifford and George E. Marcus (Berkeley: University of California Press, 1986): 100.

5. Ibid, 120–121.

6. Edgar and Sedgwick, *Key Concepts*, 13.

7. O'Fahey, "Umm Kwakiyya," 709.

8. Chimamanda Ngozi Adichie, "The Danger of a Single Story," TED Ideas Worth Spreading, 2009, https://www.ted.com/talks/chimamanda_adichie_the_danger_of_a_single_story/transcript?language=en.

9. Rex Seán O'Fahey, *The Darfur Sultanate: A History* (New York: Columbia University Press, 2008.)

10. For detailed analysis of framing and context, see Mieke Bal and Sherry Marx-MacDonald, *Travelling Concepts in the Humanities: A Rough Guide* (Toronto: University of Toronto Press, 2002).

11. Achille Mbembe, *On the Postcolony* (Oakland: University of California Press, 2001), 102.

12. Aimé Césaire, *Discourse on Colonialism* (New York: New York University Press, 2001); Frantz Fanon, *Black Skin, White Masks* (New York: Grove Press, 2008); Simon Gikandi, "Cultural Translation and the African Self: A (Post)colonial Cast Study," *Interventions* 3, no. 3 (2001): 355–375; Abdel Khaliq Mahgoub, *Marxism and the Quandaries of the Sudanese Revolution*, 2nd ed. (Azza Books: Khartoum, 1972); Mbembe, *On the Postcolony*; Albert Memmi, *The Colonizer and the Colonized* (London: Routledge, 2013); V. Y. Mudimbe, *The Invention of Africa: Gnosis, Philosophy, and the Order of Knowledge* (Bloomington: Indiana University Press, 1988); Derek Walcott, *Omeros* (New York: Farrar, Straus and Giroux, 2014); and Tukufu Zuberi and Eduardo

Bonilla-Silva, eds., *White Logic, White Methods: Racism and Methodology* (Lanham, MD: Rowman & Littlefield, 2008).

13. Gikandi, "Cultural Translation," 355.

14. Veena Das, *Life and Words: Violence and the Descent into the Ordinary* (Oakland: University of California Press, 2006), 8.

15. "Shingles," Mayo Clinic, https://www.mayoclinic.org/diseases-conditions/shingles/symptoms-causes/syc-20353054, accessed June 2018.

16. Enrique Dussel, *Twenty Theses in Politics* (Durham, NC: Duke University Press, 2008), 30.

17. "Author's International Literary Award 'for All Sudanese,'" *Dabanga* (April 20, 2017), https://www.dabangasudan.org/en/all-news/article/author-s-international-literary-award-for-all-sudanese.

18. From my field journal.

19. Oscar Handlin, *The Uprooted: The Epic Story of the Great Migrations That Made the American People* (Philadelphia: University of Pennsylvania Press, 2002), 269–270.

20. Martin F. Manalansan IV, *Global Divas: Filipino Gay Men in the Diaspora* (Durham, NC: Duke University Press, 2003), 48, 190.

21. Khachig Tölölyan, "Rethinking Diaspora(s): Stateless Power in the Transnational Moment," *Diaspora: A Journal of Transnational Studies* 5, no. 1 (1996): 3.

22. Edward W. Said, "Representing the Colonized: Anthropology's Interlocutors," *Critical Inquiry* 15, no. 2 (1989): 205–225.

23. Nancy Armstrong and Leonard Tennenhouse, eds., *The Violence of Representation (Routledge Revivals): Literature and the History of Violence* (London: Routledge, 2014). The book does not address Darfur specifically; rather the essays consider how language, and specifically writing, has been an important tool of domination, and hence violence.

24. Mwenda Ntarangwi, *Reversed Gaze: An African Ethnography of American Anthropology* (Champaign: University of Illinois Press, 2010), 13.

25. Roger Sanjek, ed., *Mutuality: Anthropology's Changing Terms of Engagement* (Philadelphia: University of Pennsylvania Press, 2014).

26. Stanley Diamond, "A Revolutionary Discipline," *Current Anthropology* 5, no. 5 (1964): 433.

27. See, for example, Michelle M. Wright, *Becoming Black: Creating Identity in the African Diaspora* (Durham, NC: Duke University Press, 2004).

28. Taussig, *Shamanism*, 7.

29. Michael Lambek, *Island in the Stream* (Toronto: University of Toronto Press, 2018), 11–12.

30. Philip Roth, *The Human Stain* (New York: Vintage, 2001), 44.

Chapter One

1. George E. Marcus, *Ethnography through Thick and Thin* (Princeton, NJ: Princeton University Press, 1998), 6.

2. James Clifford, "On Ethnographic Allegory," in *Writing culture: The Poetics and Politics of Ethnography* (Berkeley: University of California Press, 1986), 99.

3. Akhil Gupta and James Ferguson, eds., *Anthropological Locations: Boundaries and Grounds of a Field Science* (Berkeley: University of California Press, 1997), 5.

4. Alex de Waal, "Counter-Insurgency on the Cheap," *London Review of Books*, August 2004, 25–27.

5. See Marilyn Strathern et al., "Out of Context: The Persuasive Fictions of Anthropology [and comments and reply]," *Current Anthropology* 28, no. 3 (1987): 251.

6. G. D. Lampen, "History of Darfur," *Sudan Notes and Records* 31, no. 2 (1950): 177.

7. Yusuf Fadl Hasan, *Sudan in Africa: Studies Presented to the First International Conference Sponsored by The Sudan Research Unit, 7–12 February 1968* (Khartoum: Khartoum University Press, 1971).

8. Rex Seán O'Fahey, *The Darfur Sultanate: A History* (London: Hurst, 2008), 3.

9. Ibid.

10. Ali A. Mazrui, "The Multiple Marginality of the Sudan," in *Sudan in Africa*, ed. Yousif Fadl (Khartoum: University of Khartoum Press, 1971), 242.

11. Sudan Special Collections, Palace Green Library, Durham University, UK, # GB-0033/ SAD.

12. O'Fahey, *The Darfur Sultanate*, 13.

13. Mohamed Sulieman, "Ethnicity from Perception to Cause of Violent Conflicts: The Case of the Fur and Nuba Conflicts in Western Sudan" (London: Institute for African Alternatives, 1997), http://new.ifaanet.org/?p=451.

14. G. D. Lampen, "The Baggara Tribes of Darfur," *Sudan Notes and Records* 16, no. 2 (1933): 97.

15. Friedrich Ratzel, quoted in Peter Probst, "Betwixt and Between: African Studies in Germany," in *The Study of Africa: Global and Transnational Engagements*, ed. Paul Tiyambe Zeleza (Dakar: CODESROA, 2007), 161.

16. Robin E. W. Thelwall, "A Linguistic Survey in El Fasher Secondary School," *Sudan Notes and Records* 52 (1971): 55.

17. Sharif Harir, "'Arab Belt' versus 'African Belt': Ethno-political Conflict in Dar Fur and the Regional Cultural Factors," in *Sudan: Shortcut to Decay* (Uppsala: Nordiska Africainstitutet, 1994), 144–185.

18. Fredrik Barth, *Ethnic Groups and Boundaries: The Social Organization of Culture Difference* (Long Grove, IL: Waveland Press, 1998).

19. Douglas Robinson, *Displacement and the Somatics of Postcolonial Culture* (Columbus: Ohio State University Press, 2013).

20. The Fragile States Index, http://fundforpeace.org/fsi/.

21. John Ryle, "The Disaster in Darfur," *New York Review of Books* 51, no. 13 (2004): 55–59.

22. Antonio Cassese, Mohamed Fayek, Hina Jilani, Dumisa Ntsebeza, and Therese Striggner-Scott, "Report of the International Commission of Inquiry on Darfur to the United Nations Secretary-General," Pursuant to Security Council Resolution 1564 (2005), 4.

23. For details see International Criminal Court, Case Information ICC-02/0501/09.

24. European-Sudanese Public Affairs Council, "The Darfur Rebels, War Crimes and Human Rights Abuses," 2005, http://www.espac.org/darfur/darfur-rebels-war-crime.asp.

25. Mahmood Mamdani, *Saviors and Survivors: Darfur, Politics, and the War on Terror* (New York: Doubleday, 2010). Mamdani took up the problem of calculating the number and causes of deaths in Mahmood Mamdani and John Prendergast, "The Darfur Debate," Columbia University, April 14, 2009, youtube.com/watch?v=yGOpfH, accessed September 1, 2009.

26. A. B. Theobald, "Dārfūr and Its Neighbours under Sultān'alī Dinār, 1898–1916," *Sudan Notes and Records* 40 (1959): 114.

27. Martin W. Daly, *Darfur's Sorrow: A History of Destruction and Genocide* (Cambridge: Cambridge University Press, 2007), 125–126.

28. Jérôme Tubiana, Victor Tanner, and Musa Adam Abdul-Jalil, *Traditional Authorities' Peacemaking Role in Darfur*, Peaceworks no. 83 (Washington, DC: United States Institute of Peace, 2012), https://www.files.ethz.ch/isn/155469/PW83.pdf, 55–56.

29. Nicholas Thomas, *Colonialism's Culture: Anthropology, Travel, and Government* (Princeton, NJ: Princeton University Press, 1994), 105.

30. Sudan Jem, *The Black Book: Imbalance of Power and Wealth in Sudan*, trans. Abdullahi Osman El-Tom (2000), available online at http://www.sudanjem.com/sudan-alt/english/books/blackbook_part1/book_part1.asp.htm.

31. It was subsequently revealed that among the authors of the book was the slain leader of one of the rebel movements in Darfur, Khalil Ibrahim (1957–2011), a Zaghawa Kobbe who had led the Justice and Equality Movement (JEM), which along with the Sudanese Liberation Movement (SLM) was responsible for instigating the Darfuri rebellion in 2003. It is worth noting that Ibrahim had been one of the most decorated jihadist members of Al-Bashir's regime, called al-Dabbaibeen (tankers) in South Sudan, where he had waged war against innocent civilians and massacred thousands. He had held a ministerial post and enjoyed handsome dividends from a government he then went on to rebel against. This history as well as his short-lived memory of his own role as genocidaire against people he deemed infidel cast doubt on his political project.

32. See, for example, Abdel Khaliq Mahgoub, *Marxism and the Quandaries of the Sudanese Revolution* (Khartoum: Azza Press, 1969).

33. Sulieman Hamid, *Darfur: The Definitive Answer* (in Arabic) (Khartoum: Elmeidan Book, 2004), 10, translation mine.

34. Ibid, 21.

35. "Sudan's Capital Gripped in Nuptials of Chad's Deby, Daughter of Darfur Militia Leader," *Sudan Tribune*, January 20, 2012, http://www.sudantribune.com/Sudan-s-capital-gripped-in,41358, accessed March 22, 2018.

36. Julie Flint and Alex de Waal, *Darfur: A New History of a Long War* (London: Zed Books Ltd., 2008). It is perhaps worth noting that the marriage of Hilal's daughter to Deby proved to many how shifting alliances are shaping the politics of the region. Darfur is no stranger to marriage as a means of mediating conflict.

37. Anthony John Arkell, "Rock Pictures in Northern Darfur," *Sudan Notes and Records* 20, no. 2 (1937): 281–287.

Chapter Two

1. Donna Haraway, "Situated Knowledges: The Science Question in Feminism and the Privilege of Partial Perspective," *Feminist Studies* 14, no. 3 (1988): 577.

2. Rex Seán O'Fahey, *The Darfur Sultanate: A History* (London: Hurst, 2008).

3. H. G. Balfour-Paul, *History and Antiquities of Darfur* (Khartoum: Sudan Antiquities Service, 1955).

4. Talal Asad, ed., *Anthropology and The Colonial Encounter* (London: Ithaca Press, 1973); Achille Mbembe, *On the Postcolony* (Oakland: University of California Press, 2001); and V. Y. Mudimbe, *The Invention of Africa* (Bloomington: Indiana University Press, 1988). See also Barnard Magubane and James C. Faris, "On the political relevance of anthropology," *Dialectical Anthropology* 9, no. 1 (1985): 91–104.

5. James Faris, *Navajo and Photography: A Critical History of Representation of an American People* (Albuquerque: University of New Mexico Press, 1996), 13.

6. J. A. Gillan, "Darfur, 1916," *Sudan Notes and Records* 22, no. 1 (1939): 25.

7. William George Browne, *Travels in Africa, Egypt, and Syria, from the Year 1792 to 1798* (London: T. Cadel and W. Davies, 1806).

8. Gustav Nachtigal, *Sahara and Sudan*, trans. Allan G. B. Fisher and Humphrey J. Fisher, vol. 2: *Kawar, Bornu, Kanem, Borku, Enned* (Berkeley: University of California Press, 1971), 334.

9. W. B. K. Shaw, "Darb El Arba'in: The Forty Days' Road," *Sudan Notes and Records* 12, no. 1 (1929): 64.

10. Browne, *Travels in Africa*, 218.

11. Ibid., 226–227.

12. Ibid., 218.

13. Ibid., 225.

14. Ibid., 210.

15. Ibid.

16. Ibid., 202–203. This representation of a manumitted slave woman as owning property and habituated to "a luxurious life" belies the reality of slavery. It is not the only distortion in Browne's account.

17. "Caffre," a variant of "kaffir," is a derogatory term typically used by colonists to refer to Africans. In this context, however, it refers to Browne as a non-Muslim.

18. Browne, *Travels in Africa*, 227–229.

19. Ibid.

20. Ibid., 229.

21. Ibid., 218.

22. James Faris, "Pax Britannica and the Sudan: SF Nadel," in *Anthropology and the Colonial Encounter*, ed. Talal Asad (London: Ithaca Press, 1975).

23. Johannes Fabian, *Out of Our Minds: Reason and Madness in the Exploration of Central Africa* (Berkeley: University of California Press, 2000), 4.

24. Muḥammad Ibn-'Umar al-Tūnisī, *Tashidh al-adhan fi sirat bilad al-Arab wa el-Sudan* (in Arabic), ed. Mahmoud Asakir and Mustafa Musaad (Cairo: Al Dar Al Masriya Lil-Ta'lif wal-Tarjama, 1965); first published in French as Mohammed Ebn-Omar El-Tounsy, *Voyage au Darfour* (Paris: B. Duprat, 1845).

25. These genealogical charts, created by the travelers, were later used in colonial accounts of the sultanate's rule.

26. As is common in polygamous marriages, the senior wife of the sultan is the most respected. Al-Tūnisī mentioned that she, the senior wife, was usually referred to as Kinana, a woman who was opinionated, trustworthy, and wise.

27. Al-Tūnisī, *Tashidh*, 159.

28. Ibid., 161.

29. Ibid., 65.

30. Ibid., 41.

31. Ibid., 61.

32. Ibid., 165.

33. Ibid.

34. Gustav Nachtigal, *Sahara and Sudan*, trans. Allan G. B. Fisher and Humphrey J. Fisher, vol. 4: *Wadai and Darfur* (Berkeley: University of California Press, 1971).

35. Ibid., 232.

36. Ibid., 346–347.

37. Ibid., 274.

38. Ibid., 349.

39. Nachtigal is referring here to Darfuris' continuing skirmishes with the Egyptian government and the Turks.

40. Declaration of Shahada from memory as evidence of Muslim faith. The full Declaration of Shahada (Islamic faith) is "There is no Allah but Allah, and Muhammad is His Prophet." By prompting Nachtigal with the first part of this statement, people attempted to get him to complete it as evidence of his understanding of the Muslim faith. Apparently he refused to do so.

41. Nachtigal, *Sahara and Sudan*, vol. 4, 268–269.

42. Ibid., 255.

43. See, for example, O'Fahey, *The Darfur Sultanate*.

44. Nachtigal, *Sahara and Sudan*, vol. 4, 315.

45. Ibid., 316.

46. Charles T. Wilson and Robert William Felkin, *Uganda and the Egyptian Soudan*, 2 vols. (London: Sampson Low, Marston, Searle & Rivington, 1882).

47. For a critique of Felkin's account, see Jörg Adelberger, "Aspects of Fur Culture or Felkin Revisited: Arkell's Discussion of a 19th Century Traveler's Report with Six Fur Prisoners at al-Fashir," *Sudanic Africa* 2 (1991): 53–77.

48. Robert W. Felkin, "Notes on the For Tribe of Central Africa," *Proceedings of the Royal Society of Edinburgh, 1884–85* (Edinburgh: Royal Society of Edinburgh, 1884–1885), fig. 2.3, 206–207. According to Felkin, the boy on whom he based these measurements had been rescued from slavery by General Charles Gordon in 1879 and was "the only representative of his tribe who, as far as I know, has reached Europe" (205).

49. Felkin, "Notes on the For Tribe of Central Africa," 224.

50. Ibid., 207–208, 210.

51. Ibid., 208.

52. Ibid., 232.

53. Marvin Harris, *Culture, Man, and Nature* (New York: Thomas Crowell, 1971), 175, 89.

54. Ibid., 89.

55. Fabian, *Out of Our Minds*.

56. Harold Alfred MacMichael, *A History of the Arabs in the Sudan: And Some Account of the People Who Preceded Them and of the Tribes Inhabiting Dárfūr*, vol. 2 (Cambridge: Cambridge University Press, 2011).

57. Asad, introduction to *Anthropology and the Colonial Encounter*, 17.

58. Nicholas B. Dirks, *Castes of Mind: Colonialism and the Making of Modern India* (Princeton: Princeton University Press, 2001), 107.

59. Anthony Hamilton Millard Kirk-Greene, "The Sudan Political Service: A Profile in the Sociology of Imperialism," *International Journal of African Historical Studies* 15, no. 1 (1982): 21–22.

60. Sir R. Wingate, "Introduction," *Sudan Notes and Records* 1, no. 1 (1918): 1. Wingate (1861–1953) was governor general of Egypt and the Sudan.

61. George W. Stocking, ed., *Colonial Situations: Essays on the Contextualization of Ethnographic Knowledge* (Madison: University of Wisconsin Press, 1991).

62. A. C. Beaton, "The Fur," *Sudan Notes and Records* 29, no. 1 (1948): 1.

63. Sudan Special Collections, Palace Green Library, Durham University, UK, SAD/Folio (759/11/3).

64. Beaton, "The Fur," 18.

65. Ibid.

66. Gillan's archive, Sudan Special Collections, Palace Green Library, Durham University (SAD #582/8/53-4).

67. Rogaia Mustafa Abusharaf, "'We Have Supped So Deep in Horrors': Understanding Colonialist Emotionality and British Responses to Female Circumcision in Northern Sudan," *History and Anthropology* 17, no. 3 (2006): 209–228.

68. John Slight, "British Perceptions and Responses to Sultan Ali Dinar of Darfur, 1915–16," *Journal of Imperial and Commonwealth History* 38, no. 2 (2010): 242.

69. Beaton, "The Fur," 7.

70. Slight, "British Perceptions and Responses to Sultan Ali Dinar," 241.

71. J. E. H. Boustead, "The Youth and Last Days of Sultan Ali Dinar: A Fur View," *Sudan Notes and Records* 22, no. 1 (1939): 150.

72. Archives of photos and captions: Sudan Special Collections, Palace Green Library, Durham University, SAD.A81/4; A4/13; A4/19; 12/3/21; 12/3/43; 12/3/48; A81/103.

73. Gillan, "Darfur, 1916," 21.

74. Ibid., 23.

75. Beaton, "The Fur," 5.

76. British justification for annexing Darfur of course extended beyond Ali Dinar's presumed treachery; for a discussion of other factors, see O'Fahey, *The Darfur Sultanate*, and Martin Daly, *Darfur's Sorrow: A History of Destruction and Genocide* (Cambridge: Cambridge University Press, 2007).

77. I reviewed his collection at the Sudan Special Collections, Palace Green Library, Durham University (SAD GB-0033).

78. In the School of Oriental and African Studies Archives, where the majority of Arkell's papers are housed, I reviewed rare manuscripts, notes, letters, reports and administrative papers (MS 210522).

79. David Zeitlyn, "Anthropology in and of the Archives: Possible Futures and Contingent Pasts. Archives as Anthropological Surrogates," *Annual Review of Anthropology* 41 (2012): 461–480. Zeitlyn writes: "Derrida and Foucault provide key starting points to understanding archives. They see archives as hegemonic, characterizing ways of thought, modes of colonization, and control of citizens. However, they also make clear that archives can be read subversively. With patience, counter-readings allow the excavation of the voices (sometimes names) of subaltern and otherwise suppressed others from the archive" (461).

80. Bernard S. Cohen, *Colonialism and Its Forms of Knowledge: The British in India* (Princeton, NJ: Princeton University Press, 1996), 8.

81. Anthony J. Arkell, "Throwing Sticks and Throwing Knives in Darfur," *Sudan Notes and Records* 22 (1939): 251–267.

82. Anthony J. Arkell, "Darfur Antiquities," *Sudan Notes and Records* 19, no. 2 (1936): 301–311. See also Anthony J. Arkell, "The Medieval History of Darfur in Its Relation to Other Cultures and to the Nilotic Sudan," *Sudan Notes and Records* 40 (1959): 44–47.

83. See descriptions of routes connecting the region to the outside world in A. J. Arkell, "The Southern Route to Kufra," *Sudan Notes and Records* 5 (1922): 130–136.

84. Arkell, "The Medieval History of Darfur in Its Relation to Other Cultures," 44.

85. A. P. G. Michelmore, "A Possible Relic of Christianity in Darfur," *Sudan Notes and Records* 15, no. 2 (1932): 272–273. See also C. G. Dupuis, "Traces of Christianity in Northern Darfur," *Sudan Notes and Records* 12, no. 1 (1929): 112–113.

86. See, for example, Basil Spence, "Darfur Province: Stone Worship among the Zaghawa," *Sudan Notes and Records* 1, no. 3 (1918): 197–199. Also Michelmore, "A Possible Relic of Christianity in Darfur." Both authors provided historical and archaeological evidence of Christianity and paganism in Darfur through the prism of the ritual practice of drawing a cross on the foreheads of newborns for blessing and protection from harm. They also noted that stone worship among Muslim Zaghawa was a practice held in veneration and awe.

87. Nachtigal, *Sahara and Sudan*, vol. 4, 349.

88. El-Sayed El-Aswad, *Religion and Folk Cosmology: Scenarios of the Visible and Invisible in Rural Egypt* (Westport, CT: Praeger, 2002), 154–155.

89. A. J. Arkell, "Māni Magic in Northern Darfur," *Sudan Notes and Records* 19, no. 2 (1936): 317–319.

90. A. J. Arkell, "The Double Spiral Amulet," *Sudan Notes and Records* 20, no. 1 (1937): 151–155.

91. Ibid.

92. Before the publication of Arkell's works in *SNR* he wrote several drafts as evidenced in his archival notes on steel and tinder in Darfur. An example of a "steel" (Plate XVIII, Fig. AI) was made by Fur at Numo near Kebkabiya in Sudan, while another was (Plate XVIII, Fig. BI) picked up in Northern Darfur among the ruins of Uri town. According to Arkell, Uri town was originally the capital of the Kanem governor of Darfur in the thirteenth century and was part of the Kanem Empire, founded by Berbers from North Africa. Based on this, Arkell predicts that the Berbers, under the empire of Kanem, introduced steel and tinder to the Sudan. Other examples of steel have been discovered, one made in Owra in Dar Masalit while another was obtained near Ain Farah in the Furnun hills of Northern Darfur. Arkell concludes his account of steel and tinder in Darfur in 1936 by explaining the method by which skilled people used steel to make fire and how only a few iron workers still know how to make good "steel" in 1935 Darfur.

93. A. J. Arkell, "Darfur Antiquities II: Tōra Palaces in Turra at the North End of Jebel Marra," *Sudan Notes and Records* 20, no. 1 (1937): 91–105.

94. Michael Welbourne, *Knowledge* (Montreal: McGill-Queens University Press, 2001), 69.

95. Musa Adam Abdul-Jalil, "The Dynamics of Ethnic Identification and Ethnic Group Relations among the People of 'Dor,' Northern Darfur, Sudan," PhD diss., Edinburgh University, 1979.

96. Sharif Abdalla Harir, "The Politics of 'Numbers': Mediatory Leadership and the Political Process among the Beri 'Zaghawa' of the Sudan," PhD diss., Department of Social Anthropology, University of Bergen, 1987.

97. Michael Barnett, *Empire of Humanity: A History of Humanitarianism* (Ithaca: Cornell University Press, 2011).

98. Author's interview with the aid worker, Khartoum.

99. Jenevieve Lloyd, "Knowledge," in *New Keywords: A Revised Vocabulary of Culture and Society, eds.* Tony Bennett, Lawrence Grossberg, and Meaghan Morris (Malden, MA: Blackwell, 2005), 195–197.

100. http://www.gamesforchange.org/game/darfur-is-dying/, accessed March 4, 2019.

101. Ibid.

102. Mahmood Mamdani, *Saviors and Survivors: Darfur, Politics, and the War on Terror* (New York: Pantheon, 2009).

103. 24 Hours for Darfur, "Darfurian Voices: Documenting Darfurian Refugees' Views on Issues of Peace, Justice, and Reconciliation," DarfurianVoices.org, https://static1.squarespace.com/static/52920ed5e4b04a0741daa89c/t/529224ffe4b049dd0ca09a3f/1385309439460/Darfurian+Voices+-+Report+-+English.pdf, accessed April 8, 2018. The report is published in collaboration with the Darfur People's Association of New York, the Darfur Rehabilitation Project, the Genocide Intervention Network, and the Lowenstein Human Rights Project at Yale Law School.

104. "Brooklyn Darfurians," https://www.youtube.com/watch?v=zJjIC2Zku7A, posted October 2007, accessed August 10, 2017.

105. https://www.facebook.com/groups/shabab.darfur/permalink/2035541733163933/.

106. An excellent account of online digital activism, Victoria Bernal's *Nation as Network* (Chicago: University of Chicago Press, 2014), demonstrates the ways in which social media platforms often serve to reproduce the social and political relations that define everyday life within the nation.

107. V. Y. Mudimbe, *The Invention of Africa: Gnosis, Philosophy, and the Order of Knowledge* (Bloomington: Indiana University Press, 1988), x.

108. Haraway, "Situated Knowledges," 577.

Chapter Three

1. Parts of this chapter appeared in Rogaia Mustafa Abusharaf, "Debating Darfur in the World," *Annals of the American Academy of Political and Social Science* 632, no. 1 (2010): 67–85.

2. Stuart Hall, *The Fateful Triangle* (Cambridge: Harvard University Press, 2017), 21.

3. The belief in bad omens featured elsewhere in the Sudan to include the crow, the pygmy ostrich, and the bustard. For details, see J. D. Macdonald, "Problematical Sudan Birds," *Sudan Notes and Records* 26, no. 2 (1945): 301–304.

4. https://www.icc-cpi.int/darfur/albashir, accessed August 13, 2018.

5. https://archive.dohadebates.com/debates/player172b.html?d=45.

6. President Al-Bashir to *Al-Sahafa* daily newspaper, August 6, 2004, 1.

7. Al-Bashir was indicted on March 4, 2009; on March 5, Sudan TV, the official government station, began a series, *What They Are Saying about the So-Called ICC* [in Arabic], lasting for about six months. Al-Bashir's defiant behavior described here was broadcast during this series.

8. Emboldened to reveal their identities, Sudanese bloggers enumerated the members of the alliance: Supporters of Salafi Jihadists, Shahada Seekers, Banner of Martyr Shahid Abel-Fatah, League of Darfur Lions, and Nosoor Al-Bashir (Al-Bashir's Eagles).

9. Here and throughout the book, quotations in italics are drawn from my field notes.

10. Edward S. Herman and Noam Chomsky, *Manufacturing Consent: The Political Economy of the Mass Media* (New York: Random House, 2010).

11. Ibrahim Hamdi, "Sudan's Bashir Vows to Try Darfur War Criminals," Reuters, April 7, 2009, www.reuters.com/article/idUSL718741.

12. From the Sudan TV series "What They Are Saying about the So-Called ICC [in Arabic]."

13. Abdal Aziz Baraka Sakin, *The Messiah of Darfur* (in Arabic), https://www.arabischesbuch.de/index.php?title=Abdal+Aziz+Baraka+Sakin+Masih+Darfur&art_no=bs15&language=en, 20–21, translation mine.

14. In Arabic the addition of the "al" serves to convey a specific meaning, although there is a debate about the correct translation, as *jinn* is neutral, and it can mean good or bad, unlike the English translation of *jinn* as the devil, Satan.

15. Mohamad Badawi, *The Harvest of Gunpowder* (in Arabic) (Cairo: Awaraq, 2015), 11, translation mine.

16. Shams E. Idris, *The Janjaweed Legend: An Excuse for Foreign Intervention and Destruction of Darfur Society* (in Arabic) (Khartoum: Al-makttabba Al-Wattania, 2007), 28, translation mine.

17. Ibid.

18. "Darfur Soldier: 'We Were Ordered to Kill and Rape,'" https://www.youtube.com/watch?v=FtSTFIOEAoc.

19. https://www.youtube.com/watch?v=-TpFozupSWo.

20. Rogaia Mustafa Abusharaf, "Cartographies of Mutuality: Lessons from Darfur," in *Mutuality: Anthropologies Changing Terms of Engagement*, ed. Roger Sanjek (Philadelphia: University of Pennsylvania Press, 2014), 130–151.

21. Sulieman Hamid, Darfur: The Definitive Answer (in Arabic) (Khartoum: El-Meidan Book, 2004). The narrative is an excerpt highlighting a particular form of knowledge counteracting genocide deniability.

22. Hamid, *Darfur*, 20, translation mine.

23. Ali A. Mazrui, "The Blood of Experience: The Failed State and Political Collapse in Africa," *World Policy Journal* 12, no. 1 (1995): 28–34.

24. Also see Ali A. Mazrui, "The Resurrection of the Warrior Tradition in African Political Culture," *Journal of Modern African Studies* 13, no. 1 (1975): 67–84.

25. These leaders came from very diverse backgrounds, including people from both so-called "Arab tribes" and "African tribes," with Massalit, Fur, Rezeigat, Taayisha, Zaghawa, Berti, Habanyia, Bani Halba, Tunjur, Dajou, Miseiryia, Ma'alyia, Ghimiz, Tama, Beni Hussein, Ziyadia, Fallata, Burno, Maidoub, Mahameed, Mahryia, Donga, Al-Feirougi, Bani Jarar, E'raighat, E'taifat, Jawam'a, Al-maima, Al-Shatyia, Owlad Rashid, Al-Shah, Al-Kadobat, and Al-Hawara, among other ethnicities.

26. Lila Abu-Lughod, *Veiled Sentiments: Honor and Poetry in a Bedouin Society* (Berkeley: University of California Press, 2016), 23.

27. Takami Kuwayama, "'Natives' as Dialogic Partners: Some Thoughts on Native Anthropology," *Anthropology Today* 19, no. 1 (2003): 8–13.

28. See Marilyn Strathern, "The Limits of Auto-anthropology," in *Anthropology at Home*, ed. Anthony Jackson (London: Tavistock, 1987), 59–67.

29. On this debate, see Carol J. Greenhouse, "Anthropology at Home: Whose Home?," *Human Organization* 44, no. 3 (1985): 261–264.

30. https://www.unocha.org/sudan, accessed June 15, 2018.

31. For the entire map with numbers of residents in the IDP camps, see https://reliefweb.int/map/sudan/sudan-darfur-idp-camps-08-may-2013, accessed June 15, 2018.

32. UNAMID Report on IDPs in Darfur, https://news.un.org/en/story/2017/11/636822-un-report-urges-sudan-address-plight-millions-displaced-people-darfur.

33. Maria Gabrielsen Jumbert and David Lanz, "Globalised Rebellion: The Darfur Insurgents and the World," *Journal of Modern African Studies* 51, no. 2 (2013): 193.

34. See "The Crushing Burden of Rape: Sexual Violence in Darfur," Médecins sans Frontières, March 8, 2005, https://www.msf.org/crushing-burden-rape-sexual-violence-darfur; "Sudan:

Darfur: Rape as a Weapon of War: Sexual Violence and Its Consequences," Amnesty International, July 18, 2004, https://www.amnesty.org/en/documents/AFR54/076/2004/en/; Tara Gingerich and Jennifer Leaning, "The Use of Rape as a Weapon of War in Darfur, Sudan," Physicians for Human Rights, October 1, 2004, https://phr.org/resources/the-use-of-rape-as-a-weapon-of -war-in-darfur-sudan/2004; and "Mass Rape in North Darfur: Sudanese Army Attacks against Civilians in Tabit," February 11, 2015, Human Rights Watch, https://www.hrw.org/report/2015 /02/11/mass-rape-north-darfur/sudanese-army-attacks-against-civilians-tabit.

35. Alan Gilbert and Josef Gugler, *Cities, Poverty and Development: Urbanization in the Third World* (Oxford: Oxford University Press, 1982), 121.

36. Nanneke Redclift and Enzo Mingione, eds., "Introduction: Economic Restructuring and Family Practices," in *Beyond Employment: Household, Gender, and Subsistence* (Oxford: Wiley-Blackwell, 1985), 2.

37. Keith Hart, "Informal Income Opportunities and Urban Employment in Ghana," *Journal of Modern African Studies* 11, no. 1 (1973): 61.

38. Adil Mustafa Ahmad and Ata Al-Hassan Al-Battahani, "Poverty in Khartoum," *Environment and Urbanization* 7, no. 2 (1995): 195–206. Also see H. Abdel Ati, "Displacement and Poverty in Khartoum: Two Faces of the Coin," in *A Report for MEAwards* (Cairo: Population Council, 2004). Further elaborations on urban poverty in the capital city were reported by the Oxfam Project in 2008; see Hassan Ahmed Abdel Ati, Idris El Tahir El Nayal, and Samah Hussein, *Evaluation of Khartoum Urban Poor Programme, Sudan*. Oxfam GB, October 1, 2008, https://policy-practice .oxfam.org.uk/publications/evaluation-of-khartoum-urban-poor-programme-sudan-119477.

39. Salman Rushdie, *Two Years Eight Months and Twenty-Eight Nights: A Novel* (New York: Random House, 2015), 26.

40. "N. Darfur to Transform IDPs Camps into Permanent Residential Areas," *Sudan Tribune*, June 14, 2018, http://www.sudantribune.com/spip.php?article65644.

41. Marc Lamont Hill, *Nobody: Casualties of America's War on the Vulnerable, from Ferguson to Flint and Beyond* (New York: Simon and Schuster, 2017), 29.

42. David Harvey, "The Right to the City," *International Journal of Urban and Regional Research* 27, no. 4 (2003): 939.

43. Anthony John Arkell, "Māni Magic in Northern Darfur," *Sudan Notes and Records* 19, no. 2 (1936): 317–319.

44. Muḥammad Ibn-'Umar al-Tūnisī, *Tashidh al-adhan fi sirat bilad al-Arab wa el-Sudan* (in Arabic), ed. Mahmoud Asakir and Mustafa Mussad (Cairo: Al Dar Al Masriya Lil-Ta'lif wal-Tarjama, 1965).

45. Alex Argenti-Pillen, *Masking Terror: How Women Contain Violence in Southern Sri Lanka* (Philadelphia: University of Pennsylvania Press, 2013), 21.

Chapter Four

1. A peace agreement between the Sudanese government and a faction of Sudan Liberation Army signed in Abuja, Nigeria, in 2006. For further information, see United Nations Peacemaker, "Darfur Peace Agreement," May 5, 2006, https://peacemaker.un.org/node/535.

2. The Prosecutor v. Bahr Idriss Abu Garda, ICC-02/05/09, https://www.google.com/search?q =bahr+abu+garda+icc&rlz=1C1EJFC_enUS809US809&oq=Bahar+Abu+Garda&aqs=chrome .2.69i57j0l2.14274j0j7&sourceid=chrome&ie=UTF-8, accessed July 29, 2012.

3. Ibid.

4. Sara Al-Mesnad, "Qatar in Conversation with Darfur: A Cultural Approach to Mediation Policy," undergraduate portfolio submitted for Culture and Politics Honors Seminar, Georgetown University, SFSQ, December 4, 2013.

5. For details about these talks, which lasted for two and a half years, see United Nations–African Union Mission in Darfur, *Doha Document for Peace in Darfur*, https://unamid.unmissions.org/doha-document-peace-darfur, accessed March 6, 2019.

6. Personal communication from Rory Miller, December 9, 2019. See also Rory Miller, *Desert Kingdoms to Global Powers: The Rise of the Arab Gulf* (New Haven: Yale University Press, 2016).

7. Carol J. Greenhouse, "Mediation: A comparative approach," *Man* 20, no. 1 (March 1985): 104.

8. Daniel Smith, *To Be a Man Is Not a One Day Job* (Chicago: University of Chicago Press, 2017).

9. At the time of their residence, implausible stories swirled within the Sudanese community about the shock these IDPs have encountered in the city. How, for example, a woman who burned incense in her hotel room and triggered the smoke alarm refused to be evacuated by the firemen who flocked to her rescue, and how another woman came to a Sheraton buffet to ask for dinner for relatives who had moved in with her. Had it not been for the kindness of the Egyptian chef, who agreed to fill trays and trays of entrees and desserts, she would have been denied the unusual request. Finally, news traveled about a Darfuri woman who attacked a Sudanese government official in a meeting. She was reported to have pulled the chair from under him when he was about to take a seat and followed up with a violent blow on his head with a crystal ashtray. Her disappearance from other community gatherings led many to confirm that she was simply under hotel arrest.

10. Akhil Gupta and James Ferguson, eds., *Anthropological Locations: Boundaries and Grounds of a Field Science* (Berkeley: University of California Press, 1997).

11. Notes from my personal journal, Doha 2009.

12. Mikhail Mikhaïlovich Bakhtin, *The Dialogic Imagination: Four Essays*, vol. 1, ed. Michael Holquist, trans. Caryl Emerson and Michael Holquist (Austin: University of Texas Press, 2010).

13. The Arab Democracy Foundation was established in 2007 at the initiative of Arab democracy advocates and with support from the State of Qatar, where the foundation is headquartered. Primarily it provides material and moral supports to Arab civil society organizations and citizens' initiatives in their efforts to prepare the countries of the region for a peaceful transition to democratic governance. The organization folded in 2016.

14. This commission was founded by King Mohammed VI on January 7, 2004, under a royal decree and charged with looking into several matters relating to reparations for political dissidents; recommending Morocco's ratification of the ICC; and ending the death penalty. For the detailed report, see United States Institute of Peace "Truth Commission: Morocco," December 1, 2004, https://www.usip.org/publications/2004/12/truth-commission-morocco. Also, for ethnographic analysis and critique, see Susan Slyomovics, *The Performance of Human Rights in Morocco* (Philadelphia: University of Pennsylvania Press, 2005).

15. Tubiana et al., *Traditional Authorities' Peacemaking Role*, 53.

16. For an excellent account of these "traditional" mediation mechanisms, see Tubiana, Tanner, and Abdul-Jalil, *Traditional Authorities' Peacemaking Role in Darfur*.

17. "They Shot at Us as We Fled: Government Attacks on Civilians in West Darfur in February 2008," Human Rights Watch, May 18, 2008, at https://www.hrw.org/report/2008/05/18/they-shot-us-we-fled/government-attacks-civilians-west-darfur-february-2008.

18. UNSC Resolution 1325, passed by the Security Council in 2001. For critique, see Christine Bell and Catherine O'Rourke, "Peace Agreements or Pieces of Paper? The Impact of UNSC Resolution 1325 on Peace Processes and Their Agreements," *International and Comparative Law Quarterly* 59, no. 4 (2010): 941–980.

19. For elaboration on the topic of resource governance, see Musa Adam Abdul-Jalil, "The Dynamics of Customary Land Tenure and Natural Resource Management in Darfur," in Land Reform, Settlement, and Cooperatives 2 (U.N. Food and Agricultural Organization, 2006).

20. Rex Seán O'Fahey, "Conflict in Darfur: Historical and Contemporary Perspectives," in *Environmental Degradation as a Cause of Conflict in Darfur, ed. Bakri Osman Saeed* (Addis Ababa: University for Peace, Africa Programme, 2006), 23–32.

21. See Alex de Waal, *Famine that Kills: Darfur, Sudan, 1984–85* (Oxford: Clarendon Press, 1989).

22. For the text of this agreement, see https://www.un.org/zh/focus/southernsudan/pdf /dpa.pdf.

23. For details about processes of sedentarization, see Lawrence A. Kuznar and Robert Sedlmeyer, "Collective Violence in Darfur: An Agent-Based Model of Pastoral Nomad/Sedentary Peasant Interaction," *Human Complex Systems: Mathematical Anthropology and Cultural Theory* 1, no. 4 (2005): 1–22.

24. The statistics mentioned reflect the assessments conducted at the time of the RAD.

25. Jeff Crisp, "Forced Displacement in Africa: Dimensions, Difficulties, and Policy Directions," *Refugee Survey Quarterly* 29, no. 3 (2010): 1–27.

26. ADF's team shared the final statement emerging from the conference with all stakeholders in the crisis, who were thereby informed of RAD's recommendations for implementing transitional justice in Darfur. Support for implementation has been anticipated from the Arab League and Arab civil society organizations, from the contribution of the International Mediation Committee on Darfur, and through the cooperation of Darfurian elites, its civil society representatives, and the ADF. There was unanimous intent to make RAD a permanent organization, with selected members to form a follow-up committee—in essence, a truth and reconciliation committee—charged with liaising among RAD's active members to enact the recommendations of the final statement. This committee commenced its activities immediately after the RAD forum under the auspices of the ADF, including implementing a plan for the remainder of the year 2009 and for future activities in Darfur, Khartoum, and Qatar. RAD itself was institutionalized until 2011, when the ADF reorganization reoriented its portfolio. The April 2009 RAD forum considered in this chapter stands as the ADF's flagship event in its series on the crisis in Darfur. Discussions among stakeholders initiated at the forum continued, and modest gains based on the recommendations are being made.

27. See Seyyed Hossein Nasr, *The Need for a Sacred Science* (London: Routledge, 2005). Nasr has defined his notion of *scientia sacra* as "none other than that sacred knowledge which lies at the heart of every revelation and is the center of that circle which encompasses and defines tradition."

28. Martha Minow, *Between Vengeance and Forgiveness: Facing History after Genocide and Mass Violence* (Boston: Beacon Press, 1998).

29. Nigel Rapport, *Social and Cultural Anthropology: The Key Concepts* (London: Routledge, 2014).

30. Roger Sanjek, ed., *Mutuality: Anthropology's Changing Terms of Engagement* (Philadelphia: University of Pennsylvania Press, 2014).

Chapter Five

1. Clifford Geertz, "Deep Play: Notes on the Balinese Cockfight," *Daedalus* 134, no. 4 (Fall 2005): 58. This quote evokes Darfuris' experience of violence since the Janjaweed's attacks on their homeland and the subsequent flight of some across the desert to Chad and of others through the Sinai into Israel.

2. Claude Lévi-Strauss, *Myth and Meaning* (London: Routledge, 2013), 49. I open with this quotation to emphasize that each element of Darfuri displacement from the Sudan can only be appreciated as a part of a larger story.

3. Taj Haroun's account first appeared on the blog of the Weiss-Livnat International MA Program in Holocaust Studies at the University of Haifa, at https://haifaholocauststudies.word press.com/2016/05/10/taj-haroun-genocide-in-darfur-asylum-seekers-in-israel/. It is based on a talk Haroun gave at the University of Haifa in 2016 and is used with his permission.

4. For an excellent overview of the burgeoning use of online methods of ethnographic research, see Roger Sanjek and Susan W. Tratner, eds., *eFieldnotes: The Makings of Anthropology in the Digital World* (Philadelphia: University of Pennsylvania Press, 2016); and Tom Boellstorff, "Rethinking Digital Anthropology," in *Digital Anthropology*, ed. Heather A. Horst and Daniel Miller (London: Berg, 2012), 39–60. Also relevant is Jenna Burrell, "The Field Site as a Network: A Strategy for Locating Ethnographic Research," *Field Methods* 21, no. 2 (May 2009): 181–199.

5. For further discussion see Annette N. Markham, "The Methods, Politics, and Ethics of Representation in Online Ethnography," in *The Sage Handbook of Qualitative Research*, 3rd ed., ed. Norman K. Denzin and Yvonna S. Lincoln (Thousand Oaks, CA: Sage, 2005), 793–820; also Liav Sade-Beck, "Internet Ethnography: Online and Offline" *International Journal of Qualitative Methods* 3, no. 2 (June 2004): 45–51.

6. R. E. Pahl, *Divisions of Labour* (Oxford: Basil Blackwell, 1984), 2.

7. Adam Ahmed, *The Nightmare of the Exile: The Story of the Refugee from Darfur Escape, Suffering and Prison* (Bloomington: Xlibris, 2015).

8. In 2007, the Israeli government enacted what was termed the Gedera-Hadera policy, according to which refugees entering Israel from Egypt were required to sign documents promising not to live or work in Israel's heavily populated central region, defined as the area north of Gedera and south of Hadera. Presumably designed to protect Israelis' economic interests, it resulted in placing increased socioeconomic burdens on the less populated peripheral areas of the country and hence was cancelled in 2009, approximately eighteen months after enactment.

9. This same woman, along with several other people I spoke with, noted appreciatively that women in Israel are treated with a respect not always found in Darfur, particularly as it pertains to gender violence. Israeli police protection extends to the Sudanese community, inhibiting domestic violence. As one man stated, "In the Sudan, men use their strength indiscriminately and without punishment, but in Israel, they can get arrested for the same behavior."

10. Yasmin Fathi, "To Be Alive," *Al-Ahram Weekly*, August 19–25, 2004, 704.

11. For an excellent description of a violent incident involving Sudanese refugees in Cairo, see Amal Hassan Fadlalla, "Contested Borders of (In)humanity: Sudanese Refugees and the Mediation of Suffering and Subaltern Visibilities," *Urban Anthropology and Studies of Cultural Systems and World Economic Development* 38, no. 1 (Spring 2009): 79–120. Also see Fateh Azzam, ed., *A Tragedy of Failure and False Expectations: Report on the Events Surrounding the Three-month Sit-in and Forced Removal of Sudanese Refugees in Cairo, September–December 2005* (Cairo: Forced Migration and Refugee Studies Program, American University in Cairo, June

2006), schools.aucegypt.edu/GAPP/cmrs/reports/Documents/Report_Edited_v.pdf (Arabic version available).

12. See Ora Nakash, Benjamin Langer, Maayan Nagar, Shahar Shoham, Ido Lurie, and Nadav Davidovitch, "Exposure to Traumatic Experiences among Asylum Seekers from Eritrea and Sudan during Migration to Israel," *Journal of Immigrant and Minority Health* 17, no. 4 (August 2015): 1280–1286.

13. Paul Atkinson, *The Ethnographic Imagination: Textual Constructions of Reality* (London: Routledge, 2014), 82.

14. "Sudan Says Rebel's Office in Israel Proves 'Foreign Hands' in Darfur," *Sudan Tribune*, March 1, 2008, http://www.sudantribune.com/spip.php?iframe&page=imprimable&id_article =26192.

15. Quoted in Haim Yacobi, "Let Me Go to the City: African Asylum Seekers, Racialization, and the Politics of Space in Israel," *Journal of Refugee Studies* 24, no. 1 (March 2011): 61.

16. Holly Buchanan, "Escape from Darfur: Why Israel Needs to Adopt a Comprehensive Domestic Refugee Law," *Chapman Law Review* 11, no. 3 (2008): 616.

17. Moshe Dayan, "Israel's border and security problems," *Foreign Affairs* 33, no. 2 (January 1955): 257.

18. Sheldon Gellar, "Forced Deportation: African Asylum Seekers as Toxic Waste," *Jerusalem Post*, October 20, 2017, https://www.jpost.com/Opinion/Forced-deportation-African-asylum -seekers-as-toxic-waste-510890.

19. Tamar Dressler, "From Darfur to Eilat: Refugees' New Life," Ynet news.com, June 17, 2007, https://www.ynetnews.com/articles/0,7340,L-3413031,00.html, accessed October 2, 2016.

20. Ruth W. Messinger, "Darfur: Never Again?," aish.com, November 20, 2004, https://www .aish.com/ci/s/48918992.html.

21. Emanuel is quoted in Shmuel Rosner, "Action-Oriented Morality: How Can Israel Turn Away Refugees from Darfur?," *Slate*, August 28, 2007, https://slate.com/news-and-politics/2007 /08/how-can-israel-turn-away-refugees-from-darfur.html.

22. "The Infiltrators," Art Agenda Announcements, May 28, 2014, https://www.art-agenda .com/announcements/186237/n-a.

23. Isaiah Berlin, "Two Concepts of Liberty," in *The Liberty Reader*, ed. David Miller (London: Routledge, 2017), 373.

24. Raymond Williams, *Marxism and Literature* (Oxford: Oxford University Press, 1977), 132.

25. For comparison, see Tovi Fenster and Ilan Vizel, "Globalization, Sense of Belonging and the African Community in Tel Aviv–Jaffa," *Hagar: Studies in Culture, Polity & Identities* 7, no. 1 (2006): 7–24.

26. Erving Goffman, *The Presentation of Self in Everyday Life* (London: Harmondsworth, 1978), 51.

27. Mahmood Mamdani, *Saviors and Survivors: Darfur, Politics, and the War on Terror* (New York: Pantheon, 2009).

28. Charles Piot, *Remotely Global: Village Modernity in West Africa* (Chicago: University of Chicago Press, 1999), 21.

29. Devaka Premawardhana, *Faith in Flux: Pentecostalism and Mobility in Rural Mozambique* (Philadelphia: University of Pennsylvania Press, 2018).

30. "Sudan: 13 Christians Arrested in Darfur, Another Church Told to Hand over Property," *World Watch Monitor*, October 17, 2018, https://www.worldwatchmonitor.org/2018/10 /sudan-13-christians-arrested-in-darfur-another-church-told-to-hand-over-property.

31. Lewis R. Gordon, *Existentia Africana: Understanding African Existential Thought* (London: Routledge, 2013).

32. Samantha Pinto, *Difficult Diasporas: The Transnational Feminist Aesthetic of the Black Atlantic* (New York: NYU Press, 2013). See also Joel Burstyner, "Israel's Pain over Darfur Refugees," *Eureka Street* 17, no. 19, October 3, 2007, 14, https://www.eurekastreet.com.au/article/israel-s-pain-over-darfur-refugees.

Chapter Six

1. Excerpted from my journal. If a quotation from a research participant recorded in my field notes journal is incorporated into the text, I do not cite it; the source is self-evident. Longer, block quotations from my field notes will be cited as such as a gesture of acknowledgment to the narrator.

2. Roger Sanjek, *Ethnography in Today's World: Color Full before Color-Blind* (Philadelphia: University of Pennsylvania Press, 2014).

3. Rogaia Mustafa Abusharaf, *Wanderings: Sudanese Migrants and Exiles in North America* (Ithaca: Cornell University Press, 2002).

4. Ferdinand Tönnies, *Gemeinschaft und Gesellschaft* (East Lansing: Michigan State University Press, 1957), cited in Colin Bell and Howard Newby, *Community Studies: An Introduction to the Sociology of the Local Community* (London: Allen and Unwin, 1971), 26.

5. Tukufu Zuberi, *Thicker than Blood: How Racial Statistics Lie* (Minneapolis: University of Minnesota Press, 2001).

6. These organizations included Sudan Human Rights Organization (Washington, DC, and California chapters); the El Sudan Center for Democracy, Peace and Civil Rights; the Darb El-Intifada; the Voice of the Democratic Alliance; Sudanese Victims of Torture Group; the National Democratic Alliance; the Sudan Opposition Group of Colorado and Texas; the Sudanese National Rally of Philadelphia and New England; and the like. On April 25, 1998, men and women gathered in front of the Canadian Parliament to voice their protest of the deaths of two hundred high school boys who drowned in the Sudan while trying to escape the Sudanese army draft. On another occasion, they supported relief efforts during the famine that hit the southern Bahr El Ghazal through their A Dollar to Save a Life Program. Sudanese migrants channeled these efforts through organizations in the United States and Canada.

7. Judging from my own knowledge of the existing social networks of Sudanese communities, I am not suggesting that affable interpersonal relationship and social obligations have dampened or ceased to exist among Darfuris vis-à-vis other Sudanese.

8. Robert L. Bee, *Patterns and Processes: An Introduction to Anthropological Strategies for the Study of Sociocultural Change* (New York: Free Press, 1974), 15.

9. Sewell Chan, "2 Darfur Refugees Are Scarred but Free," *New York Times*, November 21, 2004, https://www.nytimes.com/2004/11/21/nyregion/2-darfur-refugees-are-scarred-but-free.html.

10. Micaela Di Leonardo, *Exotics at Home: Anthropologies, Others, and American Modernity* (Chicago: University of Chicago Press, 1998).

11. Cultural Orientation Resource Center, "Refugees from Darfur: Their Background and Resettlement Needs," COR Center Refugee Backgrounder, 2011, http://www.culturalorientation.net/library/publications/refugees-from-darfur-refugee-backgrounder.

12. Samuel P. Huntington, "The Clash of Civilizations?" *Foreign Affairs* 72, no. 3 (Summer 1993): 22–49.

13. Sidney W. Mintz and Richard Price, *African-American Religion: An Anthropological Perspective* (Boston: Beacon Press, 1992), 47. The authors' explanation of complex kinship systems and the terminologies of fictive kin among African American slaves are markedly apt for Darfuri refugees; see chap. 6, "Kinship and Sex Roles," 61–80.

14. Maurice Eisenbruch, "The Mental Health of Refugee Children and Their Cultural Development," *International Migration Review* 22, no. 2 (1988): 282–300.

15. Cultural Orientation Resource Center, "Refugees from Darfur," 4.

16. Mintz and Price, *African-American Religion*, 66.

17. Michelle Theriault Boots, "Sudanese Refugees Living in Anchorage Have Their Vehicles Vandalized," *Anchorage Daily News*, March 29, 2015, https://www.adn.com/anchorage/article/darfurian-refugees-wake-find-cars-covered-graffiti-telling-them-leave-alaska-police/2015/03/30/.

18. Excerpted from my journal.

19. Excerpted from my journal.

20. Excerpted from my journal.

21. Yagoub is here referring to his mother. The Arabic term he used, *hajja*, translated literally as "pilgrim," is an honorific term for older women; *haj* is the term used for older men. Both typically refer to someone who has made a pilgrimage to Mecca.

22. Excerpted from my journal.

23. Excerpted from my journal.

24. Excerpted from my journal.

25. Excerpted from my journal.

26. See, for example, Mahmood Mamdani, *Saviors and Survivors: Darfur, Politics, and the War on Terror* (New York: Pantheon, 2009).

27. Alex de Waal, "Darfur and the Failure of the Responsibility to Protect," *International Affairs* 83, no. 6 (2007): 1039–1054.

28. The Rwandan hotelier whose shelter of hundreds of people from the 1994 Rwandan genocide was the subject of the movie *Hotel Rwanda* starring Don Cheadle, who later became part of the Save Darfur Not on Our Watch campaign.

29. "Celebrities, Activists Rally against Darfur Genocide," *USA Today*, May 1, 2006, 1.

30. Excerpted from my journal.

31. Excerpted from my journal.

32. Jean Muteba Rahier, Percy C. Hintzen, and Felipe Smith, eds., *Global Circuits of Blackness: Interrogating the African Diaspora* (Urbana: University of Illinois Press, 2010).

33. Sidney W. Mintz, *The Birth of African-American Culture: An Anthropological Perspective* (Boston: Beacon Press, 1992), 26.

34. Excerpted from my journal.

35. Christopher Ingraham, "14 Baltimore Neighborhoods Have Lower Life Expectancies than North Korea," *Washington Post*, April 30, 2015, https://www.washingtonpost.com/news/wonk/wp/2015/04/30/baltimores-poorest-residents-die-20-years-earlier-than-its-richest/?noredirect=on&utm_term=.7995235d75f6.

36. Elijah Anderson, *Streetwise: Race, Class, and Change in an Urban Community* (Chicago: University of Chicago Press, 2013), 56.

37. Bernard M. Magubane, *The Ties that Bind: African-American Consciousness of Africa* (Trenton, NJ: Africa World Press, 1987), 128.

38. Daoud Hari, *The Translator* (New York: Random House, 2008), 66.

39. Askia Muhammad, "Sudanese President Answers Questions on Darfur," *The Final Call* 26, May 14, 2007, www.finalcall.com/artman/publish/World_News_3/Sudanese_president_an swers_questions_on_Darfur_3474.shtml.

40. Excerpted from my journal.

41. Excerpted from my journal.

42. Excerpted from my journal.

43. Excerpted from my journal.

44. "Confronting Rape and Other Forms of Violence against Women in Conflict Zones Spotlight: DRC and Sudan," Hearing Before the Subcommittee on African Affairs and the Sub-committee on International Operations and Organizations, Democracy, Human Rights, and Global Women's Issues of the United States Senate Committee on Foreign Relations, 111th Cong. (2009) (statement of Niemat Ahmadi, Darfuri liaison officer), 35–38. In conversations with fe-male lawyers working in the Gender Unit of the Sudanese Ministry of Justice, I learned of their efforts to address gender-based violence through collaborations with other organs of the state as well as civil society organizations and especially through broad-based efforts at community education. Fundamentally the unit seeks to raise awareness of several legislative actions adopted by the government to create a measure of redress for victims of gender-based violence and ac-countability for perpetrators.

45. The Sudan is a patrilineal society. Killing men and boys cuts off lines of descent and thus becomes a form a genocidal ethnic cleansing.

46. Excerpted from my journal.

47. Jean-Paul Sartre, *The Emotions: Outline of a Theory*, trans. B. Frechtman (New York: Citadel, 1948), 52.

Postscript

1. Orhan Pamuk, *Other Colors: Essays and a Story* (Vancouver, WA: Vintage, 2008), 327.

2. G. Deleuze and F. Guattari, *Capitalism and Schizophrenia* (New York: Viking Press, 1977), 232–241.

3. Richard Sorabji, *Emotion and Peace of Mind: From Stoic Agitation to Christian Temptation* (New York: Oxford University Press, 2000).

4. A scene I described in my journal of a demonstration in Khartoum carried live by Al Jazeera TV, April 2019.

5. Grant Farred, *What's My name? Black Vernacular Intellectuals* (Minneapolis: University of Minnesota Press, 1997).

6. D. H. Lawrence, *The Complete Poems of D. H. Lawrence* (Ware, Hertfordshire, UK: Words-worth Editions, 1994), 480.

7. Mohammed Terwis, YouTube, https://www.youtube.com/watch?v=QKkGAfs_YWA.

8. "Sudan's al-Burhan Says Darfur Victims Have the Right to Resort to ICC," *Sudan Tribune*, December 19, 2019, https://www.sudantribune.com/spip.php?article68733.

Bibliography

24 Hours for Darfur. "Darfurian Voices: Documenting Darfurian Refugees' Views on Issues of Peace, Justice, And Reconciliation." *DarfurianVoices.org*. https://static1.squarespace.com /static/52920ed5e4b04a0741daa89c/t/529224ffe4b049dd0ca09a3f/1385309439460/Dar furian+Voices+-+Report+-+English.pdf.

Abdel Ati, Hassan Ahmed. "Displacement and Poverty in Khartoum: Two Faces of the Coin." In *A Report for MEAwards* (Cairo: Population Council, 2004).

Abdel Ati, Hassan Ahmed, Idris El Tahir El Nayal, and Samah Hussein. *Evaluation of Khartoum Urban Poor Programme, Sudan*. Oxfam GB, October 1, 2008. https://policy-practice.oxfam .org.uk/publications/evaluation-of-khartoum-urban-poor-programme-sudan-119477.

Abdul-Jalil, Musa Adam. "The Dynamics of Customary Land Tenure and Natural Resource Management in Darfur." In *Land Reform, Settlement, and Cooperatives* 2, 9–23. UN Food and Agricultural Organization, 2006.

———. "The Dynamics of Ethnic Identification and Ethnic Group Relations among the People of 'Dor', Northern Darfur, Sudan." PhD diss., Edinburgh University, 1979.

Abdul-Jalil, Musa Adam, Azzain Mohammed, and Ahmed Yousuf. "Native Administration and Local Governance in Darfur: Past and Future." In *War in Darfur and the Search for Peace*, edited by Alex de Waal, 39–68. London: Justice Africa Pages, 2007.

Abu-Lughod, Lila. *Veiled Sentiments: Honor and Poetry in a Bedouin Society*. Berkeley: University of California Press, 2016.

Abusharaf, Rogaia Mustafa. "Cartographies of Mutuality: Lessons from Darfur." In *Mutuality: Anthropologies Changing Terms of Engagement*, edited by Roger Sanjek, 130–151. Philadelphia: University of Pennsylvania Press, 2014.

———. "Circuits of Knowledge Production." In *Networks of Knowledge Production in Sudan: Identities, Mobilities, and Technologies*, edited by Sondra Hale and Gada Kadoda, 79–97 (Lanham, MD: Lexington, 2016).

———. "A Darfur-Doha Encounter: A Sufi Mystic Whirling Trance for Peace." *Black Renaissance/Noire* 11, no. 1 (2011): 73–89.

———. "Debating Darfur in the World." *Annals of the American Academy of Political and Social Science* 632, no. 1 (2010): 67–85.

———. *Wanderings: Sudanese Migrants and Exiles in North America.* Ithaca: Cornell University Press, 2002.

———. "'We Have Supped So Deep in Horrors': Understanding Colonialist Emotionality and British Responses to Female Circumcision in Northern Sudan." *History and Anthropology* 17, no. 3 (2006): 209–228.

Adam, I. M. "Twenty-Five Muslims in Mayo Accused of Apostasy." *Al-Tiar*, December 11, 2015.

Adelberger, Jörg. "Aspects of Fur Culture or Felkin Revisited: Arkell's Discussion of a 19th Century Traveler's Report with Six Fur Prisoners at al-Fashir." *Sudanic Africa* 2 (1991): 53–77.

Adichie, Chimamanda Ngozi. "The Danger of a Single Story." *TED Ideas Worth Spreading*, 2009. https://www.ted.com/talks/chimamanda_adichie_the_danger_of_a_single_story/transcript ?language=en.

Ahmad, Adil Mustafa, and Ata Al-Hassan Al-Battahani. "Poverty in Khartoum." *Environment and Urbanization* 7, no. 2 (1995): 195–206.

Ahmadi, Niemat. Statement. In *Confronting Rape and Other Forms of Violence against Women in Conflict Zones Spotlight: DRC and Sudan: Hearing Before the Subcommittee on African Affairs and the Subcommittee on International Operations and Organizations, Democracy, Human Rights, and Global Women's Issues of the United States Senate Committee on Foreign Relations*, 35–38 111th Cong. (2009).

Ahmed, Adam. *The Nightmare of the Exile: The Story of the Refugee from Darfur Escape, Suffering, and Prison.* Bloomington: Xlibris, 2015.

Al-Mesnad, Sara. "Qatar in Conversation with Darfur: A Cultural Approach to Mediation Policy." Undergraduate portfolio submitted for Culture and Politics Honors Seminar. Georgetown University, December 4, 2013.

Amnesty International. *Darfur: Rape as a Weapon of War: Sexual Violence and its Consequences.* Mafhoum.com, July 19, 2004. http://www.mafhoum.com/press7/203S30.htm.

Anderson, Elijah. *Streetwise: Race, Class, and Change in an Urban Community.* Chicago: University of Chicago Press, 2013.

Argenti-Pillen, Alex. *Masking Terror: How Women Contain Violence in Southern Sri Lanka.* Philadelphia: University of Pennsylvania Press, 2013.

Arkell, Anthony John. "Darfur Antiquities." *Sudan Notes and Records* 19, no. 2 (1936): 301–311.

———. "Darfur Antiquities II: Tōra Palaces in Turra at the North End of Jebel Marra." *Sudan Notes and Records* 20, no. 1 (1937): 91–105.

———. "The Double Spiral Amulet." *Sudan Notes and Records* 20, no. 1 (1937): 151–155.

———. "Māni Magic in Northern Darfur." *Sudan Notes and Records* 19, no. 2 (1936): 317–319.

———. "The Medieval History of Darfur in Its Relation to Other Cultures and to the Nilotic Sudan." *Sudan Notes and Records* 40 (1959): 44–47.

———. "Rock Pictures in Northern Darfur." *Sudan Notes and Records* 20, no. 2 (1937): 281–287.

———. "The Southern Route to Kufra." *Sudan Notes and Records* 5 (1922): 130–136.

———. "Throwing Sticks and Throwing Knives in Darfur." *Sudan Notes and Records* 22 (1939): 251–267.

Arkell, Anthony John. Papers. Sudan Archive. Durham University Library. http://reed.dur.ac.uk /xtf/view?docId=ark/32150_s18c97kq43c.xml;query=Arkell;brand=default#1

Armstrong, Nancy, and Leonard Tennenhouse, eds. *The Violence of Representation: Literature and the History of Violence.* London: Routledge, 2014.

Asad, Talal, ed. *Anthropology and The Colonial Encounter.* London: Ithaca Press, 1973.

Atkinson, Paul. *The Ethnographic Imagination: Textual Constructions of Reality.* London: Routledge, 2014.

Azzam, Fateh, ed. *A Tragedy of Failure and False Expectations: Report on the Events Surrounding the Three-month Sit-in and Forced Removal of Sudanese Refugees in Cairo, September–December 2005.* Cairo: Forced Migration and Refugee Studies Program, American University in Cairo, June 2006.schools.aucegypt.edu/GAPP/cmrs/reports/Documents/Report_Edited_v.pdf.

Badawi, Mohamad. *The Harvest of Gunpowder.* Translated by Rogaia Abusharaf. Cairo: Awaraq, 2015.

Bakhtin, Mikhail Mikhaĭlovich. *The Dialogic Imagination: Four Essays.* Edited by Michael Holquist. Translated by Caryl Emerson and Michael Holquist. Austin: University of Texas Press, 2010.

Bal, Mieke, and Sherry Marx-MacDonald. *Travelling Concepts in the Humanities: A Rough Guide.* Toronto: University of Toronto Press, 2002.

Balfour-Paul, H. G. *History and Antiquities of Darfur.* Museum Pamphlet no. 3. Khartoum: Sudan Antiquities Service, 1955.

Barnett, Michael. *Empire of Humanity: A History of Humanitarianism.* Ithaca: Cornell University Press, 2011.

Barth, Fredrik. *Ethnic Groups and Boundaries: The Social Organization of Culture Difference.* Long Grove, IL: Waveland Press, 1998.

Beaton, A. C. "The Fur." *Sudan Notes and Records* 29, no. 1 (1948): 1–39.

Bee, Robert L. *Patterns and Processes: An Introduction to Anthropological Strategies for the Study of Sociocultural Change.* New York: Free Press, 1974.

Bell, Christine, and Catherine O'Rourke. "Peace Agreements or Pieces of Paper? The Impact of UNSC Resolution 1325 on Peace Processes and Their Agreements." *International and Comparative Law Quarterly* 59, no. 4 (2010): 941–980.

Bell, Colin, and Howard Newby. *Community Studies: An Introduction to the Sociology of the Local Community.* London: Allen and Unwin, 1971.

Berlin, Isaiah. "Two Concepts of Liberty." In *The Liberty Reader*, edited by David Miller, 369–389. London: Routledge, 2017.

Bernal, Victoria. *Nation as Network.* Chicago: University of Chicago Press, 2014.

Boellstorff, Tom. "Rethinking Digital Anthropology." In *Digital Anthropology*, edited by Heather A. Horst and Daniel Miller, 39–60. London: Berg, 2012.

Boots, Michelle Theriault. "Sudanese Refugees Living in Anchorage Have their Vehicles Vandalized." *Anchorage Daily News*, March 29, 2015. https://www.adn.com/anchorage/article/darfurian-refugees-wake-find-cars-covered-graffiti-telling-them-leave-alaska-police/2015/03/30/.

Boustead, J. E. H. "The Youth and Last Days of Sultan Ali Dinar: A Fur View." *Sudan Notes and Records* 22, no. 1 (1939): 149–153.

"Brooklyn Darfurians." YouTube video, 9:27. Posted by "24hoursfordarfur," October 2, 2007. https://www.youtube.com/watch?v=zJjIC2Zku7A.

Browne, William George. *Travels in Africa, Egypt, and Syria, from the Year 1792 to 1798.* London: T. Cadel and W. Davies, 1806.

Buchanan, Holly. "Escape from Darfur: Why Israel Needs to Adopt a Comprehensive Domestic Refugee Law." *Chapman Law Review* 11, no. 3 (2008): 602–632.

Burrell, Jenna. "The Field Site as a Network: A Strategy for Locating Ethnographic Research." *Field Methods* 21, no. 2 (May 2009): 181–199.

Burstyner, Joel. "Israel's Pain over Darfur Refugees." *Eureka Street* 17, no. 19 (October 2007). https://www.eurekastreet.com.au/article/israel-s-pain-over-darfur-refugees.

Cassese, Antonio, Mohamed Fayek, Hina Jilani, Dumisa Ntsebeza, and Therese Striggner-Scott. *Report of the International Commission of Inquiry on Darfur to the United Nations Secretary-General.* Pursuant to Security Council Resolution 1564 (2005).

Césaire, Aimé. *Discourse on Colonialism.* New York: New York University Press, 2001.

Chan, Sewell. "2 Darfur Refugees Are Scarred but Free." *New York Times*, November 21, 2004, https://www.nytimes.com/2004/11/21/nyregion/2-darfur-refugees-are-scarred-but-free.html.

Clifford, James. "On Ethnographic Allegory." In *Writing Culture: The Poetics and Politics of Ethnography*, edited by James Clifford and George E. Marcus, 98–121. Berkeley: University of California Press, 1986.

Cohen, Bernard S. *Colonialism and Its Forms of Knowledge: The British in India.* Princeton, NJ: Princeton University Press, 1996.

Crisp, Jeff. "Forced Displacement in Africa: Dimensions, Difficulties, and Policy Directions." *Refugee Survey Quarterly* 29, no. 3 (2010): 1–27.

Cultural Orientation Resource Center. *Refugees from Darfur: Their Background and Resettlement Needs.* COR Center Refugee Backgrounder, no. 6. 2011. http://www.culturalorientation.net/library/publications/refugees-from-darfur-refugee-backgrounder.

Dabanga. "Author's International Literary Award 'for All Sudanese.'" *Radio Dabanga*, April 20, 2017. https://www.dabangasudan.org/en/all-news/article/author-s-international-literary-award-for-all-sudanese.

Daly, Martin W. *Darfur's Sorrow: A History of Destruction and Genocide.* Cambridge: Cambridge University Press, 2007.

"Darfur Soldier: 'We Were Ordered to Kill and Rape.'" YouTube video, 3:07. Posted by *The Guardian*, Mar 4, 2009. https://www.youtube.com/watch?v=FtSTFIOEAoc.

Darfur Youth Coalition for Separation. "Darandoka Boys." Facebook, August 25, 2018. https://www.facebook.com/groups/shabab.darfur/permalink/2035541733163933/.

Das, Veena. *Life and Words: Violence and the Descent into the Ordinary.* Oakland: University of California Press, 2006.

Dayan, Moshe. "Israel's Border and Security Problems." *Foreign Affairs* 33, no. 2 (January 1955): 250–267.

De Waal, Alex. "Counter-Insurgency on the Cheap." *London Review of Books* 26, no. 15 (August 5, 2004). https://www.lrb.co.uk/the-paper/v26/n15/alex-de-waal/counter-insurgency-on-the-cheap.

———. "Darfur and the Failure of the Responsibility to Protect." *International Affairs* 83, no. 6 (2007): 1039–1054.

———. *Famine that Kills: Darfur, Sudan, 1984–85.* Oxford: Clarendon Press, 1989.

Deleuze, G., and F. Guattari. *Capitalism and Schizophrenia.* New York: Viking Press, 1977.

Di Leonardo, Micaela. *Exotics at Home: Anthropologies, Others, and American Modernity.* Chicago: University of Chicago Press, 1998.

Diamond, Stanley. "A Revolutionary Discipline," *Current Anthropology* 5, no. 5 (1964): 432–437.

Dirks, Nicholas B. *Castes of Mind: Colonialism and the Making of Modern India.* Princeton: Princeton University Press, 2001.

Dressler, Tamar. "From Darfur to Eilat: Refugees' New Life." *Ynetnews*, June 17, 2007. https://www.ynetnews.com/articles/0,7340,L-3413031,00.html.

Dupuis, C. G. "Traces of Christianity in Northern Darfur." *Sudan Notes and Records* 12, no. 1 (1929): 112–113.

Dussel, Enrique. *Twenty Theses in Politics*. Durham, NC: Duke University Press, 2008.

Edgar, Andrew, and Peter Sedgwick. *Key Concepts in Cultural Theory*. London: Routledge, 2005.

Eisenbruch, Maurice. "The Mental Health of Refugee Children and Their Cultural Development." *International Migration Review* 22, no. 2 (1988): 282–300.

El-Aswad, El-Sayed. *Religion and Folk Cosmology: Scenarios of the Visible and Invisible in Rural Egypt*. Westport, CT: Praeger, 2002.

El-Tounsy, Mohammed Ebn-Omar. *Voyage au Darfour*. Paris: Chez B. Duprat, 1845.

European-Sudanese Public Affairs Council. *The Darfur Rebels, War Crimes and Human Rights Abuses*. 2005. http://www.espac.org/darfur/darfur-rebels-war-crime.asp.

Fabian, Johannes. *Out of Our Minds: Reason and Madness in the Exploration of Central Africa*. Berkeley: University of California Press, 2000.

Fadlalla, Amal Hassan. "Contested Borders of (In)humanity: Sudanese Refugees and the Mediation of Suffering and Subaltern Visibilities." *Urban Anthropology and Studies of Cultural Systems and World Economic Development* 38, no. 1 (Spring 2009): 79–120.

Fanon, Frantz. *Black Skin, White Masks*. New York: Grove Press, 2008.

Faris, James. *Navajo and Photography: A Critical History of Representation of an American People*. Albuquerque: University of New Mexico Press, 1996.

———. "Pax Britannica and the Sudan: SF Nadel." In *Anthropology and the Colonial Encounter*, edited by Talal Asad, 153–172. London: Ithaca Press, 1975.

Farred, Grant. *What's My Name? Black Vernacular Intellectuals*. Minneapolis: University of Minnesota Press, 1997.

Fathi, Yasmin. "To Be Alive." *Al-Ahram Weekly*, August 19–25, 2004, 704.

Felkin, Robert W. "Notes on the For Tribe of Central Africa." *Proceedings of the Royal Society of Edinburgh, 1884–85*. Edinburgh: Royal Society of Edinburgh (1884–1885).

Fenster, Tovi, and Ilan Vizel. "Globalization, Sense of Belonging and the African Community in Tel Aviv–Jaffa." *Hagar: Studies in Culture, Polity & Identities* 7, no. 1 (2006): 7–24.

Flint, Julie, and Alex De Waal. *Darfur: A New History of a Long War*. London: Zed Books Ltd., 2008.

Fragile States Index. "Measuring Fragility: Risk and Vulnerability in 178 Countries." https://fragilestatesindex.org/.

Games for Change. "Darfur Is Dying." http://www.gamesforchange.org/game/darfur-is-dying/.

Geertz, Clifford. "Deep Play: Notes on the Balinese Cockfight." *Daedalus* 134, no. 4 (Fall 2005): 56–86.

Gellar, Sheldon. "Forced Deportation: African Asylum Seekers as Toxic Waste." *Jerusalem Post*, October 20, 2017. https://www.jpost.com/Opinion/Forced-deportation-African-asylum-seekers-as-toxic-waste-510890.

Gikandi, Simon. "Cultural Translation and the African Self: A (Post)colonial Cast Study." *Interventions* 3 no. 3 (2001): 355–375.

Gilbert, Alan, and Josef Gugler. *Cities, Poverty and Development: Urbanization in the Third World*. Oxford: Oxford University Press, 1982.

Gillan, J. A. "Darfur, 1916." *Sudan Notes and Records* 22, no. 1 (1939): 1–25.

Gingerich, Tara, and Jennifer Leaning. *The Use of Rape as a Weapon of War in Darfur, Sudan*. U.S. Agency for International Development/OTI: October 1, 2004. https://phr.org/wp-content/uploads/2004/10/darfur-rape-as-a-weapon-2004.pdf.

Goffman, Erving. *The Presentation of Self in Everyday Life.* London: Harmondsworth, 1978.

Gordon, Lewis R. *Existentia Africana: Understanding African Existential Thought.* London: Routledge, 2013.

Greenhouse, Carol J. "Anthropology at Home: Whose Home?" *Human Organization* 44, no. 3 (1985): 261–264.

———. "Mediation: A Comparative Approach," *Man* 20, no. 1 (March 1985): 90–114.

Gupta, Akhil, and James Ferguson, eds. *Anthropological Locations: Boundaries and Grounds of a Field Science.* Berkeley: University of California Press, 1997.

Haifa Holocaust Studies. "Taj Haroun: Genocide in Darfur & Asylum Seekers in Israel." *Holocaust Studies in Haifa,* May 10, 2016. https://haifaholocauststudies.wordpress.com/2016/05/10/taj -haroun-genocide-in-darfur-asylum-seekers-in-israel/.

Hall, Stuart. *The Fateful Triangle.* Cambridge: Harvard University Press, 2017.

Hamdi, Ibrahim. "Sudan's Bashir Vows to Try Darfur War Criminals." *Reuters,* April 7, 2009. www.reuters.com/article/idUSL718741.

Hamid, Sulieman. *Darfur: The Definitive Answer.* Translated by Rogaia Abusharaf. Khartoum: Elmeidan Book, 2004.

Handlin, Oscar. *The Uprooted: The Epic Story of the Great Migrations That Made the American People.* Philadelphia: University of Pennsylvania Press, 2002.

Haraway, Donna. "Situated Knowledges: The Science Question in Feminism and the Privilege of Partial Perspective." *Feminist Studies* 14, no. 3 (1988): 575–599.

Hari, Daoud. *The Translator.* New York: Random House, 2008.

Harir, Sharif. "'Arab Belt' versus 'African Belt': Ethno-political Conflict in Dar Fur and the Regional Cultural Factors." In *Shortcut to Decay: The Case of Sudan,* edited by Sharif Harir and Terje Tvedt, 144–185. Uppsala: Nordiska Africainstitutet, 1994.

———. "The Politics of 'Numbers': Mediatory Leadership and the Political Process among the Beri 'Zaghawa' of the Sudan." PhD diss., Department of Social Anthropology, University of Bergen, 1987.

Harris, Marvin. *Culture, Man, and Nature.* New York: Thomas Crowell, 1971.

Hart, Keith. "Informal Income Opportunities and Urban Employment in Ghana." *Journal of Modern African Studies* 11, no. 1 (1973): 61–89.

Harvey, David. "The Right to the City." *International Journal of Urban and Regional Research* 27, no. 4 (2003): 939–941.

Hasan, Yusuf Fadl. *Sudan in Africa: Studies Presented to the First International Conference Sponsored by The Sudan Research Unit, 7–12 February 1968.* Khartoum: Khartoum University Press, 1971.

Herman, Edward S., and Noam Chomsky. *Manufacturing Consent: The Political Economy of the Mass Media.* New York: Random House, 2010.

Hill, Marc Lamont. *Nobody: Casualties of America's War on the Vulnerable, from Ferguson to Flint and Beyond.* New York: Simon and Schuster, 2017.

Human Rights Watch. "Mass Rape in North Darfur: Sudanese Army Attacks against Civilians in Tabit." Human Rights Watch: February 11, 2015. https://www.hrw.org/report/2015/02/11 /mass-rape-north-darfur/sudanese-army-attacks-against-civilians-tabit.

———. *They Shot at Us as We Fled: Government Attacks on Civilians in West Darfur in February 2008.* Human Rights Watch: May 18, 2008. https://www.hrw.org/report/2008/05/18 /they-shot-us-we-fled/government-attacks-civilians-west-darfur-february-2008.

Hunt, Kasie. "Celebrities, Activists Rally against Darfur Genocide." *USA Today*, May 1, 2006. http://usatoday30.usatoday.com/news/washington/2006-04-30-darfurrally_x.htm.

Huntington, Samuel P. "The Clash of Civilizations?" *Foreign Affairs* 72, no. 3 (Summer 1993): 22–49.

Idris, Shams E. *The Janjaweed Legend: An Excuse for Foreign Intervention and Destruction of Darfur Society*. Translated by Rogaia Abusharaf. bookmark Khartoum: Al-makttabba Al-Wattania, 2007.

Ingraham, Christopher. "14 Baltimore Neighborhoods Have Lower Life Expectancies than North Korea." *Washington Post*, April 30, 2015. https://www.washingtonpost.com/news/wonk/wp/2015/04/30/baltimores-poorest-residents-die-20-years-earlier-than-its-richest/?noredirect=on&utm_term=.7995235d75f6.

International Criminal Court. "Decision on the Prosecution's Application for a Warrant of Arrest against Omar Hassan Ahmad Al Bashir." ICC-02/05-01/09. March 4, 2009. https://www.icc-cpi.int/CourtRecords/CR2009_01517.PDF.

Jumbert, Maria Gabrielsen, and David Lanz. "Globalised Rebellion: The Darfur Insurgents and the World." *Journal of Modern African Studies* 51, no. 2 (2013): 193–217.

Kirk-Greene, Anthony Hamilton Millard. "The Sudan Political Service: A Profile in the Sociology of Imperialism." *International Journal of African Historical Studies* 15, no. 1 (1982): 21–22.

Kuwayama, Takami. "'Natives' as Dialogic Partners: Some Thoughts on Native Anthropology." *Anthropology Today* 19, no. 1 (2003): 8–13.

Kuznar, Lawrence A., and Robert Sedlmeyer. "Collective Violence in Darfur: An Agent-Based Model of Pastoral Nomad/Sedentary Peasant Interaction." *Human Complex Systems: Mathematical Anthropology and Cultural Theory* 1, no. 4 (2005): 1–22.

Lambek, Michael. *Island in the Stream*. Toronto: University of Toronto Press, 2018.

Lampen, G. D. "The Baggara Tribes of Darfur." *Sudan Notes and Records* 16, no. 2 (1933): 97–118.

———. "History of Darfur." *Sudan Notes and Records* 31, no. 2 (1950): 177–209.

Lawrence, David Herbert. *The Complete Poems of D. H. Lawrence*. Ware, Hertfordshire, UK: Wordsworths, 1994.

Lloyd, Jenevieve. "Knowledge." In *New Keywords: A Revised Vocabulary of Culture and Society*. Edited by Tony Bennett, Lawrence Grossberg, and Meaghan Morris, 195–197. Malden, MA: Blackwell, 2005.

Lévi-Strauss, Claude. *Myth and Meaning*. London: Routledge, 2013.

"Looking for Omar Al-Bashir." YouTube video, 0:36. Posted by "Mohamed Osman," October 5, 2013. https://www.youtube.com/watch?v=-TpF0zupSWo.

Macdonald, J. D. "Problematical Sudan Birds." *Sudan Notes and Records* 26, no. 2 (1945): 301–304.

MacMichael, Harold Alfred. *A History of the Arabs in the Sudan: And Some Account of the People who Preceded Them and of the Tribes Inhabiting Dárfúr*, vol. 2. Cambridge: Cambridge University Press, 2011.

Magubane, Bernard M. *The Ties that Bind: African-American Consciousness of Africa*. Trenton, NJ: Africa World Press, 1987.

Magubane, Bernard, and James C. Faris. "On the Political Relevance of Anthropology." *Dialectical Anthropology* 9, no. 1 (1985): 91–104.

Mahgoub, Abdel Khaliq. *Marxism and the Quandaries of the Sudanese Revolution*. Khartoum: Azza Press, 1969.

Mamdani, Mahmood. *Saviors and Survivors: Darfur, Politics, and the War on Terror*. New York: Pantheon, 2009.

Mamdani, Mahmood, and John Prendergast, "The Darfur Debate." Columbia University, April 14, 2009. youtube.com/watch?v=yGOpfH.

Manalansan, Martin F., IV. *Global Divas: Filipino Gay Men in the Diaspora*. Durham, NC: Duke University Press, 2003.

Marcus, George E. *Ethnography through Thick and Thin*. Princeton, NJ: Princeton University Press, 1998.

Markham, Annette N. "The Methods, Politics, and Ethics of Representation in Online Ethnography." In *The Sage Handbook of Qualitative Research*, 3rd ed., edited by Norman K. Denzin and Yvonna S. Lincoln, 793–820. Thousand Oaks, CA: Sage, 2005.

Mayo Clinic Staff. "Shingles." *Mayo Clinic*. https://www.mayoclinic.org/diseases-conditions /shingles/symptoms-causes/syc-20353054.

Mazrui, Ali A. "The Blood of Experience: The Failed State and Political Collapse in Africa." *World Policy Journal* 12, no. 1 (1995): 28–34.

———. "The Multiple Marginality of the Sudan." In *Sudan in Africa*, edited by Yousif Fadl, 240–255. Khartoum: University of Khartoum Press, 1971.

———. "The Resurrection of the Warrior Tradition in African Political Culture." *Journal of Modern African Studies* 13, no. 1 (1975): 67–84.

Mbembe, Achille. *On the Postcolony*. Oakland: University of California Press, 2001.

Médecins sans Frontières (MSF) International. "The Crushing Burden of Rape: Sexual Violence in Darfur." March 8, 2005. https://www.msf.org/crushing-burden-rape-sexual-violence-darfur.

Memmi, Albert. *The Colonizer and the Colonized*. London: Routledge, 2013.

Messinger, Ruth W. "Darfur: Never Again?" *Aish.com*, November 20, 2004. https://www.aish .com/ci/s/48918992.html.

Michelmore, A. P. G. "A Possible Relic of Christianity in Darfur." *Sudan Notes and Records* 15, no. 2 (1932): 272–273.

Miller, Rory. *Desert Kingdoms to Global Powers: The Rise of the Arab Gulf*. New Haven: Yale University Press, 2016.

Minow, Martha. *Between Vengeance and Forgiveness: Facing History after Genocide and Mass Violence*. Boston: Beacon Press, 1998.

Mintz, Sidney W. *The Birth of African-American Culture: An Anthropological Perspective*. Boston: Beacon Press, 1992.

Mintz, Sidney W., and Richard Price. *African-American Religion: An Anthropological Perspective*. Boston: Beacon Press, 1992.

Mudimbe, V. Y. *The Invention of Africa: Gnosis, Philosophy, and the Order of Knowledge*. Bloomington: Indiana University Press, 1988.

Muhammad, Askia. "Sudanese President Answers Questions on Darfur." *The Final Call*, May 14, 2007. www.finalcall.com/artman/publish/World_News_3/Sudanese_president_answers_ques tions_on_Darfur_3474.shtml.

Nachtigal, Gustav. *Sahara and Sudan*. Vol. 2, *Kawar, Bornu, Kanem, Borku, Enned*. Translated by Allan G. B. Fisher and Humphrey J. Fisher. Berkeley: University of California Press, 1971.

———. *Sahara and Sudan*. Vol. 4, *Wadai and Darfur*. Translated by Allan G. B. Fisher and Humphrey J. Fisher. Berkeley: University of California Press, 1971.

Nakash, Ora, Benjamin Langer, Maayan Nagar, Shahar Shoham, Ido Lurie, and Nadav Davidovitch. "Exposure to Traumatic Experiences among Asylum Seekers from Eritrea and Sudan during Migration to Israel." *Journal of Immigrant and Minority Health* 17, no. 4 (August 2015): 1280–1286.

Nakhwah. "Arab Democracy Foundation (ADF)." http://www.nakhwah.org/en/organizations /697-Arab-and%20Democracy-Foundation-ADF.

Nasr, Seyyed Hossein. *The Need for a Sacred Science*. London: Routledge, 2005.

Ntarangwi, Mwenda. *Reversed Gaze: An African Ethnography of American Anthropology*. Champaign: University of Illinois Press, 2010.

O'Fahey, Rex Seán. "Conflict in Darfur: Historical and Contemporary Perspectives." In *Conference Proceedings: Environmental Degradation as a Cause of Conflict in Darfur*, edited by Bakri Osman Saeed, 23–32. Addis Ababa: University for Peace, Africa Programme, 2006.

———. *The Darfur Sultanate: A History*. London: Hurst, 2008.

———. "Umm Kwakiyya or the Damnation of Darfur." *African Affairs* 106, no. 425 (October 2007): 709–717.

Pahl, R. E. *Divisions of Labour*. Oxford: Basil Blackwell, 1984.

Pamuk, Orhan. *Other Colors: Essays and a Story*. Vancouver, WA: Vintage, 2008.

Pinto, Samantha. *Difficult Diasporas: The Transnational Feminist Aesthetic of the Black Atlantic*. New York: NYU Press, 2013.

Piot, Charles. *Remotely Global: Village Modernity in West Africa*. Chicago: University of Chicago Press, 1999.

Premawardhana, Devaka. *Faith in Flux: Pentecostalism and Mobility in Rural Mozambique*. Philadelphia: University of Pennsylvania Press, 2018.

Probst, Peter. "Betwixt and Between: African Studies in Germany." In *The Study of Africa*, vol. 2: *Global and Transnational Engagements*, edited by Paul Tiyambe Zeleza, 157–188. Dakar: CODESROA, 2007.

Rahier, Jean Muteba, Percy C. Hintzen, and Felipe Smith, eds. *Global Circuits of Blackness: Interrogating the African Diaspora*. Urbana: University of Illinois Press, 2010.

Rapport, Nigel. *Social and Cultural Anthropology: The Key Concepts*. London: Routledge, 2014.

Redclift, Nanneke, and Enzo Mingione, eds. "Introduction." In *Beyond Employment: Household, Gender, and Subsistence*, 1–11. Oxford: Wiley-Blackwell, 1985.

ReliefWeb. "Sudan: Darfur IDP Camps (08 May 2013)." May 16, 2013. https://reliefweb.int/map /sudan/sudan-darfur-idp-camps-08-may-2013.

"The Return of Asad Africa." YouTube video, 2:16. Posted by "Mohammed Terwis," June 16, 2015. https://www.youtube.com/watch?v=QKkGAfs_YWA.

Robinson, Douglas. *Displacement and the Somatics of Postcolonial Culture*. Columbus: Ohio State University Press, 2013.

Rosner, Shmuel. "Action-Oriented Morality: How Can Israel Turn Away Refugees From Darfur?" *Slate*, August 28, 2007. https://slate.com/news-and-politics/2007/08/how-can-israel -turn-away-refugees-from-darfur.html.

Roth, Philip. *The Human Stain*. New York: Vintage, 2001.

Rushdie, Salman. *Two Years Eight Months and Twenty-Eight Nights: A Novel*. New York: Random House, 2015.

Ryle, John, "The Disaster in Darfur." *New York Review of Books* 51, no. 13 (2004): 55–59.

Sade-Beck, Liav. "Internet Ethnography: Online and Offline." *International Journal of Qualitative Methods* 3, no. 2 (June 2004): 45–51.

Said, Edward W. "Representing the Colonized: Anthropology's Interlocutors." *Critical Inquiry* 15, no. 2 (1989): 205–225.

Sakin, Abdal Aziz Baraka. *The Messiah of Darfur*. Translated by Rogaia Abusharaf. https://www.arabischesbuch.de/index.php?title=Abdal+Aziz+Baraka+Sakin+Masih+Darfur&art_no=bs15&language=en.

Sanjek, Roger. *Ethnography in Today's World: Color Full before Color-Blind*. Philadelphia: University of Pennsylvania Press, 2014.

———, ed. *Mutuality: Anthropology's Changing Terms of Engagement*. Philadelphia: University of Pennsylvania Press, 2014.

Sanjek, Roger, and Susan W. Tratner, eds. *eFieldnotes: The Makings of Anthropology in the Digital World*. Philadelphia: University of Pennsylvania Press, 2016.

Sartre, Jean-Paul. *The Emotions: Outline of a Theory*. Translated by B. Frechtman. New York: Citadel, 1948.

Shaw, W. B. K. "Darb El Arba'in: The Forty Days' Road." *Sudan Notes and Records* 12, no. 1 (1929): 63–71.

Slight, John. "British Perceptions and Responses to Sultan Ali Dinar of Darfur, 1915–16." *Journal of Imperial and Commonwealth History* 38, no. 2 (2010): 237–260.

Slyomovics, Susan. *The Performance of Human Rights in Morocco*. Philadelphia: University of Pennsylvania Press, 2005.

Smith, Daniel. *To Be a Man Is Not a One Day Job*. Chicago: University of Chicago Press, 2017.

Sorabji, Richard. *Emotion and Peace of Mind: From Stoic Agitation to Christian Temptation*. New York: Oxford University Press, 2000.

Spence, Basil. "Darfur Province. Stone Worship among the Zaghawa." *Sudan Notes and Records* 1, no. 3 (1918): 197–199.

Stocking, George W., ed. *Colonial Situations: Essays on the Contextualization of Ethnographic Knowledge*. Madison: University of Wisconsin Press, 1991.

Strathern, Marilyn. "The Limits of Auto-anthropology." In *Anthropology at Home*, edited by Anthony Jackson, 59–67. London: Tavistock, 1987.

Strathern, Marilyn, M. R. Crick, Richard Fardon, Elvin Hatch, I. C. Jarvie, Rix Pinxten, Paul Rabinow, Elizabeth Tonkin, Stephen A. Tyler, and George E. Marcus. "Out of Context: The Persuasive Fictions of Anthropology [and Comments and Reply]." *Current Anthropology* 28, no. 3 (1987): 251–281.

Sudan Jem. *The Black Book: Imbalance of Power and Wealth in Sudan*. Translated by Abdullahi Osman El-Tom. Last modified on March 22, 2018. http://www.sudanjem.com/sudan-alt/english/books/blackbook_part1/book_part1.asp.htm.

Sudan Tribune. "N. Darfur to Transform IDPs Camps into Permanent Residential Areas." June 14, 2018. https://www.sudantribune.com/spip.php?article65644.

———. "Sudan Says Rebel's Office in Israel Proves 'Foreign Hands' in Darfur." March 1, 2008. https://www.sudantribune.com/spip.php?iframe&page=imprimable&id_article=26192.

———. "Sudan's al-Burhan says Darfur Victims have the Right to Resort to ICC." December 19, 2019, https://www.sudantribune.com/spip.php?article68733.

———. "Sudan's Capital Gripped in Nuptials of Chad's Deby, Daughter of Darfur Militia Leader." January 21, 2012. https://www.sudantribune.com/Sudan-s-capital-gripped-in,41358.

Suliman, Mohamed. *The Inversion of Ethnicity from Perception to Cause of Violent Conflicts: The Case of the Fur and Nuba Conflicts in Western Sudan*. London: Institute for African Alternatives, 1997. http://new.ifaanet.org/?p=451.

Symons, Donald. "A Critique of Darwinian Anthropology." *Ethnology and Sociobiology* 10, no. 1–3 (1989): 131–144.

Taussig, Michael T. *Shamanism, Colonialism, and the Wild Man: A Study in Terror and Healing.* Chicago: University of Chicago Press, 1987.

Thelwall, Robin E. W. "A Linguistic Survey in El Fasher Secondary School." *Sudan Notes and Records* 52 (1971): 46–55.

Theobald, A. B. "Dārfūr and Its Neighbours under Sultān'alī Dinār, 1898–1916." *Sudan Notes and Records* 40 (1959): 113–120.

Thomas, Nicholas. *Colonialism's Culture: Anthropology, Travel, and Government.* Princeton, NJ: Princeton University Press, 1994.

Tölölyan, Khachig. "Rethinking Diaspora(s): Stateless Power in the Transnational Moment." *Diaspora: A Journal of Transnational Studies* 5, no. 1 (1996): 3–36.

Tönnies, Ferdinand. *Gemeinschaft und Gesellschaft.* East Lansing: Michigan State University Press, 1957.

Tubiana, Jérôme, Victor Tanner, and Musa Adam Abdul-Jalil. *Traditional Authorities' Peacemaking Role in Darfur.* Washington: US Institute of Peace, 2012.

Tūnisī, Muḥammad Ibn-'Umar al-. *Tashidh al-adhan fi sirat bilad al-Arab wa el-Sudan.* Edited by Mahmoud Asakir and Mustafa Mussad. Cairo: Al Dar Al Masriya Lil-Ta'lif wal-Tarjama, 1965. This is an Arabic translation of Mohammed Ebn-Omar El-Tounsy, *Voyage au Darfour* (Paris: Chez B. Duprat, 1845). It has also been translated into English as Muḥammad Ibn-'Umar al-Tūnisī, *In Darfur: An Account of the Sultanate and Its People.* Edited and translated by Humphrey Davies (New York: New York University Press, 2018).

United Nations. "Darfur Peace Agreement." https://www.un.org/zh/focus/southernsudan/pdf/dpa.pdf

United Nations–African Union Mission in Darfur. *Doha Document for Peace in Darfur.* https://unamid.unmissions.org/sites/default/files/ddpd_english.pdf.

United Nations High Commissioner for Human Rights (OHCHR) and the African Union–United Nations Hybrid Operations in Darfur (UNAMID). *The Human Rights Situation of Internally Displaced People in Darfur, 2014–2016.* n.d. http://www.ohchr.org/Documents/Countries/SD/UNAMID_OHCHR_situation_Darfur2017.docx.

United Nations Office for the Coordination of Humanitarian Affairs. "Sudan." Last modified January 13, 2020. https://www.unocha.org/sudan.

United States Institute of Peace. "Truth Commission: Morocco." December 1, 2004. https://www.usip.org/publications/2004/12/truth-commission-morocco.

Walcott, Derek. *Omeros.* New York: Farrar, Straus and Giroux, 2014.

Welbourne, Michael. *Knowledge.* Montreal: McGill-Queens University Press, 2001.

Williams, Raymond. *Marxism and Literature.* Oxford: Oxford University Press, 1977.

Wilson, Charles T., and Robert William Felkin. *Uganda and the Egyptian Soudan.* 2 vols. London: Sampson Low, Marston, Searle & Rivington, 1882.

Wingate, F. R[eginald]. "Forward." *Sudan Notes and Records* 1, no. 1–2 (1918): 1–2.

World Watch Monitor. "Sudan: 13 Christians Arrested in Darfur, Another Church Told to Hand Over Property." October 17, 2018. https://www.worldwatchmonitor.org/2018/10/sudan-13-christians-arrested-in-darfur-another-church-told-to-hand-over-property.

Wright, Michelle M. *Becoming Black: Creating Identity in the African Diaspora.* Durham, NC: Duke University Press, 2004.

Yacobi, Haim. "Let Me Go to the City: African Asylum Seekers, Racialization, and the Politics of Space in Israel." *Journal of Refugee Studies* 24, no. 1 (2011): 47–68.

Zeitlyn, David. "Anthropology in and of the Archives: Possible Futures and Contingent Pasts. Archives as Anthropological Surrogates." *Annual Review of Anthropology* 41 (2012): 461–480.

Zuberi, Tukufu. *Thicker than Blood: How Racial Statistics Lie*. Minneapolis: University of Minnesota Press, 2001.

Zuberi, Tukufu, and Eduardo Bonilla-Silva, eds. *White Logic, White Methods: Racism and Methodology*. Lanham, MD: Rowman & Littlefield, 2008

Index